Oñati International Series
in Law and Society

European Democracies Against Terrorism

Governmental policies and intergovernmental cooperation

Edited by Fernando Reinares

A Series published for
THE OÑATI INTERNATIONAL INSTITUTE
FOR THE SOCIOLOGY OF LAW

Ashgate

DARTMOUTH
Aldershot UK • Burlington USA • Singapore • Sydney

Published by
Dartmouth Publishing Company Limited
Ashgate Publishing Limited
Gower House
Croft Road
Aldershot
Hants GU11 3HR
England

Ashgate Publishing Company
131 Main Street
Burlington, VT 05401-5600 USA

Ashgate website: http://www.ashgate.com

British Library Cataloguing in Publication Data
European democracies against terrorism : governmental
 policies and intergovernmental cooperation. – (Oñati
 international series in law and society)
 1. Terrorism – Government policy – Europe
 I. Reinares, Fernando
 363.3'2'094

Library of Congress Cataloging-in-Publication Data
European democracies against terrorism : governmental policies
 and intergovernmental cooperation / Fernando Reinares, ed.
   p. cm. — (Oñati international series in law and society)
   ISBN 0-7546-2015-8 (hbk.) — ISBN 0-7546-2019-0 (pbk.)
   1. Terrorism – Government policy – European Union
 countries. 2. Terrorism – Prevention – International
 cooperation. I. Reinares-Nestares, Fernando. II. Series.
 HV6431.E85 1999
 363.3'2'094—dc21   99-15645
                                                              CIP

ISBN 0 7546 2015 8 (Hbk)
ISBN 0 7546 2019 0 (Pbk)

Typeset by Manton Typesetters, Louth, Lincolnshire, UK.
Printed and bound in Great Britain by MPG Books Ltd, Bodmin, Cornwall.

Contents

Introduction

FERNANDO REINARES

Terrorism, as practised by small clandestine organizations with the alleged intention of affecting the structure and distribution of power, both at a national or international level, has been particularly notorious in Western Europe since the late 1960s. Most of that violence was perpetrated by underground groups having insurgent orientations, irrespective of their concrete ideological inspiration, but some had vigilante leanings instead. Though the duration and intensity of such lasting phenomenon has varied from one country to the other, it has generally produced important political and social consequences. In spite of its limited scope when compared with other manifestations of organized collective violence, terrorism can nonetheless exert a severe impact on the fundamental processes common to democratic regimes in the advanced industrial societies of Europe as well as elsewhere. For instance, systematic and sustained terrorist activity not only recurrently violates human rights, it also impedes the free exercise of civil liberties, alters the normal functioning of official institutions, hinders the management of public affairs by elected authorities or disrupts the autonomous development of civil society. Combined with other factors likely to strain or overload the political system, terrorism becomes a risk, if not exactly a threat, to the stability of liberal democracies, in particular those undergoing a process of consolidation. Any legitimately constituted government is thus expected to readily and persistently confront such an aggressive challenge to both the existing tolerant political order and the monopoly of physical coercion over a given territory claimed by the state.

Even when the formation of terrorist organizations is typically preceded by disruptive collective mobilizations which undergo successive stages of radicalization, to the extent that some cautious proactive intervention is somewhat feasible for authorities concerned, democratic governments rather more often have to intervene once illegal violence has been dramatically initiated. Still, terrorism poses serious dilemmas for executives trying to formulate and implement consistent policies aimed at neutralizing the phenomenon. Governmental responses, in the context of democratic regimes, are normally conditioned by currents of domestic public opinion, legal guarantees enjoyed by the citizens, the various state institutions involved and even those articulated interests eventually active in the sector of internal security. As to those liberal democracies known in highly industrialized societies, anti-terrorist policies have tended to include some strictly political decisions aimed at peacefully regulating social conflicts or affecting the internal cohesion of armed clandestine organizations, the enactment of legislations intended to deter extremists from resorting to a repertoire of terrorism and favour law enforcement operations, and a number of other specialized responses to be undertaken by state security agencies, these latter two increasingly adopted in a context of cooperation between countries due to the transnationalized character of the challenge. Such initiatives, which sometimes lead to differential results in terms of relative utility, depending on their own nature and the situational conditions, often also display coincidences as to their effectiveness across countries. It may nevertheless be asserted that measures generally considered most useful against terrorism and least dangerous to the fabric of open societies are those taken under the rule of law and in accordance with the principles of liberal democracies.

In the first part of this multidisciplinary book, contributors describe and examine elements of different internal security policies adopted and developed by several Western European governments, over the past three decades, in order to counter the challenge of terrorism. Bruce Hoffman and Jennifer Morrison-Taw, for instance, elaborate a national plan for successfully countering terrorism, based on a comparative study of seven selected past and present experiences, specifying four crucial elements: the existence of a functioning overall command and coordination structure; a mixture of legitimizing measures adopted by the authorities to build public trust and of adequate sensitive legislation; coordination within and between national intelligence services; and collaboration among governments and security forces of different countries. David Bonner focuses his chapter precisely on the security legislation enacted in the United Kingdom as part of the broad governmental policy implemented to face terrorist challenges, critically assessing the effectiveness of such measures and examining the influence on law of the European Commission and Court of Human Rights, as well as of the European Court of Justice, with respect to cases brought before them, relating all those issues to the constitutional order existing and reflecting also on the peace process in Northern Ireland. Daniel Hermant and Didier Bigo enter into some epistemological debate with respect to the very

notion of terrorism, before devoting their contribution to the analysis
of relevant changes observed with respect to state responses against
armed clandestine organizations in France, from the middle 1970s
until the 1990s, a rather notorious shift in severity taking into account the previous existence of generalized popular as well as elite
beliefs holding the myth of a revolutionary past and thus reluctant to
criminalize the use of political violence even within democracies.

Spain is the case study dealt with in the chapter which I co-
authored with Oscar Jaime-Jiménez, where we analyse the escalation
of terrorist violence during the transition from authoritarian rule in
the second half of the 1970s and its subsequent continuous decline
following the consolidation of a new democracy through the 1980s,
stressing the relative impact of diverse governmental measures implemented to counter such type of violence, providing an informed
evaluation on the counterproductive effects of illegal police intervention, and emphasizing finally the importance of international
cooperation, mainly bilateral among analogous and contiguous
democratic regimes. Luciana Stortoni-Wortmann explores, in the
concluding chapter of this first part of the book, dedicated to
governmental policies in Western Europe, the remarkable evolution
of police response to terrorism in Italy since the end of the 1960s
until well into the 1980s, describing the main developments in
specialized methods adopted by state security agencies and explaining them through the interplay of a particularly influential set of
variables, such as the dynamics of leftwing and rightwing violence
itself, changing structural and functional features of the national
internal security field, or reactions coming from institutions and
actors located within a political system so dramatically affected by
the campaigns of several armed clandestine organizations.

However, contemporary terrorism is not a form of political violence confined within the limits of particular state jurisdictions. It
tends to cross established frontiers and has increasingly become an
evolving transnational phenomenon, as previously noted. Either
because terrorist organizations decide to mobilize resources outside
the country of reference where they repeatedly carry out their armed
activities or because they deliberately look for targets in national
territories other than the one they come from. Due to these and
other relocating circumstances, often facilitated by the complexities
of our world system and innovations associated with the globaliza-
tion process, governmental anti-terrorist policies applied within
definite domestic boundaries are objectively constrained in their
possible effects. For this reason, bilateral or multilateral interna-

tional cooperation is of the greatest importance in the prevention and control of such actual or potential menace not only to the stability of democratic regimes but to the basic equilibrium of entire geopolitical regions as well. In this sense, the second part of the book precisely analyses problems and perspectives surrounding inter-governmental cooperation against terrorism, transnationalized or properly international, as developed within the framework of the European Union.

Peter Chalk, for instance, assesses both positive and negative implications for counterterrorism derived from the provisions about cooperation between member states in the fields of justice and home affairs contained in the Treaty on European Union, provisions also known as the third pillar, focusing his chapter not only on advances in the common approach to shared internal security concerns but also on some serious issues likely to render problematic the necessary democratic acceptability of collaborative intergovernmental action in law enforcement and judicial matters. Monica den Boer openly addresses the question of whether or not the existing Treaty on European Union is adequate to deal with the reinforcement of cooperation against terrorism, since due to several historical and political reasons the member states have trouble in tackling such criminal phenomenon in a homogenous manner, so that in order to improve counterterrorism the third pillar structure and decision making process has to be reviewed or enhancements could otherwise be possible adjacent to the official instruments, as suggested in this chapter. Malcolm Anderson furthermore argues that effective and continuing cooperation in that field is almost impossible to achieve because there must be substantial agreement between governments of the member states on political rather than criminal law enforcement objectives, and because mutual assistance is also complicated by the diverse contexts in which transnational violence takes place, the difficulty of conceptualizing terrorism, the problematic legal basis of counterterrorism, differing articulation of the security agencies involved in different countries, and the unwillingness of national authorities to share intelligence. In the concluding chapter of this second part and of the volume as a whole, Ronald D. Crelinsten and Iffet Özkut examine how certain definitional and operational changes in the area of counterterrorism may relate to the official treatment of immigrants, refugees and asylum seekers in a European Union where the population of member states is increasingly concerned over security but tends to ignore endogenous potential threats, a fact moving the authors to explore alternatives

to technological solutions which may engender unintended consequences and supplant other potentially more effective approaches
at the level of social policies pertaining to the promotion of human
rights.

Considerable academic effort has already been dedicated to the
normative and empirical analysis of state responses to terrorism in
the context of liberal democracies. However, this volume contains
distinctive and original contributions to the theme. On the one hand,
it offers highly valuable information, not easily accessible through
secondary sources, and updated case studies most relevant for all
scholars, working in a number of fields within the social sciences,
interested in the phenomenon of contemporary terrorism and, more
concretely, in the analysis of various measures usually adopted as
part of anti-terrorist governmental policies. On the other hand, beyond the experiences of bilateral cooperation or the assessment of
less developed multilateral agreements, this book provides not only
an accurate description of the counterterrorism possibilities existing
within the European Union, but also substantial evaluative considerations about those factors likely to obstaclize advances in judicial
or police cooperation on the matter, as well as about problems
concerning the democratic legitimacy of intergovernmental cooperation in this area of internal security defined as common to all member
states. Accordingly, the collection would also appeal to professionals
in the area of public security and like persons holding office in
concerned branches of regional, national or community administrations. *European Democracies against Terrorism*, the title of this volume
as well as of the multidisciplinary workshop held at the International
Institute for the Sociology of Law in Oñati, Basque Country of Spain,
where the papers now assembled were originally presented, deliberately stresses the antagonism between arranged civic tolerance and
coercive tyrannical elitism. Indeed, liberal democracies in general, old
and new European democracies in particular, will continue facing the
challenge of terrorism in the future, an expression of violence which
may be undergoing significant modifications at the turn of the century. Hence the importance of contributing to a better understanding
and appropriate estimation of interventions that can be adapted at
governmental level and joint measures to be introduced in the realm
of intergovernmental cooperation.

Part I
Governmental Policies

1 A Strategic Framework for Countering Terrorism

BRUCE HOFFMAN AND
JENNIFER MORRISON-TAW

Introduction

The strategies and tactics used by governments throughout the world to counter terrorism have varied widely, from such highly visible actions as declarations of states of siege or martial law, enactment of anti-terrorist legislation, and strengthening of judicial powers, to less visible measures such as the establishment of computerized data banks, enhanced intelligence capabilities and covert operations. Some of these countermeasures, such as Italy's use of so-called 'penitence laws', have been more successful than others. Some have not only failed, like Britain's short-lived policy of interning terrorist suspects in Northern Ireland during the 1970s, but have proved counterproductive, alienating the public from the authorities and further polarizing an already fractured political environment. Other government countermeasures, such as amnesties and offers of cash rewards for information, have had mixed results.

Methodological Problems and Challenges in Assessing the Effectiveness of Various Countries' Individual Use of Countermeasures against Terrorism

However, while much attention has been focused on the individual experiences of various countries in coping with their respective terrorist or insurgent problems,[1] relatively little research has been devoted either to broad, systematic, comparative analyses or to developing a methodology to evaluate the success of these countermeasures and their relevance to other countries with similar problems.

One approach to redressing this lacuna in terrorism and insurgency research has been the attempts to capture, through the use of models or other quantitative analytical aids, the effects of the various countermeasures used by governments and thereby to develop a methodology or criteria to gauge the success or failure of counter-measures. Although the use of quantitative methods in the social sciences has grown and some of these approaches have yielded useful results in a number of fields, terrorism and insurgency research un-fortunately are not among them. To date, three key quantitative studies of these phenomena have been produced: an unpublished doctoral dissertation that examined, respectively, the effects of Brit-ain's, Italy's and West Germany's counterterrorist measures between 1970 and 1985 (Sobieck, 1990); a research effort undertaken at the behest of the US government that primarily used quantified data derived from case studies of the counterterrorist campaigns waged by Israel, France and Colombia (Hayes, 1982); and a similar study prepared for the US Department of State's Office of Long Range Assessment and Research (subsequently published by a private aca-demic press) that embraced a broad, systematic comparative approach in analysing the effects of counterterrorist measures in mostly urban environments in Uruguay, Cyprus, Northern Ireland, Spain and Italy (Hewitt, 1984). Despite some individually interesting conclusions, each study revealed serious shortcomings in attempting to model or quantify the effects of counterterrorist measures.

In his unpublished doctoral dissertation, Sobieck, for example, attempts to use statistics to determine the effectiveness of various governmental policies in deterring terrorist violence. Although he acknowledges problems of data collection, collation and analysis, there are additional difficulties evident in his approach. Sobieck chooses to use changes in governmental policies as his independent variable and frequency of terrorist activity as his dependent vari-able. This implies that governmental policies are determined independently of terrorist activity, although, to the contrary, and as Sobieck points out repeatedly in his text, governmental policies actually change in direct response to terrorist activity. Although he intends to show how changes in governmental policy can inhibit terrorist activity, what Sobieck does is describe a cycle: the govern-ment imposes increasingly stringent policies to deter continuing or increasing terrorist activities; this continues to the point at which terrorists respond by curtailing their activities. The stringency of the policy, however, is determined by the level of terrorist activity, clearly indicating that the change in policies is not an independent variable. Moreover, the existence of such an upward spiral in ter-rorist activity and governmental response, combined with the fact that no policy has completely deterred terrorism in any of Sobieck's case studies, suggests that terrorism may again increase despite existing policies, leading to a situation in which the government must impose yet more stringent counterterrorist policies.

Sobieck's results are also relative: in Northern Ireland, for example, where the most stringent governmental policies of all the case studies were imposed, the rate of terrorism is nonetheless higher than in both West Germany and Italy. Political situation, culture, socioeconomic factors, religious antagonism and so on, would therefore seem to be more sufficiently explanatory independent variables for the rate of terrorist activity than governmental policy, which could perhaps be better characterized as an 'intervening variable' (that is, one which seems to correlate to culture/politics/history in so far as the 'same' policies, according to Sobieck, are implemented differently in each case study).

Finally, Sobieck's use of time-series analysis, with which he compares the rate of terrorism before and after the implementation of a given policy, is also problematic. Sobieck does not use a control group (a state, for example, which in the same time period did not impose a given policy to counter extant terrorism, in comparison with a state which, in the same time period, did impose the given policy to counter extant terrorism) to test the viability of other explanations for changes in the rate of terrorism. Therefore he has determined that the rate of terrorism overall decreased in the three case studies after the imposition of harsher anti-terrorist policies, but has not tested to see if the decrease in terrorism could be explained otherwise. As a hypothetical example, the incidence of terrorism worldwide could have decreased as weapons and terrorist 'tools of the trade' became less accessible internationally. Had Sobieck used an outlying case study (outside the 1970–85 time frame he chose for his three main case studies), his conclusions could have been tested against general trends of the period. The trouble with this approach, though, is a familiar one pertaining to terrorism research in general: the paucity of empirical data.

Hayes' work as part of a US government-sponsored research effort avoids the problem of attributing terrorist behaviour entirely to governmental policies by explicitly identifying and incorporating into his analyses what he calls 'ecological events': those 'things' (that is, socioeconomic, political factors) that can be expected to influence terrorist behaviour but are not government policy-relevant.[2] Nonetheless, terrorist behaviour is still the dependent variable in Hayes' analysis. As in Sobieck's work, this is a simplification that fails to take into account the cycle in which terrorism drives policy, which, in turn, affects terrorism.

One drawback of Hayes' work is that it only measures the effectiveness of government policies of which terrorists are aware; Hayes' emphasis is on changing terrorist behaviour rather than on studying the overall effectiveness of a counterterrorist campaign which can include policies aimed at apprehending and punishing (combating) terrorists as well as at changing their behaviour (anti-terrorism).[3] Finally, Hayes' conclusions cannot be broadly generalized: indeed, they are surprisingly case-specific. For example, he found that, whereas concessionary policies in Colombia appeared to be associated with decreases in terrorism over time, similar policies in France and Israel actually led to increased terrorism. In contrast, firm, non-concessionary policies in these two countries were in fact responsible for decreases in terrorism (Hayes, 1982: 1–6).

These kinds of analyses can be made without relying on complex statistics as well as by using fewer simplifying assumptions than Hayes does in his equations. Indeed, Hayes had to extrapolate from and quantify reality in order to create statistical models, leaving his conclusions even less rooted in reality than simple observations. This can be an extremely useful technique, yet, with Hayes' small sample size, and the numbers of intervening variables he had to deal with, as well as the complex relationship between terrorism and policy making, use of statistical analysis is misleading. Moreover, without qualitative analysis that ties such conclusions to more general counterterrorist policy making, they are merely descriptive.

Christopher Hewitt's quantitative studies, which were originally prepared for the US Department of State are somewhat more sophisticated, and rely less on statistics. He thus avoids some of the dangers of simplification that Sobieck and Hayes run into. He does, however, quantify violence (a difficult endeavour) in order to conduct similar time-series analyses. Thus, like Sobieck and Hayes, Hewitt measures changes in the level of violence after various governmental policies are implemented.

One of the advantages of Hewitt's work over Sobieck and Hayes is that he takes a variety of factors into account, most importantly, the type of terrorist group (nationalist, leftist, and so on) and the type of state in which the terrorism is occurring (for example, democratic or authoritarian). Nor does Hewitt assume that the independent variable is governmental policies (Hewitt, 1984). He points out, for example, that emergency powers are usually made more severe in direct response to an increase in violence. In other words, policy becomes the dependent variable, driven by the terrorist actions. Hewitt also points out that it is difficult to isolate the individual effects of a single policy, given that a government usually uses more than one emergency power simultaneously.

All in all, Hewitt's statistical work is a good example of the way in which a quantitative approach can be used to support analysis. But, because it has little broad predictive quality, and must be used in association with qualitative data collection and analysis,[4] it suggests that quantitative analysis at this stage in its development must remain a supportive tool rather than the basis for explanations and predictions about the effectiveness of various counterterrorist and counterinsurgency policies.

The common weakness of these quantitative methods when applied to terrorism is a reflection of the fact that this form of violent subversion erupts at various times in various places as the result of an often idiosyncratic combination of factors and conditions, including socioeconomic, political, ethnic, historical and psychological factors, to name but a few. By the same token, the governments and security apparatuses confronted by these threats often vary just as widely, from the most liberal to the most authoritarian, and, even within democracies, frequently span both extremes of the ideological spectrum.

Given this inherent incompatibility of the respective conditions of individual countries which gives rise to terrorism, the inapplicability of certain countermeasures used by repressive regimes to democratic governments, and the widely varying composition and character of both individual terrorist and insurgent organizations as well as national military, security and police forces, the pursuit of a single, analytical methodology to determine the effectiveness of individual counterterrorist and counterinsurgency measures that can be applied generally to an almost unlimited range of different countries and governments is a futile quest. This is not to suggest that constructive comparisons cannot be made across a number of cases or that an overall framework for an effective strategic counterterrorist/counterinsurgency plan, based on the individual experiences of several case studies, cannot be developed.

Methodological Approach

This chapter summarizes a qualitative analysis of seven key case studies of counterterrorist[5] campaigns waged in Europe, Africa

and Asia between the 1950s and the 1980s. The research reported
here was originally conducted at the RAND Corporation for the US
Department of State between 1991 and 1992. It examined specifically the three key British counterterrorist campaigns of the 1940s
and 1950s, involving Malaya, Kenya and Cyprus; the more recent
struggle in Northern Ireland; the urban terrorist dimension of the
1965–80 Rhodesian conflict; and the counterterrorist[6] experiences
of Germany and Italy during the 1970s and 1980s.[7] Its purpose was
to identify lessons and experiences that may be regarded as the
essential prerequisites to developing a comprehensive and coherent
national counterterrorist plan. The report's conclusions are based
on the analysis of the countermeasures' apparent success or failure
and on certain broad general trends that would support their use in
countries similarly afflicted by violence and subversion. Each case
study included a detailed historical analysis so that key idiosyncratic factors – such as leadership and personal charisma, the nature
and origins of terrorist grievances and demands, the extent of popular support, and the rapidity and nature of government responses –
could be examined systematically and analysed comparatively.

The drawbacks of this particular type of approach compared
with a quantitative one are obvious. In this approach, no single
variable can be determined to account for effective counterterrorist
measures across all the cases. Moreover, no single factor can be
identified to explain the success or failure of a given measure. These
weaknesses notwithstanding, this type of study nonetheless offers a
significant advantage in that its results can be practically applied.
The assumption behind the study was that a country facing a
terrorist campaign today could therefore extrapolate from these
cases to its own situation, taking into account the various factors
that make some measures more effective than others, alongside the
considerations that suggest the probability of success.

The report's most important conclusion was arguably that individual application of selected tactics and policies without a
comprehensive national plan can prolong a conflict or even lead to
complete failure. As simple and obvious as this point is, historically
it has more often been ignored or forgotten than followed. The
three British counterterrorist campaigns during the 1950s are cases
in point. In each successive campaign, the same mistakes in organization and intelligence were repeated, with the lessons of the earlier
conflict seemingly ignored. Mistakes made in Malaya, for example,
were made again in Northern Ireland more than two decades later,
undermining Britain's initial response to the growing violence in

that province. And in Rhodesia's prosecution of its urban counterterrorist campaign during the 1960s and 1970s, the same pattern was repeated, despite the fact that the Rhodesian approach was based on the British model of the 1950s.

We concluded in the study that a national plan should acknowledge four elements crucial to a successful counterterrorism campaign. The first element is *an effective overall command and coordination structure*. A functioning command and coordination structure should be in place before terrorist violence erupts, to detect and respond to the first signs of unrest and subversion. The lack of such a structure not only gives the initiative to the terrorists, but allows confusion to develop among the security forces about their respective roles and responsibilities, leading to competition, duplication of effort, and inefficient collection and dissemination of intelligence. If such a structure is not already in place, it must be erected as soon as the violence begins and not only maintained but continually refined and adapted. The most effective structure will also be one led by an individual with responsibility and authority over all elements and aspects of the counter-terrorism campaign.

Second, *'legitimizing' measures must be taken by the government to build public trust and support, combined with anti-terrorist legislation sensitive to public sentiments.* 'Legitimizing' measures are needed to build public confidence in the government and support for the counterterrorist campaign, as is anti-terrorist legislation that is sensitive to public concerns over potential civil liberties infringements and restrictions. Legitimizing measures can encompass a wide variety of actions and legislation:

- political concessions to ethnic or religious minorities;
- economic measures to ameliorate housing and employment inequities or deficiencies;
- defensive steps to protect the public from terrorist reprisals.

The circumstances in a given country will determine which measures will most effectively improve government–civilian relations. Such measures are necessary to

- deprive the terrorists of legitimacy,
- undermine their claims as a viable alternative to the government,
- negate popular support or sympathy for the terrorists,
- redress any popular grievances that may indirectly fuel unrest or be exploited for anti-government purposes.

At the same time, anti-terrorist legislation must aid the government in the capture and prosecution of terrorists, but must not alienate the general population. The role of the civilian population in the success or failure of a terrorist campaign is crucial and cannot be underestimated. Indeed, short of the complete suppression of civil liberties, a government cannot hope to defeat a terrorism campaign using coercive measures alone. If, as in Cyprus during the 1950s, the majority of the population supports the terrorists and the government can offer no inducements to break this bond, success, much less victory, will prove elusive.

The third crucial element is *coordination within and between intelligence services*. There must be a centralized intelligence service that detects early terrorist activity and coordinates information gathering and dissemination among the military, police and other security services. The success of a campaign will rest, not only on the type and quality of information gathered, but on the timely and effective dissemination of that information to all relevant branches of the counterterrorism effort. Given the nature of these types of conflicts and the characteristics of the enemy, the emphasis must of course be on the cultivation and exploitation of human intelligence sources (HUMINT).

Finally, there must be *collaboration among governments and security forces of different countries*. Collaboration between governments is essential to prevent terrorist use of cross-border bases and sanctuaries or uninhibited transnational movement by terrorists and their supporters. Such cooperation will also facilitate the coordination and sharing of intelligence collection and dissemination, as well as the efficacious processing of extradition requests. For example, terrorists operating in Western Europe during the 1970s and early 1980s were able to find political refuge in France, East European countries and the Middle East, and this seriously hampered counterterrorist efforts.

It should be emphasized, however, that these four elements must be applied discriminately, within a carefully coordinated framework designed to emphasize the governments' strengths and exploit the terrorists' weaknesses.[8] Let us briefly consider why these four elements have proved so critical to success in various counterterrorist campaigns.

Command and Coordination Structure

In most of the case studies reviewed in this study, no adequate command and coordination structure was in place when the terrorist campaigns began. Nor were the initial efforts to construct one expeditious or effective. Governments not only had to recognize their deficiencies in command and coordination, they had also to go through a process of trial and error before finally developing adequate command and coordination structures. The initially uncoordinated responses gave terrorists invaluable time to establish themselves within society and consolidate their efforts while the security forces got themselves organized.

Accordingly, without such a unified and coordinated structure, the security forces will inevitably not be able to cooperate as effectively and efficiently as possible, and intelligence will not be disseminated adequately. More importantly, the creation of a command and coordination structure makes possible the development of a unified plan and provides the means with which to carry it out. As the British discovered in Malaya, Kenya and Cyprus during the 1950s, once they had a command and coordination structure and had appointed a single individual to direct it, they were able to emphasize the aspects of the campaign that were most critical. Elsewhere, however, the variegated bureaucracies of democratically elected governments made such a process impossible: elected officials could not be entirely replaced by appointed 'supremos'; entrenched agencies and ministries could not be eliminated or superseded; and governments had to be careful lest they validate terrorists' claims and prove themselves overly repressive and/or incompetent.

Indeed, in a democracy, the government cannot delegate too much power and authority to its security forces without inevitably threatening civil liberties; but retaining too much power and authority can paralyse or impede a counterterrorist campaign through bureaucratic lethargy or redundancy. Although appointing a single leader to head a counterterrorism campaign, as Great Britain did in Malaya, Kenya and Cyprus, reduces internal security force competition, leads to more efficient collection, analysis and dissemination of intelligence, and allows the development and effective prosecution of a single, unified plan, such a position is incompatible with democracy. In Italy, where a single head of operations could not possibly be appointed, the most effective countermeasures resulted directly from the formation of special anti-terrorist units (with members drawn from both the state police and the *carabinieri*) headed by an individual with complete authority only over their operations. Yet even this small-scale version of a 'supremo' was problematical, despite its success against the terrorists: the Italian police forces, judiciary and legislature all expressed grave concern that, since there was no effective monitoring of these units' activities, they could easily subvert constitutionally guaranteed civil rights.

However, within the constraints that accompany democracy, a government can certainly make constructive adjustments to the command and coordination structure. Intelligence should be centralized, so that a single office functions as a clearing house for the collation, analysis and effective dissemination of all intelligence. Each security force should have representatives in that office to direct the most relevant materials to the tactical forces best suited to act on that intelligence. Cooperation among the security forces can also be improved by joint training and the creation of specific joint operations centres. Ultimately, the head of state or his specific representative should be responsible for making command decisions and, indeed, for developing a unified plan, with clearly defined roles for each service. Finally, whatever command and control structure is implanted at the federal levels of government should be reproduced throughout the sub-federal levels of government as well, so that civil administration, security forces, intelligence-gathering organizations and the judiciary are adequately represented at every level.

Effective Anti-terrorist Legislation and Measures to Build Public Trust

The importance of good government–civilian relations in a successful counterterrorism campaign must not be underestimated. Terrorists cannot ultimately succeed against the government without support from the general population; when the government responds effectively to the political and economic needs of the population, terrorism has a much less fertile environment in which to grow. When, however, the government is not responsive, if the conflicting interests of the government and the population are completely immutable and popular dissatisfaction is allowed to grow, with few or no political concessions offered, terrorists are more likely to find both active and tacit anti-government support within the population. This will severely compromise intelligence gathering and can also be exploited for propaganda purposes by the terrorists. In Malaya and Kenya, where Great Britain both recognized and responded to public concerns and interests, the counterterrorist campaigns were extremely successful. In contrast, whilst Rhodesian operations were tactically successful, the country nonetheless lost the struggle because of the government's refusal or inability to acknowledge the interests of the majority black population. Therefore legislation that acknowledges the need for public support can play an extremely positive role in a counterterrorism campaign.

In addition, legislation that offered lighter or even commuted sentences to terrorists who abandoned their struggle and joined forces with the government, for example, proved extremely effective in Malaya, Kenya and Italy. Unfortunately, however, legislation during a counterterrorism campaign too often takes on an altogether different character. In most of the case studies examined here, emergency regulations, laws and other legislation that aided the security forces and facilitated operations against terrorists were deemed essential. In some cases, capital punishment was decreed for mere possession of firearms and explosives, or membership in a terrorist organization. Provisions for detaining or interning terrorists and suspected terrorists without trial for prolonged periods were promulgated, and requirements for warrants to arrest persons or search houses and commercial property were suspended. A variety of collective punishments and measures were defined, including levying fines, closing businesses, imposing curfews, and wholesale removal and resettling of local populations. Powers to deport persons connected in some way with terrorism, to control the sale and movement of food and other goods, and to exercise censorship over the press were also accorded to the various governments discussed here.

Many of the emergency measures were designed to allow governments greater flexibility or severity in prosecuting and punishing both terrorists and their sympathizers than would have been possible under non-emergency legislation. A number of the measures, however, were specifically intended to impede active or passive civilian aid to the terrorists. Such measures proved in many cases to be double-edged. Although they were effective in slowing actual aid to the terrorists, they also often inconvenienced the civilian population; the public, resenting such impositions, increased both its passive and active support for the terrorists. Such measures also allowed the terrorists to portray themselves as the 'true defenders' of the people. Moreover, much of the legislation did not meet international standards, such as those set by the 1977 Geneva Protocol on the Protection of Victims of Non-external War. Indeed, there is a fine line between the imposition of emergency measures and the restriction of civil rights, and in each of the cases discussed, the relevant governments had to address this issue.

Building solid relations with the public is one of the keys to a successful counterterrorist campaign. Poor relations will inevitably prolong, if not thwart, a government's struggle against its terrorist opponents. Intelligence becomes much more difficult to gather; measures directed at the terrorists often become focused on the population at large, and the government must spend precious resources either courting the public, having already alienated it, or punishing it with increasingly repressive measures. Bad relations can also completely undermine the effectiveness of even a sound command and coordination structure (as in Cyprus, for example); good relations give the authorities a margin for error that can buy critical time in the counterterrorist struggle.

Public relations thus become a serious battleground, especially where the terrorists seek, not to gain territory, but to affect government policies. Governments must take the struggle for public sympathy and support as seriously as any other: as was done in Malaya, special government information offices should be created expressly for the purpose of disseminating propaganda, divining and responding to the interests of the public, and using psychological warfare against the terrorists. Such measures should begin early in the campaign and be continued without respite. They also require predetermined points of concession and acceptable incentives, so that the government can act in a timely and unified manner.

The potentially counterproductive role that anti-terrorist legislation can play in the battle for public support must also be taken into consideration. Thus, even though the imposition of emergency laws, enactment of new legislation and changes in the judicial process can be extremely effective tools in the fight against terrorism, they must be developed carefully to avoid impinging upon civil liberties and thereby engendering popular resentment. Where such legislative and judicial changes were heavy-handed, as for example in Rhodesia and Germany, they had few positive effects on the counterterrorism campaigns. Moreover, in some respects they proved counterproductive, triggering public condemnation which the terrorists manipulated to legitimize their own position. In Italy, on the other hand, although some legislation increased the power of the police and the judiciary, it was the penitence and dissociation laws that really broke terrorists' power and gave the government the upper hand. Finally, in Northern Ireland, the government noted the fine line between repression and effective legislation but nonetheless ignored it, inciting drastic increases in terrorist recruitment and violence against the security forces.

A government's priority should therefore be to develop consistent legislation and policies. Italy's inconsistent policy response to the Red Brigades' first kidnapping in the mid-1970s, for example, made this a viable tactic for the terrorists, who learned that at the least such an action would throw the government into public confusion. Indeed, in each of the cases examined here, the development of legislation and governmental policy responses to terrorism was ad hoc rather than pre-emptive or preventive; yet now that certain legislation has proved effective in these countries, appropriate versions of it could be adopted elsewhere early enough to have preventive effects. But it must be adopted with the understanding that there is frequently a trade-off between strong anti-terrorist legislation and government's good relations with the public. Moreover, the tendency to use harsh legislative measures in a counterterrorism campaign often reflects a government's unwillingness to accept that terrorist demands are often radical reflections of broader concerns within the populace. When the government is unwilling to make concessions, provide incentives or acknowledge valid popular grievances, the counterterrorism campaign is condemned to eventual failure: it will rely on the tactical skills of the operations force, functioning with only limited intelligence; it will require expensive, long-term repressive measures to prevent a resurgent threat; and it will most likely alienate the international community, leading possibly to sanctions such as those imposed against Rhodesia.[9]

Centralized Intelligence

Appropriate use of information, the key to any successful counterterrorism campaign, depends on three tasks: the acquisition, proper analysis and, perhaps most important, coordination and dissemination of intelligence. This triad can be accomplished only by establishing a centralized, cooperative and integrative intelligence organization that can channel information effectively to the security forces engaged in tactical operations. Each of the case studies examined here reflects the critical importance of intelligence: in each, campaign success was directly proportional to the emphasis placed on intelligence.

Indeed, unless other elements of the counterterrorist campaign are in place and functioning, a government will not be able to emphasize intelligence adequately. A well-organized command and coordination structure and recognition of the public's role in a counterterrorist campaign are prerequisites for the development of an effective intelligence system. Of the basic elements of a successful counterterrorism campaign, intelligence is the one most dependent on the effective functioning of all the others.

Thus, where a formal command and coordination structure was instituted and the public was assiduously cultivated as a source of information, counterterrorist campaigns were successful. Where even one of these elements was missing, the counterterrorist campaign either reached stalemate or failed completely. In Rhodesia, for example, where the command and coordination structure was not fully in place until late in the campaign, the creation of a single authority was impossible, and the government was unable to obtain information on, or the cooperation of, the black majority population: intelligence, consequently, was sparse and dissemination ineffective. In Germany, Cyprus and Northern Ireland, the governments often maladroitly alienated the population, while the bureaucratically entrenched command and coordination structures hindered intelligence efforts. Only in Malaya and Kenya, where a colonial government had the flexibility to adapt organizationally to the needs of the campaign, were the intelligence requirements almost completely fulfilled.

The Italian experience stands alone as an example of the way other elements of a counterterrorist campaign can compensate for the lack of a single element. Italy relied on extensive legislative measures to undermine the terrorist organizations and gave less emphasis to either counterterrorist tactical operations or intelligence. Indeed, unlike Germany, which has relied on bulky data-gathering structures that generated criticism from the public and, perhaps more significantly, were often easily circumvented by the terrorists, the Italians wrote legislation that brought the intelligence directly to them, in the form of terrorist confessions. Such a strategy takes into account the constraints a democracy faces. One could argue, however, that the Italian case is somewhat anomalous in that success was achieved against the terrorists, not through intelligence efforts, but through the enactment of effective legislative and political and economic measures, leading to increased public support.

Finally, in none of the cases was there any evidence of a coordinated intelligence structure in place prior to the terrorist campaign's commencement and escalation. Had it been, it is possible that none of the security situations would have deteriorated as seriously or, in some cases, as completely as they did. In every instance, recognition of the severity of the threat went unnoticed or unacknowledged until it was too late, owing respectively to superficial intelligence gathering and insufficient dissemination. Governments must therefore create and take seriously intelligence capabilities that will give timely warning of any potential internal threats.

Foreign Collaboration

Foreign collaboration in counterterrorist campaigns has been sporadic at best. Individual countries often have political, economic or diplomatic interests that affect their efforts to cooperate with other countries.

Of the cases examined here, the British efforts in Malaya, Kenya and Cyprus require little discussion in terms of foreign collaboration, which only took the form of continued international trade and diplomatic ties with Britain. Rhodesia, on the other hand, despite having sanctions imposed on it by much of the world, nonetheless received concrete support from South Africa for most of the conflict. Rhodesia, in turn, supported the Portuguese counterinsurgency efforts in neighbouring Mozambique. And foreign collaboration has played an important, if often uneven, role in the counterterrorist campaigns in Northern Ireland, Germany and Italy.

Foreign collaboration in counterterrorist campaigns is capricious, depending completely on the individual political and economic interests of the countries involved and, to a lesser extent, on the personalities and relationships between political leaders as well as senior police, military and security service personnel. South Africa, for example, actively aided the Rhodesians until Pretoria decided that the Rhodesians could not win and halted the aid. The South African government was even willing to pressure the Rhodesians to accept a black majority government – despite the fact that such a concept was anathema to it – in an effort to save itself and curry favour with the United States.

The value of foreign collaboration also depends on the circumstances facing a given country: it can be merely helpful, or it can be critical to the success of an entire counterterrorist campaign. All campaigns, for example, can benefit from shared research and intelligence, mutual extradition agreements and concrete aid. But foreign collaboration will be especially critical wherever terrorists can base themselves in neighbouring countries to stage cross-border attacks. When terrorists receive supplies and training from foreign countries, collaboration can aid interdiction[10] and, in admittedly rare cases (when sufficient pressure can be brought to bear), result in the cessation of external support. And when countries suffer a great deal of imported terrorism, whether against their indigenous populations or against foreign nationals, collaboration with the countries in which the terrorists are based will be critical.

Creation of Special Counterterrorist Forces

Although special response units, like those developed by the British, Rhodesians, West Germans and Italians, tend to capture the official as well as the popular imagination, in most terrorist campaigns their function is often more preventive than reactive and, when employed on covert intelligence-gathering/offensive operations, can often be controversial. Their very existence helps determine the kinds of actions terrorists will take. In Rhodesia, for example, after the government's response units had proved themselves operationally effective and were widely publicized, there were very few attempts to mount an urban terrorism campaign. After the West German GSG 9 unit's brilliant success at Mogadishu, the nature of terrorist attacks in West Germany changed, making GSG 9 almost obsolete and relegating it mostly to internal and external training missions. Yet the creation and maintenance of such units is an extremely costly deterrent to terrorism, in terms of both highly trained manpower and resources. Less expensive preventive measures include public awareness campaigns, extensive police patrolling and improved access control in public places. Such measures were originally used by the British in Northern Ireland and were very successfully adopted in Rhodesia. Moreover, such measures can be subsidized by businesses, and they require the positive involvement of the community in its own defence – a step that can also lead to improved relations between the public and the security forces. Thus special counterterrorist forces are rarely used over the long term for their original purpose (responding to terrorist actions) nor are they necessarily always the most cost-effective means by which to prevent terrorist attacks. It may therefore be prudent to balance their relative deterrent value in counterterrorist campaigns with more day-to-day security force responsibilities.

Conclusion

Clearly, counterterrorist campaigns vary as widely as the circumstances in which they occur. Even within the limits of this study, when we examined cases in Europe, Asia and Africa, spanning the period from the 1950s to the 1980s, with governments ranging from colonial to democratic, four common elements emerged which, used singly or in combination, successful campaigns contain regardless of geographic regions, time periods, and political systems:

1. an effective overall command and coordination structure;
2. confidence-building or 'legitimizing' measures and anti-terrorist legislation developed to weaken the terrorists while strengthening public support for the government;
3. coordination within and between intelligence services;
4. foreign collaboration amongst governments and security forces.

It should be emphasized that a successful national plan for a counterterrorist campaign need not be developed in a vacuum. Previous campaigns in a variety of circumstances, time periods and regions have yielded 'lessons learned' that can be applied to current strategic planning. Attention to these lessons can help a government battling terrorists to avoid mistakes made in past counterterrorist campaigns and, equally importantly, can help that government to recognize the basic strategic elements that, transcending time and place, apply to any successful campaign.

Lessons learned, of course, vary in character. Those at the tactical and operational levels are not always relevant or equally applicable to different situations. Those at the strategic level vary as well: lessons from a counterterrorist campaign in which a single leader had complete authority or major political concessions were possible will not necessarily apply to a campaign in which democratic checks and balances or immutable political interests prevent flexibility of action. The cases examined in this study range from conflicts in British colonial possessions, where 'supremos' wielded complete authority over the government and the military, to counterterrorism campaigns in Northern Ireland, Germany and Italy, where measures against terrorists were constrained by both civil liberties legislation and public concern, where concessions to terrorist demands would have indicated undesirable weakness and where, in some instances, among already unsteady democratic systems, the effects might have led to further domestic political anarchy.

In ideal circumstances, all four elements will be present in a government's strategy. Administrative and operational control would be vested in one overall commander; the value of maintaining good relations with the public would not be underestimated or neglected and would be reflected in the development of explicit and balanced anti-terrorist legislation; intelligence would be centralized to allow for efficient and expeditious collection, analysis and dissemination; and governments would cooperate to inhibit transnational terrorist operations.

Since ideal circumstances are unlikely to exist, however, it is critical for governments planning counterterrorist campaigns to be able to play to their strengths. Thus a democratic government will clearly be unable to endow a single leader with power over the military and civil administration or pursue intelligence or counterterrorist operational activities as rigorously or repressively as a government less cognizant of civil liberties would do. On the other hand, a democratic government can, for example, emphasize the development of thoughtful legislation that reflects popular concerns without capitulating to terrorists.

Regardless of the nature of the government, the need for an effective command and coordination structure pervades the other elements of a successful national plan. Where coordination is lacking between or within these elements, the campaign will be plagued by redundancy, inefficiency and discontinuity. This held true for each of the cases examined here. When a clear chain of command and practical coordination was established – whether in the campaign as a whole or within an integral element such as intelligence collection, collation and dissemination – the successful resolution of the conflict was more quickly achieved. When such a command and coordination structure was lacking, campaigns foundered, citizens were alienated both by inconsistent government policies and (perhaps most importantly) by the government's inability to protect them, and terrorists easily exploited the situation to entrench themselves firmly within the population.

In countries like Germany and Italy, public opposition to centralized security force command structures (in response to the memories of what had happened there in the 1930s and 1940s) severely inhibited coordination. Too much coordination is believed to raise the prospect of Orwellian state control; but too little coordination can hamstring a government into near-paralysis, thus reinforcing precisely those elements that seek to undermine democracy. In such a situation, intelligence and operational coordination are still possible, but what must then take precedence are the other elements of the counterterrorism campaign. Coordinated public relations campaigns and non-partisan, creative and timely legislation can compensate for inadequate intelligence or an ineffective overall command structure. This was the case in Italy, where the Red Brigades were arguably conquered more by innovative legislation than by well-coordinated and well-orchestrated counterterrorist operations. Where the two coincide, as they did during Great Britain's exceptional campaign in Malaya, resourceful legislation and a well-conceived command structure make a powerful combination.

Depending on the circumstances, adequate and coordinated intelligence can be as useful to a counterterrorist campaign as an effective command structure or attention to public relations. In the cases examined here, excluding Italy, governments that placed an emphasis on intelligence conducted their campaigns much more successfully than those that did not. HUMINT is especially important in terrorism, where the enemy is indistinguishable from the general population. Rhodesia's operational successes, though not sufficient to counterbalance the political struggle the government finally lost, were due in large part to human intelligence. Human intelligence also served Great Britain well in Kenya and Malaya. In Cyprus, on the other hand, where Great Britain could obtain little information from a recalcitrant population, and where the terrorists infiltrated the government more successfully than the government could infiltrate the terrorist movement, the scarcity of human intelligence almost completely undermined operations.

Intelligence, though, is as sensitive an issue as centralization. National intelligence, military intelligence and police intelligence frequently exist as separate entities, usually for separate purposes. These agencies' objectives, training, and modus operandi are different, and bureaucratic competition and institutional rivalry between them often inhibit coordination. National intelligence is basically outward-looking and less relevant to internal, domestic affairs, although it is useful when terrorists conduct operations from foreign bases. Military intelligence tends to be up-to-the-minute operational information geared to discerning enemy orders of battle and intentions. Police intelligence, in contrast, involves social and political information that defines the operational environment and operates under the rule of law if it is to be used in court. In a terrorist campaign, both 'environmental' and operational intelligence are clearly necessary if the military is to be able to distinguish its enemies from the population at large and then engage them successfully without alienating the general public. In democracies, concern over civil liberties violations often makes gathering information on citizens difficult, and sharing that data with other agencies nearly impossible. This can obviously also severely handicap operational capabilities.

Effective collaboration between governments can deprive terrorists of their access to bases outside the country where their struggle is being fought. RAF operations in West Germany, for example, would have been severely constrained had the group been unable to take refuge in East Germany. The Rhodesian conflict would have been much different had the terrorists been unable to mount cross-border operations from bases in Zambia and Mozambique. The same certainly is true of Provisional IRA operations both in Northern Ireland and in England from secret locations in the Republic of Ireland. The power of foreign collaboration was clearly demonstrated during the war against Iraq: intelligence services from regions as diverse as Europe and the Middle East – including such traditional adversaries as Israel's Mossad and Syrian intelligence agencies – mounted an unprecedented global counterterrorist security effort that reportedly thwarted planned operations, pre-empted scheduled attacks and hindered reconnaissance, logistical supply and transnational terrorist movements.

Special counterterrorist forces can also give the government a significant advantage over terrorists. Such forces are primarily a deterrent to various types of terrorist operations, making actual employment of the forces rarely necessary. There are drawbacks, however, to the creation of such forces: they are expensive to maintain; they siphon off the best policemen or soldiers into a force that is rarely employed; disparities in pay between special counterterrorist forces and regular police forces create new sources of discontent and morale problems among services; and, though some perceive such forces as perhaps the most effective weapon in a government's counterterrorist arsenal, others perceive them as little more than government 'hit teams' and a threat to civil liberties.

There is of course no guarantee that any of these countermeasures, even when uniformly and consistently applied, will assure decisive victory. Nor can these countermeasures be duplicated exactly from case to case; individual governments will have to determine how best to create special counterterrorist forces, legislation, command structures and so on, suited to their circumstances. Yet, when compared across the case studies examined here, the utility of these four elements is evident. They can thus serve as a broad guideline in future counterterrorism planning.

It would be foolish to close a discussion of the historical lessons learned from past counterterrorist campaigns without making reference to some of the changes that have occurred in the nature and character of terrorism during more recent times and assessing (briefly) their possible impact on future government responses. In particular, two key trends suggest that we may have to revise our notions of the stereotypical terrorist organization and, in turn, the counter-measures needed to combat this threat:

- the proliferation of terrorist groups motivated by a religious imperative and, related to this,
- the overall diffusion of the terrorist threat as evidenced by the increasing involvement of 'amateur' terrorists alongside their more easily identified 'professional' counterparts.

In these respects, the situation that unfolded in France during the summer and autumn of 1995 arguably encapsulates the new challenges posed by terrorism and the difficulties of response in the post-cold war era. While the French government flexed its strategic muscle testing nuclear devices in the South Pacific and 'showed off' its conventional military prowess in such disparate world 'hot-spots' as Bosnia and Rwanda, back home metropolitan France stood anxious and frustrated (*Le Figaro*, 1995; Berkhan, 1995; Macintyre, 1995c). Between July and October, a handful of terrorists, using bombs fashioned from four-inch nails wrapped around camping-style cooking gas canisters, killed eight people and wounded more than 180 others. Some 32 000 soldiers, police and customs officials were mobilized, who checked the identities and documents of nearly three million people, of whom 70 000 were detained for further questioning (Macintyre, 1996). France's borders were significantly tightened and its continued participation in the seven-nation Schengen 'open borders' agreement was put in doubt. Harsh new anti-terrorism laws were also introduced, strengthening existing legislation specifically enacted after a previous bombing campaign in 1986 (*Reuters News Media*, 1995; Ibrahim, 1995).[11]

Still the bombings continued. Indeed, not until early October did any group even claim credit for the bombings, when the radical Armed Islamic Group, or GIA, a militant Algerian Islamic organization, took responsibility for the attacks. Moreover, it threatened to intensify the bombing campaign unless the French President, Jacques Chirac, cancelled a forthcoming meeting with his Algerian counter-part at the United Nations' 50th anniversary celebration, closed the

French legation in Algiers, severed all economic and diplomatic links with Algeria and publicly denounced that country's impending national elections. They also gave the president three weeks in which to convert to Islam ('Chirac *soumets-toi*') or face the consequences (*New York Times*, 1995; Macintyre, 1995a). This was an affront to any nation's sovereignty and right to pursue its own foreign policies, and France, not surprisingly, refused to accede to virtually all the demands.[12]

Notwithstanding the thousands of security forces deployed, the borders tightened and legislation strengthened, the challenge in combating this threat was immense (Raufer, 1995). French authorities, for example, believe that, while 'professional' terrorists may have perpetrated the initial bombings, like-minded 'amateurs' – that is, entirely self-motivated operatives or unsophisticated imitators drawn from within France's large and increasingly restive Algerian expatriate community – were responsible for at least some of the subsequent attacks (Bell, 1995; Sage, 1995a; 1995b; Smith, 1995; Whitney, 1995; *Intelligence Newsletter*, 1995). Accordingly, if correct, this meant that the campaign could continue even if the original masterminds of the bombings were all apprehended. In addition, they facilitated the campaign 'metastasizing' beyond the small cell of professionals who ignited it, striking a responsive chord among disaffected Algerian youths in France and thereby increasing exponentially the aura of fear and, arguably, the terrorists' coercive power as well.

Thus the vast military might of a modern nation-state was temporarily rendered nugatory. Its extensive security apparatus, consisting of specially-trained gendarmes, even when acting from previously scripted, high-level emergency plans and supported by the full weight of the government's well-oiled bureaucratic machine of prosecutors and magistrates, soldiers and intelligence operatives, was effectively stymied. While this is certainly not the first time in history that a great power has been frustrated by an exponentially smaller adversary (and may be recalled as a fairly inconsequential example at that), France's experience is nonetheless instructive on a number of levels. Accordingly, the situation that arose in France may be a harbinger or model for future terrorist campaigns.

In conclusion, governments now arguably face new problems and new challenges in developing effective countermeasures that are likely to render combating terrorism even more difficult than it was in the past. In such circumstances, security force responses and resources obviously will have to be more flexible and innovative than they have ever been. While new challenges and new threats will ineluctably require new responses and new approaches, these countermeasures can be effectively developed and built upon from the lessons from previous experiences. The wheel should not have always to be reinvented; nor should certain inherent prerequisites to effective counterterrorism campaigns based on past experience be ignored or forgotten.

Notes

1   Although previous research conducted by the Santa Monica, California-based RAND Corporation – such as Hanon Alon (1980) – may be seen as having laid the groundwork for such a methodology, it focused on the experiences of only one country.

2   One of the findings of Hayes' study was that these 'ecological events' do indeed have effects on terrorism.

3   Of course, many policies are intended to serve both functions. Arrests and incarceration are intended as much to deter future terrorism by modifying potential terrorist behaviour as to punish perpetrators of terrorist acts. On the other hand, observation and infiltration of terrorist groups have a single purpose: to capture terrorists.

4   Throughout his work, and in his final chapter, Hewitt applies his quantitative findings to more qualitative findings in order to develop meaningful analyses.

5   It is perhaps worthwhile to pause here and consider the differences between terrorism and insurgency and countering each. Both terrorists and insurgents wish to demonstrate to a given population that its government is inadequate or illegitimate, but the two groups take somewhat different approaches: whereas terrorists wish to draw government and public attention to certain issues, insurgents are interested in seizing and holding territory. Often, however, terrorists and insurgents share similar tactics. This chapter therefore applies the same sets of principles to both counterterrorism and counterinsurgency campaigns, on the assumption that the principles outlined here can be effectively applied in either situation.

6   The term 'counterterrorism' is distinguished in this study from the term 'anti-terrorism'. The former refers to apprehending and punishing (combating) terrorists, the latter to changing or preventing terrorist behaviour and to physical security measures as well.

7   This chapter will make reference to both West Germany, which
        faced an onslaught of terrorism in the early 1970s and began to
        develop responses, and today's reunified Germany, where until
        recently the main terrorist groups persisted and counterterrorist
        capabilities are still in place. The two will be differentiated by
        context and will not be used interchangeably.

8   Many writers have offered lists of the 'principles' of counterinsur-
        gency or counterterrorism: Frank Kitson and Julian Paget are
        particularly notable among them. The RAND Corporation study
        differed from previous offerings in so far as it applied these well-
        known but often ignored principles to a variety of case studies
        spanning regions, time periods and types of governments. Com-
        parison amongst case studies yields lessons about the crucial
        relationship between a government's capabilities and the relative
        utility of each of the above elements in a national counterterrorist
        or counterinsurgency campaign. See Frank Kitson (1977; 1971),
        Julian Paget (1967) and R.W. Komer (1972). Julian Paget's admo-
        nitions for integration, organization, and the advantages of popular
        support in particular, apply to every aspect of a counterinsurgency
        or counterterrorism campaign.

9   Perhaps the best example of this is South Africa, where, after
        decades of violence and repression, the white-dominated govern-
        ment was finally forced to acknowledge the political interests of
        the black majority population. Arguably, the radical changes that
        have occurred in South Africa in recent years would not have taken
        place without the constant struggle of the insurgents in the African
        National Congress and other black political movements.

10   Indeed, a classic example of such foreign cooperation occurred on
        12 January 1987, when Bashir al-Khodur, a Lebanese national,
        was arrested at Milan's airport after 20 pounds of plastic explo-
        sives and several detonators were found in his possession. The
        following day, Mohammed Ali Hamadei – one of the Hezbollah
        terrorists wanted for the June 1985 hijacking of a TWA aircraft
        (and the murder of an American Navy diver on board) – was
        arrested at Frankfurt airport after explosives were discovered in his
        suitcase. Hamadei's apprehension subsequently led to the arrest of
        his brother, Abbas, a long-time West German resident, on 26 Janu-
        ary. The Hamadeis and al-Khodur were reportedly part of a new
        deployment of Shi'a extremists sent to Italy, West Germany and
        France both as active terrorists and as 'sleepers'. Information passed
        by the West German security services to its French counterparts

subsequently led to the arrest in March of eight members of a Hezbollah network based in France, who included six Tunisians, a Lebanese national and an Iranian citizen of Armenian extraction. They admitted to having ties with Iran's secret service and further investigation revealed that members of this cell had been responsible for the series of terrorist bombings that shook Paris in September 1986, killing eight people and wounding more than 150 others. The effect of this blow to the Hezbollah infrastructure in France was staggering: the number of international terrorist incidents in that country dropped from 40 in 1986 to only 15 in 1987. See Karen Gardela and Bruce Hoffman (1990: 20).

11   The wave of bombings that shook Paris during 1986 began in February with an explosion in a shopping centre that killed eight people and culminated the following September with a nine-day terrorist rampage that killed another eight people and wounded more than 150 others. Following the first incident, a group calling itself the Committee of Solidarity with the Arab and Middle East Political Prisoners claimed credit for the bombing and demanded the release of three terrorists imprisoned in France. After the French government refused to accede to this demand, three more bombings occurred in February, two more the following month, and five in September.

12   Chirac did, however, cancel his meeting with his Algerian counterpart, President Zeroual, much to the chagrin of the Algerian government (Macintyre and Bone, 1995; Macintyre, 1995b).

References

Alon, Hanon. 1980. *Countering Palestinian Terrorism in Israel: Toward a Policy Analysis of Countermeasures*. Santa Monica: The RAND Corporation, N-1567-FF.

Bell, Susan. 1995. '16 hurt in Paris nail-bomb blast'. *Times* (London), 18 August.

Berkhan, Med. 1995. 'Islamists: The Division of Europe'. *Le Point* (Paris), 2 September.

Gardela, Karen and Bruce Hoffman. 1990. *The RAND Chronology of International Terrorism for 1987*. Santa Monica: RAND Corporation R-3890-RC.

Hayes, Richard E. 1982. *The Impact of Government Behavior on Frequency, Type, and Targets of Terrorist Group Activity*. McLean: Defense Systems.

Hewitt, Christopher. 1984. *The Effectiveness of Counter-Terrorist Policies*. Lanham: University Press of America.

Ibrahim, Youssef. 1995. 'Chirac Orders French Borders Tightened to Combat Bombings'. *New York Times*, 6 September.

Intelligence Newsletter. 1995. 'Terrorism: Political Backdrop to Paris Attacks'. Paris, 26 October.

Kitson, Frank. 1971. *Low Intensity Operations*. London: Faber & Faber.

Kitson, Frank. 1977. *Bunch of Five*. London: Faber & Faber.

Komer, R.W. 1972. *The Malayan Emergency in Retrospect: Organization of a Successful Counterinsurgency Effort*. Santa Monica: RAND Corporation, R-957-ARPA.

Le Figaro. 1995. 'St Michel Bomb: Islamist Connection Most Likely'. Paris, 27 July.

Macintyre, Ben. 1995a. 'Algerians admit to French bombings'. *Times* (London), 9 October.

Macintyre, Ben. 1995b. 'Chirac ordered by terrorists to cut links with Algeria'. *Times* (London), 19 October.

Macintyre, Ben. 1995c. 'Parisians face up to security failure'. *Times* (London), 19 October.

Macintyre, Ben. 1996. 'French police seize bombs and rifles in Paris dawn raids'. *Times* (London), 20 February.

Macintyre, Ben and James Bone. 1995. 'Meeting of French and Algerian leaders called off'. *Times* (London), 23 October.

New York Times. 1995. 'Algerian Group Says It Planted Bombs in France'. New York, 8 October.

Paget, Julian. 1967. *Counter-Insurgency Campaigning*. London: Faber & Faber.

Raufer, Xavier. 1995. 'Terrorism: The Secret Memorandum'. *Le Vif/L'Express* (Paris), 13 October.

Reuters News Media. 1995. 'French Gov't Seeks Tighter Anti-Terrorism Law'. *Reuters News Media* (World-Wide Web), 25 October, 5:32pm EDT.

Sage, Adam. 1995a. 'Paris faces autumn of terror as fifth bomb is discovered'. *Times* (London), 5 September.

Sage, Adam. 1995b. 'French hold 40 in hunt for bomb terrorists'. *Times* (London), 12 September.

Smith, Alex Duval. 1995. 'Police fight "war" in French suburbs'. *Guardian* (London), 1 November.

Sobieck, Steven. 1990. 'Democratic Responses to Revolutionary Terrorism: A Comparative Study of Great Britain, Italy and West Germany'. PhD thesis submitted to the Claremont Graduate School, Claremont.

Whitney, Craig R. 1995. 'French Police Arrest Suspected Leader of Islamic Militant Group'. *New York Times*, 3 November.

The Authors

Bruce Hoffman is Director of the RAND Washington Office and head of its terrorism research. He is also editor-in-chief of the journal, *Studies in Conflict and Terrorism*. Previously, he was Reader in International Relations and Director of the Centre for the Study of Terrorism and Political Violence at St Andrews University, Scotland.

Jennifer Morrison-Taw is a contributing editor of the journal, *Studies in Conflict and Terrorism*.

2 The United Kingdom's Response to Terrorism: the Impact of Decisions of European Judicial Institutions and of the Northern Ireland 'Peace Process'

DAVID BONNER

Introduction

This chapter considers facets of, and general themes in, the United Kingdom's response to terrorism, defined in security legislation as the use of violence for political ends (including any use of violence for the purpose of putting the public in fear). It examines the response of the European Commission and Court of Human Rights and of the European Court of Justice (ECJ) to cases brought before them arguing that certain aspects of that response are incompatible with, respectively, the European Convention on Human Rights (ECHR) and the legal regime of the European Community (EC). Such external supervision is especially important given a United Kingdom legal and constitutional order lacking an overriding Bill of Rights limiting the legislative power of a Parliament dominated by the executive, in a context in which United Kingdom courts have only relatively recently unequivocally accepted the supremacy of EC law over statute. Finally, the chapter proffers some thoughts on current and possible future impacts on security legislation and policy of the Northern Ireland 'peace process' (a continuing process of uncertain outcome – despite the agreement reached on Good Friday, 1998 – aimed at securing an end to violence, and the sociopolitical causes which spawn and sustain it, through a settlement reached in all-inclusive talks embracing even parties previously supportive of the use of violence to achieve political ends).

The United Kingdom consists of mainland Great Britain (England, Wales and Scotland) and of Northern Ireland (the six counties in the north-eastern corner of the island of Ireland). Until 1922, the whole island formed part of the United Kingdom, but the remaining 26 counties now form the Republic of Ireland, the constitution of which laid claim to Northern Ireland as part of its national territory. The Irish government recognizes that such unity can only be attained by peaceful persuasion and with the consent of a majority of the people of Northern Ireland (a majority at present being in favour of continued union with Great Britain as an integral part of the United Kingdom) and made appropriate changes to the territorial claim in its constitution, since the 'peace process' seemed to have produced an overall political settlement.

As regards the security legislation examined here, the more extreme departures from the norm apply only in Northern Ireland. But legislative responses, once peculiar to Northern Ireland, are often adapted for the mainland. Within Great Britain, the various police forces (43 in England and Wales alone), some with special units, constitute the anti-terrorist personnel, with the lead intelligence role now being taken by MI5 (the security service) searching for a new role/raison d'être with the demise of the cold war. In Northern Ireland, its police force, the Royal Ulster Constabulary (RUC), with paramilitary equipment and special units, is in charge of operations, assisted particularly in border areas (such as the so-called 'bandit country' of South Armagh) by British Army units (for example, the Special Air Service – SAS), some of which are themselves accused of perpetrating a form of terrorism. A variety of United Kingdom intelligence agencies ('military' and 'civilian'), competing sometimes to the detriment of overall effectiveness, have operated in Northern Ireland.

Terrorist Challenges Shaping the United Kingdom Response

Since 1968, the United Kingdom has experienced several terrorist challenges which have prompted and moulded its response, which draws also on its experience with 'terrorist' emergencies in its withdrawal from colonial empire and with earlier violent manifestations of the troubled relationship between Britain and Ireland.

International Terrorism

'International terrorism' is political terrorism '(i) directed at foreigners or foreign targets; (ii) concerted by governments or factions of more than one state; or (iii) aimed at influencing the policies of a foreign government' (Wilkinson, 1986: 182). The United Kingdom has been the victim of acts of international terrorism, involving the hijacking and destruction of its aircraft abroad, the kidnapping and killing of its nationals abroad, and bombings and assassinations and attempted assassinations in the United Kingdom by foreign terrorist groups, mostly connected with the Middle East (see, for a more detailed list of acts, Walker, 1992: 22–4). Some of this terrorism has been sponsored by foreign governments (such as Libya and Iran) which have liquidated or sought to liquidate expatriate opponents of the regime living in the United Kingdom. Much of this terrorism has been combated by the police, albeit with special units, deploying the ordinary law of the land, although since 1984 special powers of arrest and extended detention without charge, once applicable only to terrorism connected with Northern Ireland affairs, have also been deployed. Some international terrorist suspects have been tried in the United Kingdom for criminal offences. Others have been deported under the security powers in the Immigration Act 1971.

Domestic Terrorism Not Concerned with Northern Ireland Affairs

There have been terrorist acts perpetrated by Scottish and Welsh nationalists, by ultra-right, racist, neo-Fascist groups, by anarchists such as the Angry Brigade, and in the form of bombings, particularly incendiary bombings of stores, and food contamination, by extreme fringe elements among campaigners for animal welfare. Apart from the creation of a statutory 'food terrorism' offence, all such terrorism has been met using the ordinary law.

Terrorism Connected with Northern Ireland[1]

The principal terrorist threat which has shaped the United Kingdom response since 1968 has been terrorism connected with Northern Ireland affairs, that is to say, connected with the question whether Northern Ireland should remain part of the United Kingdom or should rather be detached to form part of an all-Ireland socialist republic.

This terrorism is perpetrated by paramilitary groups on both sides of a sectarian divide, in a context in which religious affiliation and political loyalties coincide: by Republicans/Nationalists (Catholics), on the one side, and by Loyalists/Unionists (Protestants) on the other. The Republican terrorist campaign has manifested itself in bombings on the mainland since 1972: the Brighton bombing in October 1984, designed to eliminate the prime minister and many of her cabinet, and the February 1991 missile attack on 10 Downing Street while John Major's cabinet was in session at the height of the Gulf War manifest a theme of attacking the highest level of government on the mainland. There have also been attacks on British diplomats, service personnel and military installations on the continent and on British diplomatic personnel and institutions in the Republic. Recent years have seen major 'successes' against economic targets, particularly in the commercial heart of the capital, in the high-profile Docklands development and in the central shopping area of Manchester; the 'dummy' mortaring of Heathrow Airport in the Spring of 1994, and more callous random attacks inflicting civilian casualties (for example, Warrington, 20 March 1993). Loyalist mainland activity has primarily been confined to the acquisition of weaponry and explosives from a fairly small group of sympathisers among Protestants in Scotland and in the north-west of England, although in 1979 an Ulster Volunteer Force (UVF) cell in Glasgow bombed two pubs frequented by Catholics. Protestant paramilitaries have crossed the border and perpetrated several terrorist attacks in the Republic of Ireland. Northern Ireland, however, has borne the brunt of the violence. More than 3000 people have been killed there in the troubles since 1969.

Such figures (each death tragic in itself) may seem small compared with other conflicts elsewhere or when compared to the normal level of violence in major American cities, but the population of Northern Ireland is only some 1.5 million. An equivalent impact for other countries can be gauged by multiplying the deaths figure by the multiple obtained by dividing the particular country's population by that of Northern Ireland. The violence in Northern Ireland has been a complex of insurgent guerrilla warfare (some of it irredentist), sectarian killings and attacks, inter- and intrafactional conflicts within both communities, kneecappings, punishment shootings and other modes of enforcing discipline both amongst members of the paramilitary groups and against perceived deviants (such as drug dealers, petty criminals or sex offenders) in the communities dominated by the paramilitaries, and activity of more traditional criminal provenance (for example, bank robberies, kidnappings and protection rackets).

On the Republican/Nationalist side, the main identifiable groups are the Provisional IRA (PIRA), the Official IRA, and the Irish National Liberation Army (INLA). Only PIRA, the most significant threat to the stability of the United Kingdom, is examined in any detail here. The Irish Republican Army (IRA) can trace a history of political violence aimed at severing the link with Britain back into the mid-nineteenth century. Practically moribund militarily in 1969, it re-emerged in the sectarian violence accompanying the political upheaval set in train with the emergence of the Civil Rights movement, principally as a defender of Catholics against sectarian attacks. It split, late in 1969, into two 'wings': the Official IRA, now following a non-sectarian political approach to the status of the province, and PIRA, firmly dedicated to the traditional physical force approach. But both groups have used violence for political ends.

PIRA's violence is aimed at producing a 'war weariness' among electorate and government in Great Britain, enhancing support for a British withdrawal from Northern Ireland. In seeking ultimately an all-Ireland socialist republic of Gaelic hue, unitary rather than federal, it also threatens the constitutional and governmental structure of the Republic of Ireland, whose government it perceives as illegitimate. In 1975, it became dominated by a Northern Ireland leadership and, since 1983, it has operated, with its political 'front', Provisional Sinn Fein (hereinafter 'Sinn Fein'), a dual strategy of seeking its all-Ireland socialist republic through 'armed struggle' (the Armalite in one hand), contesting elections, taking seats at local government level in both parts of Ireland, and being willing to take seats at parliamentary level in the Republic but not in the United Kingdom (the ballot paper in the other hand). The PIRA ceasefires have seen Republican violence maintained by INLA and two further splinter groups: by the Continuity IRA, said to be the military wing of Republican Sinn Fein, a body which split from Sinn Fein in the mid-1980s, and, more worryingly, by what the authorities claim is the military arm of the 32 County Sovereignty Committee opposed to Sinn Fein involvement in the political negotiations of the peace process: the Real IRA.

Militarily, PIRA is well armed and equipped – an experienced terrorist organization able to call, beyond a smaller group of some 300 activists, on a wider range of support of varying degrees (such as turning a blind eye), some willing, some intimidated. As a British military intelligence expert, General Glover, put it in 1978:

There are still areas within the province, both rural and urban, where the terrorists can base themselves with little risk of betrayal and can count on active support in emergencies. The fear of a possible return to Protestant rule and oppression will underpin this kind of support for the Provisionals for many years to come. Loyalist action could quickly awaken it to a much more volatile level. (Cited in Coogan, 1995: 211)

PIRA was initially organized along conventional army lines of brigades and companies, but changes were made as this proved increasingly cumbersome and insecure, and it now appears to be a mixture of 'companies' and so-called 'Active Service Units' (ASUs). 'Company' work consists mainly of 'policing' operations in the areas dominated by PIRA. ASUs carry out operations and attacks in Northern Ireland, in Great Britain and in mainland Europe. Conscious of the need for security, the ASUs operate a cell system of four people, only one of whom is in contact with higher authority, as a mechanism to minimize damage if operatives are caught. PIRA trains its activists in techniques of resisting interrogation. It deploys a security unit to search out, interrogate and execute informers, and has successfully operated an amnesty system for those informers who voluntarily disclose their activities and for those 'supergrasses' who withdrew their statements and evidence, thus reducing the effectiveness of that counterterrorist strategy which had clearly damaged PIRA and other paramilitary groups in the short period of its full operation.

Financially, PIRA has a strong base, with sophisticated money-laundering operations. Its annual income is variously estimated at between £3 and £7 million sterling, generated, mainly in Northern Ireland, from robbery, extortion, defrauding government and the EC, from direct collections and subscriptions, and from a variety of business operations (cheap fare taxis in West Belfast, social clubs, video shops) of varying degrees of legitimacy, which also offer opportunities for 'laundering' money. 'Laundering' is here used to denote the process whereby proceeds and profits from criminal enterprises are converted through business and financial institutions into respectable funds, properties and accounts. Some money and materials have come from Libya and from Irish–American groups in the USA. The resources are used to support ASUs and their dependants, and to fund the operations of Sinn Fein. The latter is said now to take the lion's share of resources. The official British assessment guiding current policy is that PIRA can be contained but not defeated militarily; there is no purely military solution. While the organization has been penetrated by informers operated by British intelligence and the RUC Special Branch, it appears that the security services have not been able to penetrate the higher echelons of PIRA.

The main terrorist paramilitary groups on the Unionist/Loyalist side of the politico-religious divide are the Ulster Volunteer Force (UVF) and the Ulster Freedom Fighters (UFF)/Ulster Defence Association (UDA). The term, 'Loyalist', may seem a strange one for groups prepared to use violence to resist the policies of the elected government. The loyalty of such groups is not to the United Kingdom government per se, but only to such governments and policies as maintain the status of Protestant Ulster as part of the United Kingdom, and the term has thus 'been associated with Protestants who have opposed concessions to the Catholic minority, condemned links between Northern Ireland and the Irish Republic, and resisted Westminster's attempts to enforce political change' (Nelson, 1984: 9). Commentators have drawn a useful distinction between two strands of thought in Unionism: Ulster Loyalist and Ulster British. Roughly speaking, the former are 'Ulster Protestants first and British second; the Ulster British are British first and only secondarily root their identity in Ulster' (Bruce, 1994: 1–2).

The UVF is an illegal, paramilitary organization, which violently opposed concessions by a moderate Ulster government to Catholics, and which, over the course of the troubles since 1968, has carried out sectarian murders (so-called 'anti-IRA action') and committed robberies and bombings, including one in Scotland.

The UFF similarly carries out sectarian attacks as anti-IRA measures. It is a 'flag of convenience' for the formerly legal paramilitary group, the UDA, enabling it to be involved in, but to disown, terrorist activity. The UDA, proscribed in Northern Ireland since August 1992, is a predominantly working-class movement which began in 1971 as a coordinating body for the great variety of Loyalist vigilante groups set up to defend Protestant areas against attack. Politically it has expressed interest in an independent Northern Ireland as well as more traditional calls for devolved government within the United Kingdom. It played a part in politically motivated strikes, one of which, in 1974, brought down the Northern Ireland Executive, wherein power was shared between Catholics and Protestants. It has facets of a political organization but also those of a Protestant 'pro-state terror' body,[2] ready to take the war to the terrorists. In the wake of proscription of the UDA and the effects of the Stevens inquiry into collusion between the security forces and the paramilitaries, the UFF reorganized itself into a more secure 'cell' structure, increased its rate of assassinations and extended their scope to Sinn Fein activists.

Although there have been violent clashes with the security forces, Loyalist violence has rather been directed against Catholics. Loyalist groups seem well-equipped in terms of weaponry. They raise finance through robberies, extortion and protection rackets, some involving apparently bona fide security firms, the operation of cheap fare taxis in working class, Protestant areas of Belfast, a variety of tax frauds connected with the construction industry and, possibly, involvement with drugs and pornography. There is evidence of collusion between Republican and Loyalist groups over demarcating their respective spheres of influence and of cash transactions between them. Money and weaponry have been supplied from sympathizers in Canada (Ontario), Scotland and north-west England, with some purchases made in Poland and South Africa. There are links between paramilitary groups and some members of the predominantly Protestant security forces, particularly the Royal Irish Regiment (formerly the Ulster Defence Regiment), but disagreements on the scale of collusion and over allegations that British intelligence has played a leading or guiding role, using Loyalist paramilitaries as proxies so that their terror becomes 'state' rather than merely 'pro-state'.[3] Clearly, the authorities have not been slow to crack down hard on the activities of Loyalist paramilitaries through internment (1972–5) and imprisonment after conviction in the ordinary or the special 'Diplock' courts. In 1978, the European Court of Human Rights rejected a claim of a policy of politicoreligious discrimination in the operation of internment without trial; the disparity in treatment resulted from the then inability of the police to operate in certain Republican areas (*Ireland* v. *United Kingdom* 1978). Although there have been shadowy contacts between members of Protestant paramilitary groups and members of mainstream Unionist political parties, there appears to be no complete analogue of the relationship between Sinn Fein and PIRA. But there are at least affiliations of view between the UVF and the Progressive Unionist Party and between the UDA and the Ulster Democratic Party, both parties coming to the fore during the 'peace process'. Bruce, the leading academic authority on Loyalist paramilitaries, comments thus on the marginal but important differences between them (pro-state terror groups) and PIRA (an anti-state terror group):

> it seems reasonable to suggest that the Loyalist paramilitaries differ from the IRA in being awkward terrorists, often unsure about what they are doing and sometimes thoroughly incompetent, and suffering in

popularity for their mistakes. In a highly condensed description, one could suggest that the Loyalist paramilitary organisations differ from the IRA in being less well-organised and less well-staffed; less selective and less skilful in their operations; less well-funded and less well-armed; more vulnerable to the policing of the security forces; more vulnerable to the propaganda work of the government's agencies; less well able to develop an enduring political programme and community base for their activities; more vulnerable to racketeering; and hence less popular with the population they claim to defend. (Bruce, 1992: 268)

The Loyalist ceasefires by the UVF and UDA/UFF have held, but the period since their declaration has seen violence carried out by an extreme splinter group, the Loyalist Volunteer Force, opposed to involvement in the political negotiations of the peace process.

The socioeconomic involvement of paramilitary groups in the community (as employer, purveyor of cheap transport or leisure facilities, or a vigilante force dealing with other criminal elements) is of concern since it may make them (particularly on the Republican side) a more acceptable part of the society they have set out to destabilize, perhaps being seen as more efficient or legitimate than the agencies of the state which ostensibly governs the areas concerned. Each group is rooted in its respective community and shares its traditional fears, concerns and political aspirations. There seems a cultural permanence, with little shortage of new recruits or leaders to replace those imprisoned. This suggests that only a political settlement acceptable to the vast majority of both communities in Northern Ireland can hope to bring lasting peace and stability. Security laws and policies can only assist in containing violence at the minimum level possible. It is important to ensure that, so far as is possible, the existence and application of such laws and policies does not retard the attainment of a political solution by exacerbating tension between the security forces and the community, increasing suspicion of government and authority, and increasing political or material support for the terrorists. Possible short-term effectiveness of a policy (such as internment without trial) may have to be traded off against acceptability or longer-term damage to the overall political strategy. Moreover, one must remember that one does not save the liberal state from terrorism by trampling roughshod on its most precious values and postulates; that may be to change the nature of the state for the worse.

The Response in Terms of Emergency or Security Legislation

Since 1968, a legislative response to the problems posed by terrorism has been to enhance the security forces' investigative and coercive powers (inevitably at some cost to civil liberties), to modify the criminal trial process in Northern Ireland and to create new criminal offences. The response by way of enabling United Kingdom courts to try certain offences committed abroad and, in certain respects, to limit the scope of the 'political offence' exception to extradition, is examined elsewhere in this book (see Chapters 6 and 8).

The security legislation is the Prevention of Terrorism (Temporary Provisions) Act 1989 (hereinafter 'PTA'), applicable (generally speaking) throughout the United Kingdom, and the Northern Ireland (Emergency Provisions) Act 1996 (hereinafter 'NIEPA 1996'), embodying more extreme measures applicable to Northern Ireland. Both Acts replaced and extended earlier legislation. The main thrust of this response is to treat terrorist acts purely as another species of crime, its perpetrators as criminals rather than political offenders/ 'freedom fighters'/soldiers/prisoners of war. The aim is to deal with such acts so far as possible through a criminal justice process, albeit a process somewhat modified to make it respond better to problems posed for it by the secret nature of terrorist groups and their ability to intimidate the community, witnesses or jurors. However, where it is perceived that a criminal process cannot work – for example, because certain evidence cannot be disclosed in court for fear of prejudicing intelligence networks, agents or informers, or where the evidence would be insufficient to meet the criminal standard of proof – resort has been had to a variety of extrajudicial, non-court-oriented executive processes (deportation, exclusion from all or part of the United Kingdom, internment without trial). At this point in particular in the security response, especially with respect to terrorism connected with Northern Ireland affairs, there is an increasing danger of marked conflict between the political response and the security measures. The key facets of the anti-terrorist legislation are six in number.

Proscription

Certain groups, including the IRA, are proscribed/banned organizations. Membership or professed membership are serious criminal offences. So are professions of support, for instance organizing a meeting in support of the IRA or parading in public to show

support for it. The rationale of these measures is largely
presentational rather than practical: to enshrine in law public ab-
horrence at the methods used by such groups to achieve political
ends in a liberal democracy. Until recently, neither members nor
supporters of such groups could be directly heard on the broadcasting media, although their words could be reported there as well as
in the press, and film of them could be dubbed using an actor's
voice, fully synchronized with the movements of the speaker's lips.
This odd, arguably counterproductive and unjustifiable restriction
on the polity's 'oxygen of information' was held valid by courts in
Great Britain and Northern Ireland and by the European Commission on Human Rights which declared the challenge inadmissible as
manifestly ill-founded, disclosing no possible breach of the qualified guarantee of freedom of expression in the Convention (see *R.* v.
Secretary of State for the Home Department, ex parte Brind 1991;
Re McLaughlin's Application, 1991; *Brind and McLaughlin* v *UK*
1994).

Stop, Question and Search in Northern Ireland
The security forces may stop any person for so long as is
necessary in order to question him with respect to his identity and
what he knows about any recent explosion or other life-endanger-
ing incident. There are powers of random search of persons and
vehicles in public places for munitions. Searches of premises (other
than dwelling houses) for munitions can be equally random. To
search a dwelling house requires reasonable suspicion but does not
need prior judicial approval. A soldier or police officer, lawfully
searching a person or place, can examine any document (other than
one reasonably believed to be legally privileged) to see if it contains
information useful to terrorists.

Stop and Search in Great Britain
The PIRA campaign of bombing British cities saw the pro-
duction of amending legislation in 1994 and 1996 to create new
powers for the police to stop and search vehicles and people on a
random basis for the purpose of preventing terrorism, to cordon off
areas in connection with a terrorist investigation and to search
without judicial authorization premises within that cordon (Criminal Justice and Public Order Act 1994, s. 81; Prevention of Terrorism
(Additional Powers) Act 1996).

Attacking Terrorist Finances and Material Assistance for Terrorism

Steps have been taken to hamper the financing of terrorism, which go beyond penalizing simple fund raising or supply and include the following: requiring security firms in Northern Ireland to be licensed by the secretary of state; releasing persons (such as bank officials or accountants) from their legal obligation of confidence where money is thought to be for terrorist groups/purposes; creating several offences in connection with possession of or dealing with terrorist money; so structuring these offences as to encourage the giving of information to the authorities about money handled that a person believes may be terrorist money, and so as to facilitate entrapment exercises or 'follow the chain' or 'sting' investigative operations, and criminalizing the withholding of information about such offences.

Both to encourage such cooperation and to deter offenders, the threshold of criminal liability, as compared with comparable offences, is lower, and sometimes the onus of proof with respect to a 'guilty mind' is passed to the defence. The authorities can deploy powers of terrorist investigation which enable access to material relevant to the investigation held even by innocent third parties, for example banks, accountants, lawyers or journalists. 'Terrorist investigation' embraces not only the financial aspect of terrorism, but also its political support, physical force or operational dimensions. The material sought may well be confidential material or have been acquired to further another public interest (as with journalistic material and the public's right to know). Access to it usually involves a judge deciding whether it is in the public interest that confidentiality be overridden and material (such as details of bank accounts or financial transactions) be produced. In emergency, a senior police officer can authorize access. In Northern Ireland, for investigations into a financial/material assistance offence, access may instead be authorized by the secretary of state, thus bypassing the safeguard of independent judicial scrutiny of applications to interfere with privacy and confidentiality. For terrorism connected with Northern Ireland affairs, the police have been able to use the threat of liability for the offence of failing to disclose information about terrorism, as a means to 'persuade' the media to hand over untransmitted film without recourse to this judicial process. Courts can forfeit money or other property held for prohibited purposes, and can restrain dealing in it when proceedings are imminent, so as, for example, to prevent it being moved out of the country. Reciprocal agreements aim to allow courts abroad to enforce UK orders against monies in the foreign jurisdiction, and those of foreign courts to be enforced against terrorist monies/properties in the UK (HC Debs, vol. 143, col. 241; see Prevention of Terrorism (Temporary Provisions) Act 1989 (Enforcement of External Orders), Order 1995, S.I. 1995, No. 760.

Wider Powers of Arrest and Extended Detention without a Criminal Charge Being Brought against the Suspect

By 'wider' is here meant wider than the powers applicable to investigating other serious non-terrorist criminal offences. Under the 'ordinary' law, individuals can only be arrested on reasonable suspicion of a specific criminal offence. Those so suspected of a serious offence may be held without charge for up to 36 hours, extendible up to 96 hours with the approval of a magistrates' court in an *inter partes* hearing.

In contrast, under the PTA, individuals can come into police detention (a) through an arrest anywhere in the UK on reasonable cause to suspect that the person is or has been concerned in the commission, preparation or instigation of acts of terrorism, or (b) after being stopped at a port/airport, generally when travelling to Great Britain from any part of Ireland or leaving Britain to go there (PTA, s.14(1), sch. 5). There is no immigration control because the UK and Ireland form a Common Travel Area, which predates and is independent of the EC regime of free movement. Police at the port/ airport have a power of random examination of travellers to see if any might be terrorists and to detain for further examination those who arouse suspicion. The powers apply to terrorism connected with Northern Ireland affairs and to international terrorism, but are still more extensively used in respect of Northern Irish than international terrorism. A person arrested or who is stopped and examined can be held for up to 48 hours on police authorization. That detention can be extended by up to a further five days (maximum seven in all) with the approval of a secretary of state.

The powers as currently formulated and operated without judicial involvement for more than a four-day period are only saved from violating the ECHR because of a derogation under Art. 15 contingent on the situation of political violence connected with Northern Ireland constituting a public emergency threatening the life of the United Kingdom (see below).

Extended detention serves several purposes: holding a suspect in safe custody pending the checking of alibis, the result of forensic tests, the translation of documents and communicating with other police forces. A prime purpose of extended detention is to enable proper questioning of the suspect in order to gain evidence of involvement in terrorism sufficient to prefer a criminal charge. Most are released without further proceedings, although the 'success rate' for the authorities is significantly higher in Northern Ireland. The power is said to be especially important there, because of local difficulties of gathering evidence by normal police methods. Witnesses able to point to the guilt of particular individuals will not appear in court for fear of the consequences for themselves and their families. So in Northern Ireland there is a heavy reliance on the obtaining of confessions from suspects as the only or the main evidence against them at their criminal trial. There has been much concern about interrogation practices there, with the European Court of Human Rights condemning practices of the British Army in 1971 as inhuman and degrading treatment violative of Art. 3 of the Convention (*Ireland* v. *United Kingdom* 1978: 81–2, 107) and evidence of serious physical abuse of suspects by RUC detectives later in the 1970s (Taylor, 1980). Enhanced supervision and other changes initially reduced the incidence of allegations of abuse but they have recently increased, and interrogation by the RUC has been the subject of criticism in UN bodies (*Review of the Operation of the Northern Ireland (Emergency Provisions) Act 1978 by the Rt. Hon. Sir George Baker OBE*, 1994, Cmnd 9222, hereinafter cited as 'Baker', paras 308–14; *The Guardian*, 29 October 1991: 3).

Persons detained under the PTA have an absolute right, after the first 48 hours, to have someone informed of their detention and to have access to legal advice. Within those first 48 hours, a senior police officer can authorize delay in exercising those rights (for example, because to grant them would be to interfere with the gathering of information about acts of terrorism), but such delay cannot extend more than 48 hours from the person's arrest. In certain cases, a very senior officer can direct that the suspect's interview with his lawyer take place within the sight and hearing of a police officer unconnected with the investigation of the case (Police and Criminal Evidence Act 1984, ss.56, 58 (England and Wales); NIEPA 1996, ss.45–7).

A Choice of Process to Deploy against a Terrorist Suspect: Criminal Charge or some Extrajudicial Executive Process

There is no specific offence of 'terrorism'. Rather, terrorists commit ordinary, serious criminal offences like murder or causing explosions. There are various special offences of support of such groups and handling their property. In Great Britain, terrorists are tried in the ordinary criminal trial process, although there will be extra security arrangements in and around the court building. In Northern Ireland, terrorist trials take place without a jury: trial by a single judge, in so-called 'Diplock courts'. This was introduced for fear of intimidation of jurors and because partisan jurors might produce perverse acquittals. A prime purpose of arrest and detention was to secure confessions. These are more readily admissible in terrorist trials in Northern Ireland than elsewhere in the United Kingdom, but only if the prosecution establishes that no torture, inhuman or degrading treatment and no violence or threat of violence was used to obtain the confession. The trial judge also has a discretion to exclude evidence not obtained by those methods if he considers it would be in the interests of justice to do so. Diplock trials have relied heavily on confessions for convictions; often the real trial is about what happened in the police interrogation centre to produce the confession.

During the first half of the 1980s, significant use was also made of accomplice/'supergrass'/converted terrorist testimony (compare Chapter 5 in the present volume). That strategy was initially successful, with many convictions, and undoubtedly hurt terrorist organizations. Later trials saw judges less happy with the quality of the evidence. The law still permits the conviction of the accused on the uncorroborated testimony of an accomplice, subject to the rule that the arbiter of fact must be warned that to do so may be dangerous, which in Northern Ireland amounts to requiring the trial judge to warn himself to take the utmost care in assessing the evidence and drawing inferences from it. The strategy may ultimately have been detrimental, further eroding public confidence in the administration of justice in Northern Ireland (Bonner, 1987: 23; Greer, 1986: 189). Dissatisfaction with trial by judge alone brought calls for collegiate (preferably three-judge) trial to increase public confidence and make for better decision making (SACHR, 1986–7, 61–2, 63–75) and for a return to jury trial, with safeguards to protect jurors against intimidation (Greer and White, 1986). It has been doubted, however, whether measures proposed would afford them sufficient protection (SACHR, 1986–7, 58–9).

Indeed, instead of major changes in that sort of direction, the government procured the enactment of legislation (Criminal Evidence (Northern Ireland) Order 1988 (NI 20); Criminal Justice and Public Order Act 1994, ss.34–9), making serious inroads into a suspect's 'right to silence' or privilege against self-incrimination, applicable right across the criminal justice spectrum and not solely to persons charged with terrorist offences. The legislation gives to a criminal court or jury powers to draw inferences from a person's failure to answer questions put to him by the police when under caution, or from his failure to give evidence at his trial. Such inferences can only count as supporting evidence: no one can be sent for trial, have a case to answer or be convicted of an offence, solely on the basis of an inference drawn from silence. The powers, thus, strictly speaking, fall short of making failure to give answers a criminal offence in itself or legally compelling someone to incriminate himself, but they may well heighten the pressure to give answers, and concern has been expressed about a danger of false confessions and possible miscarriages of justice (Greer, 1995: 207–12). The powers enable inferences to be drawn in a number of contexts.

The first context is where the accused relies in court on a particular fact in his defence, but had, when questioned by the police under caution, when charged or when officially informed that he might be prosecuted, unreasonably failed to mention that fact at that time. The second situation is where the accused, having properly been asked by the police to do so, failed to account for incriminating objects, substances or marks found on or about him or in the place where he was arrested, or failed to account for his presence at a particular place at the time of his arrest. But here, inferences may only be drawn where the police reasonably believe that his suspicious whereabouts or the presence of the object, mark or substance found on him show his criminal involvement in a particular offence, and the police must have informed him of this and asked for an explanation. The third context in which adverse inferences may be drawn is where the accused chooses not to give evidence at his trial, having been told that he has the opportunity to do so and warned that proper inferences can be drawn from his failure to do so. Concern has been expressed that use of accomplice evidence may undergo some revival, with attempts to use it uncorroborated other than by inferences drawn from the accused's silence, giving rise to a risk of producing unreliable convictions, with detrimental effects on public confidence in the administration of justice (Greer, 1995: 207–12).

Four executive, non-judicial processes have been used in the last two decades:

1. with respect to aliens, refusal of entry to the United Kingdom or deportation from it under the immigration laws on national security grounds, a process used mainly against international terrorist suspects, although it could be used against some Irish citizens suspected of IRA terrorism;

2. exclusion from the United Kingdom of Irish citizens under the anti-terrorist legislation as suspected IRA terrorists;

3. exclusion from Great Britain under that legislation of British citizens connected with Northern Ireland as suspected IRA/Loyalist terrorists, a form of internal exile;

4. the internment without trial of terrorist suspects, a process only used in Northern Ireland (1971–5) and now in abeyance. In the absence of a public emergency threatening the life of the nation within the meaning of Art. 15, internment without trial violates Art. 5 of the ECHR (*Ireland* v. *United Kingdom* 1978: 89–90).

These processes may be effective in removing terrorists from circulation in a particular community, but are less satisfactory than a criminal justice process because they involve varying degrees of interference with an individual without being seen to prove anything against him. Even when decisions are based on good intelligence from the police and security forces, that may well fall short of establishing proof of that person's guilt of a serious criminal offence. The processes ought to be subject to binding review by a judicial body, rather than merely to reference to an adviser or advisers.[4] But exclusion of citizens from one part of a *United* Kingdom is arguably counterproductive, emphasizing Northern Ireland as a place apart to which the government is less committed than it is to Great Britain; in other words, the solution has become part of the problem, contributing further to the suspicion and division that fuels the conflict. That this was the case with internment without trial was eventually conceded and that process was abandoned in 1975. Calls for its reintroduction on a selective, limited basis have been resisted on the grounds that it would alienate a significant sector of the community in Northern Ireland and that any further appearance of repression might increase the flow of funds from sympathizers abroad.

Exclusion as such probably does not breach the United Kingdom's obligations under the ECHR (being an interference with free movement rights not ratified by the United Kingdom, rather than a deprivation of liberty), but actual detention of British citizens pending the making or the execution of an exclusion order arguably does, in the absence of a valid public emergency derogation (see Bonner, 1985, 200–204; for analogous restriction on movement of a Mafia suspect, *Ciulla* v. *Italy* 1989, and compare *Raimondo* v. *Italy* 1994 with respect to Protocol Four). Thankfully, in March 1998, Parliament rendered non-operational the exclusion order process, although powers remain in the statute book capable of rapid executive reintroduction with subsequent parliamentary approval.

The Political Dimension: the 'Hearts and Minds' Aspect of Combating Terrorism

The main public stance of successive governments has been that terrorists are criminals, not freedom fighters, and that there are to be no negotiations with them, concessions to them or amnesties for them. Government will not give in to terrorist blackmail since this only serves to increase terrorism and terrorist demands. This was reflected in ministerial refusal publicly to deal with Sinn Fein's elected representatives until a PIRA ceasefire and, formerly, in the bleak position of British hostages in the Lebanon. This firm approach, however, has not been consistently applied over the last three decades. Discussions with Sinn Fein, seen by government as representing PIRA, preceded the formal announcements in the Downing Street declaration of December 1993 and the PIRA and Loyalist ceasefires in August and October 1994, respectively, and formed a key part of the peace process.

Combating terrorism has not only a security dimension but also political, economic, social and psychological dimensions, the so-called 'hearts and minds' aspects. The United Kingdom's part in promoting conflict resolution of disputes that generate terrorism is inevitably greater in its own domestic sphere, although its colonial past connection with some of the areas involved and its Commonwealth and EC membership may give it a degree of influence elsewhere. Its political response to Northern Ireland terrorism is aimed at achieving a political solution to the divisions of Northern Ireland in the form of constitutional structures to reconcile the mutually inconsistent and conflicting traditions, aspirations and identities of divided communities, while according a consultative role to the Irish government, in order to provide stable, accountable government in the hope that this will help reduce the 'water' of grievance-generated community support in which the terrorist 'fish' swim. Steps to the same end have also been taken to try to meet legitimate grievances with reforms in voting and the electoral boundary system, housing allocation, public sector complaints and discrimination-monitoring mechanisms, and by providing 'fair employment' legislation to try to combat politicoreligious discrimination in employment. Various socioeconomic measures have been taken since 1970, involving a massive inflow of government money to improve Northern Ireland's beleaguered economy and stimulate investment and employment, and to provide social security. But the economy remains depressed and unemployment high, particularly in Catholic areas. Overall lack of success prior to the peace process testifies to the intractability of the problem: concessions to one side tend to alienate or antagonize the other, and such problems have bedevilled the political negotiations of the peace process and continue to threaten acceptance and full implementation of the 'Good Friday' settlement.

Themes in The United Kingdom Response

The legal and political responses manifest a number of themes, not all of which are complementary or consistent. One theme is 'normalization', that anti-terrorist or emergency laws should approximate as closely as circumstances permit to normal or ordinary law. This has been reflected in the increase in situations in which powers require reasonable suspicion for their exercise, in the extension, albeit in modified form, to those detained under the terrorism provisions, of rights of access to lawyers and to have someone informed of the person's detention, and in the internal review of the necessity of detention before the issue of the secretary of state's extension of detention beyond 48 hours. But the tendency to exclude the judiciary from key decisions, and the exclusion of citizens from part of the realm, both run markedly counter to this theme. And, in part, the degree of assimilation with ordinary laws is apparent only because they have moved further in the direction of the emergency regime.

A second and related thread in policy is that of 'criminalization', a shorthand term for a policy which aims to treat terrorists as criminals rather than political offenders or freedom fighters, and which seeks to remove them from circulation in the community through a modified criminal prosecution approach, designed to make them more amenable to conviction and to subjection to a prison regime which aims to treat them in the same way as other criminals convicted of serious crimes. The policy is reflected in the judicial and legislative modifications of the political offence bar to extradition, and in the implementation of agreements of the 'extradite or submit to prosecution' model, examined in Chapters 6 and 8 in this book. In Northern Ireland, execution of this policy has involved extensive modifications to the trial process. The pursuit of this 'criminalization' strategy there brought the demise of the draconian policy of internment/detention without trial. But clearly the executive processes of exclusion and analogous action (refusal of entry, deportation) under the immigration legislation as means of removing suspects from circulation in a particular community conflict with this supposedly dominant theme in policy. They do, however, reflect a theme common to emergency powers of using executive processes, generally not judicially reviewable, to cure the inability of the criminal process to cope.

A third facet, particularly evident in the investigative stage of the criminal process and in the deployment of the security powers of exclusion, refusal of entry or deportation, is a general antipathy to, but some degree of ambivalence about, the protective role of the judiciary as a scrutinizer of executive action: a policy of the marginalization of the judiciary; that is, tending to exclude them from involvement other than in adjudicating on the guilt or innocence of the suspect at trial. The judiciary have aided this by refusing to deploy powers of judicial review as fully and creatively as possible and, reportedly, by refusing to become the agency for making decisions under the terrorism legislation on the extension of detention without charge beyond 48 hours. The ambivalence in attitude can be seen, in that, in contrast, at least in Great Britain, they have been given a central role in sanctioning the deployment of the search and seizure provisions with respect to terrorist investigations. In Northern Ireland, the secretary of state can and does bypass them in relation to investigations into the financing of terrorism.

A further theme is that of international cooperation, reflected in the TREVI group, the third pillar of European Union, aviation security, the 'extradite or submit to prosecution' international agreements (see Chaptes 6 and 8) and in the restraint and confiscation provisions with respect to the financing and proceeds of terrorism. There is also a 'hearts and minds' aspect (policies designed to reduce support for terrorism and enhance support for government and those willing to work for change solely by constitutional means – the peace process being but the latest stage in that). But drastic departures from liberal values enshrined in the European Convention and other human rights' instruments, or from standards accepted as fundamental by the polity, can exacerbate the political problems by fuelling community discontent and distrust, hindering further prospects for a political settlement and affecting international cooperation. The security legislation and its implementation needs to be appraised carefully with that in mind.

The Response of European Judicial Institutions

In a liberal democracy, anti-terrorist policies should comply with the rule of law, not only in the sense of a pure principle of legality, but also in the sense that the rules, legally enacted, should comply with basic human rights and freedoms. In the United Kingdom, with a constitutional system lacking an overriding bill of rights, ensuring that that is done lies primarily with the actors in the political process shaping the making of legislation, although there is also some room for the courts to import such values in the interpretation and application of legislation. But, until October 2000, if aggrieved individuals wished to challenge clear legislative rules as having violated rule of law/human rights values, they must have looked beyond the merely domestic legal order of the United Kingdom.

Two legal regimes of particular relevance are considered here. The first regime (chronologically) is the ECHR, which sets out a wide range of essentially 'first generation' human rights and freedoms, but which has the disadvantage of not as yet being incorporated into United Kingdom law, so that, although it can be prayed in aid by litigants, and the courts can take it into account in interpreting ambiguous provisions of United Kingdom law, ultimately a clearly worded statute will prevail, even if clearly violative of the ECHR, leaving litigants to invoke the machinery of the ECHR as a regional system of human rights protection by petitioning the European Court of Human Rights under Article 34 (until late 1998, by way of the European Commission on Human Rights).[5] If a breach is found by the Court (or until 1999 by the Committee of Ministers of the Council of Europe, endorsing the Commission's report on the merits of the case), there is then an international legal duty on the state to remedy the breach, for example by paying compensation and changing its law or practice.

The second legal regime is the law of the EC, which is rather thinner on relevant human rights values, but has the advantage of being incorporated into United Kingdom law so that it can be relied on by individuals in United Kingdom courts as against governmental entities, but, more importantly, so that it will prevail over other conflicting legal norms, including Acts of Parliament.

The Response of the ECHR

A wide range of issues concerning the United Kingdom's anti-terrorist law and policy have been raised through the machinery of the ECHR: the use of lethal force by the security forces in Northern Ireland (*Stewart* v. *UK* 1984; *Farrell* v. *UK* 1982, 1984; *Kelly* v. *UK* 1993) and in Gibraltar (*McCann and Others* 1995); whether governmental security policies go far enough towards protecting the right to life of the community in Northern Ireland (*W* v. *UK* 1983; *M* v. *UK and Ireland* 1986); interrogation practices of the security forces (*Ireland* v. *UK* 1978; *Donnelly* v. *UK* 1975); internment without trial and politico-religious discrimination in its operation (*Ireland* v. *UK* 1978); prison conditions during the 'dirty' or 'blanket' protest which preceded hunger strikes as a mode of winning political prisoner/special category status for those convicted of terrorist offences (*McFeeley* v. *UK* 1980); powers of examination of travellers at ports/airports (*McVeigh* v. *UK* 1981); whether exclusion orders infringe the right to family life of those excluded (*Ryan* v. *UK* and *Morrey* v. *UK*, both cited in Walker, 1992: 96); various aspects of the regimes of arrest and extended detention of terrorist suspects (see *Fox, Campbell and Hartley* 1990; *Brogan* 1988; *Brannigan and McBride* 1993; all against *UK*; *Murray* v. *UK* 1994, upholding an army arrest power under s.14 of NIEPA 1978); broadcasting restrictions covering members of terrorist organizations and their supporters/apologists (*Brind and McLaughlin* v. *UK* 1994); and, most recently, access to a lawyer during police questioning and the suspect's right to silence as an aspect of a fair criminal trial (*Murray* v. *UK* 1996; *The Guardian*, 9 February 1996; *The Independent*, 1 March 1996; European Court of Human Rights 1996). This chapter highlights here only those cases which raise issues about the security/emergency powers delineated in the third section of this chapter which have reached the stage of final decision by the Court or (until 1999) the Committee of Ministers.

Powers of examination of travellers at ports and airports

The Commission in *McVeigh* (1981) upheld these as permissible deprivations of liberty within Art. 5(1)(*b*) which allows the lawful arrest and detention of a person in order to secure the fulfilment of a legal obligation, in this case the obligation to submit to examination at the ports. It took into account that the obligation arose only in the limited circumstances of travel across a clear geographical or political boundary, and that the purpose of examination was limited and directed to an end of obvious public importance in the context of a serious and continuing threat from organized terrorism. The security check was seen as important in controlling terrorist movement, and resort to detention was legitimate where suspicions were aroused requiring examination in a depth not practicable at the port. The search, questioning, fingerprinting and photographing of the applicants were legitimate interferences with their right to private life, justified under Art. 8(2) as measures in accordance with law which were necessary in a democratic society for the prevention of crime. The retention of fingerprints, photographs and information obtained from the suspects, kept separate from criminal records where the detainee did not have a criminal record, and reserved exclusively for use in the fight against terrorism, was similarly held necessary in the interest of public safety and for the prevention of crime, since intelligence and forensic material may be of critical importance in the detection of terrorist offenders. Refusal to allow two of the applicants to contact their wives was, however, a breach of their right to family life under Art. 8(1) not legitimated by the 'clawback' provisions of Art. 8(2). The government has since introduced better rights, within limits, for detainees to have someone informed of the fact of their detention and to have legal assistance, but rights with respect to the latter have been criticized in *Murray* v. *UK* (1996).

McVeigh (1981) was decided in terms of the ECHR as normally applicable: no 'public emergency' derogation was then in operation, but the Commission interpreted the Convention mindful of a need to allow some leeway to states to deal with terrorism, an approach endorsed by the Court in other cases examined below.

Internment without trial

The regimes of internment without trial, operative in Northern Ireland from August 1971 to December 1975, were one subject of *Ireland* v. *UK* (1978): such regimes are compatible with the ECHR only during a public emergency threatening the life of the nation, otherwise violating Arts 5(1)(c) and (3) which sanction deprivation of liberty only for the purpose of bringing the person arrested and detained into the criminal process. At the time the requisite emergency existed, a matter unsurprisingly not contested by the Irish government which might want to resort to similar powers if threatened by paramilitary violence connected with the affairs of Northern Ireland. Despite two of the regimes being subject only to an 'adviser' system of review, the Court, weakening the due process protection it thought important in *Lawless* v. *Ireland* (1961), held that in the circumstances the measures did not go beyond the limits warranted by the exigencies of the situation. Worryingly, for a body charged with the protection of human rights, it accorded the state a very wide margin of appreciation ('the latitude which signatory states are permitted in their observance of the Convention': Jones, 1995) almost tantamount to rendering European supervision of the situation a merely formal exercise, a pattern repeated in *Brannigan and McBride* (1993). Its decision formulated scant guidance for decision makers.

Arrest and extended detention without charge

The Court has considered two such regimes: in *Brogan* (1988) and in *Brannigan and McBride* (1993), it examined that under the PTAs, delineated in the third section of this chapter, while in *Fox, Campbell and Hartley* (1990) it considered that under NIEPA 1978, now abandoned, which had sanctioned the arrest of a person on mere suspicion of being a terrorist and his detention for up to 72 hours.

Fox, Campbell and Hartley (1990) establishes that, whatever the legal formulation of an arrest power, arrest and detention which is in fact based on 'mere' (albeit honest) as opposed to 'reasonable suspicion' is not compatible, absent an Art. 15 emergency, with Art. 5 of the Convention. *Brogan* (1988) affirms that the PTAs' formulation requiring reasonable suspicion of involvement in terrorism, rather than of a specific criminal offence, is, despite its vagueness, sufficiently in line with that Article's concept of 'offence', although in that case the facts were such that the detainees were being questioned after their arrest about specific offences. Neither case altogether clarifies whether, absent an Art. 15 emergency, the arrest of an individual for questioning for general intelligence purposes, rather than for purposes of attempting to gain enough evidence to bring him within the criminal process (a major criticism of the operation of the powers), is compatible with the Convention (Finnie, 1989: 703; 1991: 288).

The main thrust of *Brogan* (1988) concerns the requirement that persons arrested on suspicion of having committed an offence (as that term is understood in Art. 5) must be brought promptly before a judge or other judicial officer or else released without charge. The decision establishes that, absent an Art. 15 emergency, detention in excess of four days without being brought before a judge or judicial officer does not comply with the notion of promptness in Art. 5(3), but lays down no maximum period for which suspects could be detained without charge without breaching the Convention as normally applicable. Instead of complying with the judgment by introducing a judicial element with respect to extensions of detention without charge beyond the initial 48-hour period in the PTA, the United Kingdom government derogated from the Convention under Art. 15 in respect of persons detained in connection with terrorism connected with Northern Ireland affairs and gave an assurance that suspects detained in connection with international terrorism would not be detained under the PTA for more than four days. That derogation was upheld as valid by the Court in *Brannigan and McBride* v. *UK* (1993). The Court's finding that the requisite emergency situation existed in the United Kingdom because of the violence within Northern Ireland and terrorist incidents connected with Northern Ireland on the mainland was, unsurprising, given the low threshold set by its test as formulated and applied in *Lawless* in 1961. The Court there defined it as 'an exceptional situation of crisis or emergency which affects the whole nation and constitutes a threat to the organised life of the community of which the State is composed'. It is for the Convention agencies to determine whether such an emergency existed. The margin of appreciation afforded to states effectively means that those agencies examine whether the government acted manifestly unreasonably or arbitrarily, whether it had sufficient reason to believe that there existed such an emergency, rather than whether the agency would have acted differently had it been faced with the decision. It involves a degree of according the state the benefit of the doubt, a presumption in its favour. Too wide a margin of appreciation may operate to the detriment of effective protection of human rights and unduly dilute the crucial element of independent European supervision (Jones, 1995: 449).

Nor was it surprising that the Court did not dwell on the fact that the government had withdrawn an earlier derogation. The withdrawal of the notice did not mean there was no emergency

strictly warranting the use of the power impugned, but merely
reflected the government's, as it turned out mistaken, legal view
that the power was compatible with Art. 5 as normally operative.

What was controversial and the subject of criticism, however, was
the Court's acceptance that the exclusion of the judiciary from extension of detention decisions was strictly required by the exigencies of
the situation. That finding involves a very wide margin of appreciation for government, since the reasons government provided (an *ex
parte* process is non-judicial and risks tarnishing the independence of
the judiciary, and material might not be discloseable to the individual, thus weakening his chances of making proper representations)
are by no means convincing and ignore the protective role of the
judge in scrutinizing proposed executive action in *ex parte* proceedings (for example, applications by the police for search warrants)
where such scrutiny is thought of as providing protection for individual interests. The judge could safely see all relevant security material
and seek to protect the individual's interests by subjecting the material to close, independent scrutiny. This would surely be better than
habeas corpus proceedings (which the Court saw as a safeguard)
which can only probe the legality of the home secretary's extension
and the reasonableness of the initial arrest (Bonner, 1989: 450–51;
Marks, 1993: 360; 1995: 69). On this aspect of the case, the dissent-
ing judgments are to be preferred (particularly those of Walsh and
Pettiti JJ). The decision gives insufficient weight to the fact of judicial
involvement in extension of decisions in civil law countries in Europe
(for example, France, Italy and Spain) and fails properly to address
the argument of Amnesty International that such judicial involvement may be invaluable in preventing abuses which can occur during
incommunicado detention (Harris *et al.*, 1995: 500). The Court,
however, has gone some way to dealing with those dangers in that
part of its recent judgment in *Murray* v. *United Kingdom* (*The Guardian*, 9 February 1996; *The Independent*, 1 March 1996; European
Court of Human Rights, 1996) dealing with denial of access to a
lawyer during the first 48 hours of detention under the PTA in
Northern Ireland.

'*Fair trial': the right to silence and access to a lawyer*

In *Murray*, the Court considered the case of someone arrested under
the PTA in a house in which a PIRA informer had been held
captive. He was denied access to a solicitor during the first 48 hours
of his detention at the police station in accordance with the delay
provisions in the emergency legislation and cautioned that adverse

inferences might be drawn from his silence during the pre-trial stage of criminal proceedings. The applicant was convicted, with the trial judge, sitting without a jury in a 'Diplock' court, drawing adverse inferences from the applicant's failure to account for his presence at the house and from his remaining silent during the trial.

The European Court of Human Rights held that, on the particular facts of this case, the drawing of adverse inferences from such silence did not violate Art. 6(1), (2) (the right to a fair criminal trial), even though the right to remain silent under police questioning and the privilege against self-incrimination lay at the heart of fair trial procedure under those provisions. Whether drawing adverse inferences from silence infringed fair procedure had to be determined on a case-by-case basis, having particular regard to the situations in which the law permitted them to be drawn, the weight attached to them by the national courts in assessing all the evidence and the degree of compulsion inherent in the situation. Here, taking account of the provisions of United Kingdom law permitting inferences to be drawn as supporting evidence only and after the suspect had been given proper warning, and having regard to the weight of evidence against the applicant, it was in this case only a matter of common sense to draw an adverse inference from his failure to give an explanation for his presence at the house. It was not unreasonable or unfair in these circumstances. However, given that such inferences could be drawn, the concept of fairness enshrined in Art. 6 mandated that the accused have access to a lawyer to take proper advice in the dilemma in which he found himself. Its denial in the first 48 hours of detention breached the rights of the accused under Art. 6(1) (the general right to a fair criminal trial) and Art. 6(3)(c) (the right to defend oneself through legal assistance).

Murray falls short of upholding the compatibility of all the interferences with the right to silence examined in the third section of this chapter, but requires a right of immediate and unconditional access to a lawyer in circumstances where the law permits adverse inferences to be drawn from silence. The delay provisions in United Kingdom law will have to be removed or else sought to be protected by a further notice of derogation under Art. 15, something only possible as regards the threat from Northern Ireland terrorism.

An overall assessment of the role of the Convention organs

In these cases, the Court and the Commission have taken primarily a 'state-oriented' rather than a 'protection of individual rights'-oriented

approach to interpretation, stretching to the limit the normal provisions of the Convention, mindful of the need for liberal–democratic
states to take action to combat a growing and serious threat to their
society and, perhaps, conscious of the wider threat to Europe as a
whole and their own states. The recent *Murray* case, however, does
indicate a stricter line with respect to access to legal advice and
shows the Court at its most comfortable in dealing with pre-trial
criminal procedure. Where Art. 15 has come into play with respect
to political violence connected with Northern Ireland affairs, the
Court and Commission have granted such a wide margin of appreciation that European supervision has been diluted to a barely
intrusive level. Doubtless this degree of deference can be explained
by the relative youth of the European system of protection, its
dependence on state consent and support, and the fact that the
emergency measures under scrutiny have been invoked by a liberal
democratic state with a democratically elected executive faced with
a degree of political violence not experienced elsewhere in Western
Europe. In contrast, in the *Greek Case* (1969), faced with the
spectre of an undemocratic junta using such powers to undermine
democracy, the Commission, arguably applying a stricter test of
emergency, found that none existed and that Greece had breached
the Convention. But, if the deferential approach taken with respect
to political violence connected with Northern Ireland is only to be
expected of conservative European judicial bodies, that is nevertheless of some concern, since it is in times of crisis and emergency that
domestic mechanisms of accountability and control are found want-
ing in providing the careful consideration which needs to be given
to civil liberties issues and rule of law values in the framing of anti-
terrorist powers. Fortunately, the decision of the Court in *Aksoy* v.
Turkey (1996) that detention for up to 15 days without access to a
court exceeded what was required by the exigencies of an emergency situation, makes clear that its willingness to defer to the state
is not unlimited, particularly where there has been widespread concern within the family of European nations about the nature of that
state and its commitment to human rights values.

The Response of the ECJ

European Union provisions on combating terrorism are contained within its third 'pillar', creating a framework for cooperation
and, if thought appropriate, joint action, in the fields of justice and
home affairs (including such matters of common interest as immigration policy, judicial cooperation in criminal matters and police

cooperation for purposes of preventing and combating terrorism) while complying with the European Convention on Human Rights. This 'pillar' so far falls outside the ambit of EC law interpreted and applied by the European Court of Justice (ECJ). But the right of free movement between member states of economically active EU citizens or those who wish to be so active (something within the first 'pillar') provides a context for challenging exclusion orders (EOs) under the PTA (and related 'security' aspects of immigration processes of denial of entry and deportation) as a means of refusing a person entry to a particular territory or of expelling him from it. The litigation produced by the reimposition of an EO on Gerry Adams, president of Sinn Fein, prohibiting him from entering Great Britain, looked set to raise interesting substantive questions for the ECJ. Adams is both a British and an Irish citizen. The United Kingdom court which considered his case and upheld the EO as valid in terms purely of 'national' law (affirming the traditional 'hands off' approach of United Kingdom courts to such 'security' matters) and in principle as within the 'public security' exceptions to free movement, decided to refer to the ECJ questions about the compatibility of the EO with rights of free movement as regards the newer Art. 8a(1) in that sphere inserted by the Maastricht Treaty (was the Article merely declaratory or did it confer rights of free movement additional to those which existed under the EEC Treaty prior to its amendment by the Treaty on European Union; did it have direct effect, whether the provisions covered situations wholly internal to a single member state, and was this such a situation) and a question of law about the proportionality principle in this case which, in relation to limitations on rights of free movement, involved freedom of speech (Adams wanted to come to Great Britain to address MPs and journalists in the House of Commons) and national security (*R. v. Secretary of State for the Home Department, ex parte Adams* 1995; *The Independent*, 27 July 1994).

However, one early effect of the first PIRA ceasefire and the current 'peace process' was the removal in October 1994 of the EO against Adams and a successful application by the secretary of state to the court to withdraw the reference and dismiss Adams's application for judicial review (*R. v. Secretary of State for the Home Department, ex parte Adams* 1995; *The Independent*, 28 April 1994). In *McQuillen*, Sedley J made no such reference to the ECJ because at that time the one in *Adams* was pending, but gave liberty to reapply if that was withdrawn (*R. v. Secretary of State for the Home Department, ex parte McQuillen* 1995, 426). In terms of substance, the matter would turn on the scope and extent of the 'public policy' and 'public security' exemptions to free movement rights: to which Articles they apply (probably across the board) and what they permit. This writer doubts whether the ECJ, if ever faced with those substantive issues, would operate a stricter level of review of executive action in the security context than that operated by United Kingdom courts or the organs of the European Convention on Human Rights (Douglas-Scott and Kimble, 1994: 524–5).

Another reference for a preliminary ruling in a case involving the PTA has, however, been disposed of by the ECJ. *Gallagher* (Case C-175/94, Judgment of the Court (Sixth Chamber), 30 November 1995, 1995 ECRI-4523), however, has so far only involved the narrower question of the mode of decision making with respect to EOs and the means for challenging them in terms of substance and merits, as distinct from pure legality, through the adviser system. The ECJ (following the Advocate General's opinion) considered Art. 9(1) of Directive 64/221/EEC (on the coordination of special measures concerning the movement and residence of foreign nationals which are justified on the grounds of public policy, public security or public health) as prohibiting, save in cases of urgency, the administrative authority from taking a decision authorizing expulsion *before* the 'competent authority' has given its opinion. Although it does not preclude that 'competent authority' from being appointed by the administrative authority which decides on refusal or expulsion, the 'competent authority' must be able to perform its duties in absolute independence, not subject to any control by the administrative authority empowered to take the measures provided for in the directive. It is for the national court to determine in the case whether the system meets these requisites.

Consequential administrative and legal changes to the process by which EO decisions are made have been effected through regulations (The Prevention of Terrorism (Exclusion Order) Regulations 1996, approved by Parliament on 14 March 1996, HC Debs, vol. 273, cols 1124–71) which retain the adviser system. Whether the adviser(s) can be a 'competent authority' remains to be seen; mere civil servants in the appropriate department clearly cannot. Unfortunately, in an area of fundamental importance to human rights, the decision in *Gallagher* has not proved a catalyst for subjecting EOs to a binding process of review by an independent judicial body. Instead, the catalyst for providing such a body with respect to national security/terrorism exclusions or deportations under the immigration legislation was the European Court of Human Rights' decision under the European Convention on Human Rights in *Chahal* (1996), responding to which forms the principal rationale of the Special Immigration Appeals Commission Act 1997.[6] That Act made no mention of exclusion orders under the PTA, anticipating the rendering non-operational in March 1998 of the whole exclusion order regime, on a principled basis, regardless of progress in the 'peace process'.

The Current Search for a Political Solution: the Impact of the Northern Ireland 'Peace Process'[7]

The Northern Ireland 'peace process' is a current political process of yet uncertain outcome, despite the Good Friday 'agreement', outlined below. It has involved the governments of the United Kingdom and of Ireland, and those political parties in Northern Ireland committed to change by peaceful means alone. It is a process which, with the good offices of the President of the United States as facilitator rather than mediator, is aimed at securing an end to violence and the sociopolitical causes which spawn and sustain it, through a settlement reached in all-inclusive talks embracing even parties previously supportive of the use of violence to achieve political ends. The process looked set to make progress with the announcement of ceasefires by PIRA (August 1994) and the Loyalist paramilitaries (October 1994) in response to clarifications of the Downing Street Declaration (December 1993). But that optimism progressively faded as the process stalled over the decommissioning of paramilitary weapons as a precondition for Sinn Fein to be admitted to all-party talks, and then suffered a severe blow with the resumption of hostilities by PIRA in February 1996 and the London and Manchester bombings. The Loyalist ceasefire has, for the main part, remained in place.

Proximity talks involving all parties other than Sinn Fein were followed by elections within Northern Ireland to elect representatives to a forum and to take part in all-party talks which began in June 1996, involving only those parties clearly renouncing violence. Despite an enhanced vote in those elections and in the May 1997 General Election, the lack of a new PIRA ceasefire meant Sinn Fein's exclusion from all-party talks. Given that no renewed ceasefire by PIRA seemed in prospect, that Loyalist paramilitaries threatened to retaliate if PIRA terrorist acts continued, that the issue of decommissioning of weapons remained unresolved, that the Loyalist marching season in 1997 further divided the two commu-

nities and witnessed a return to a form of 'ethnic cleansing', and
that the parties all seemed to be as far apart as ever on desired
substantive outcomes, there was an understandable mood of pessi-
mism about the prospects for success through the talks. However,
the General Election produced a Labour government with no need
to rely on Unionist political parties for support in the House of
Commons, headed by a prime minister committed to change and
with a dynamic secretary of state for Northern Ireland in Dr Mo
Mowlam. That government, and its Irish counterpart, made a crucial concession that decommissioning of arms, rather than being a
precondition of the admission of Sinn Fein to the talks, could
instead proceed in parallel with its admission (the 'twin track'
initiative). A new PIRA ceasefire came in response to a call from
Sinn Fein's leader, Gerry Adams, in July 1997. Sinn Fein, having
signed up to the Mitchell principles on non-violence, was admitted
to the political talks on 9 September 1997. The Ulster Unionists
joined them a week later. So the political talks, under the chairman-
ship of former American Senator George Mitchell, proceeded with
the inclusion of all parties save Dr Paisley's Democratic Unionist
Party and Mr McCarteney's United Kingdom Unionist Party, which
chose not to participate.

The United Kingdom response to these first PIRA and Loyalist
ceasefires saw a cautious easing of security measures, but the continuance in force of the bulk of the emergency or security legislation,
because, despite the ceasefires, the paramilitaries retained intact
their structure, organization and arsenals and their capacity to
strike whenever they chose, and some powers were in any event
needed to protect against international terrorism. In September
1994, the broadcasting restrictions were lifted. In October that
year, all remaining closure orders on border roads in Northern
Ireland were rescinded and the exclusion orders on Gerry Adams
and Martin McGuinness, the Sinn Fein leaders, were lifted. By
February 1995, the Northern Ireland secretary had revoked all the
exclusion orders made by him, while, by March 1996, only 33 of
those imposed by the Home Secretary remained. The latter's reluctance to revoke more stemmed from a fear that those covered by
them posed a security threat to the mainland and might take the
opportunity afforded by any removal of their order to prepare for a
resumption of hostilities. The presence of the army on the streets of
Northern Ireland was greatly reduced, the Northern Ireland civilian
search unit was disbanded and many vehicle control zones were
removed, the number of house searches declined by 75 per cent, the

number of detentions under the PTA substantially declined on both sides of the Irish Sea and the London police forces were able to scale down the high-profile armed patrols they had been operating in central London. The remission rate for prisoners in Northern Ireland was increased from one-third to one-half of sentence.

Despite the continuance of punishment beatings and shootings on both sides of the sectarian divide and the murder in Northern Ireland of a number of alleged drug dealers by Direct Action Against Drugs (thought to be a flag of convenience for PIRA), a mood of optimism prevailed in a situation of 'partial peace'. The ending of the PIRA ceasefire in February 1996 saw enhanced security powers given to the police on the mainland and a range of security restrictions were reimposed in Northern Ireland. With the reinstatement of the PIRA ceasefire in July 1997, a range of measures were relaxed. Many de-escalatory steps taken during the initial ceasefire had in any event remained in place (for example, the reopening of all closed border roads). But the march of progress towards normalization can only be at a pace consistent with changes in the level of violence. It has not yet been possible to introduce a judicial element into review of extended detention without charge decisions under the PTA. But the indications were that internment without trial would be removed from the statute book rather than merely remaining non-operational but readily reinvokable. In addition, by October 1997 all exclusion orders had been lifted and that security regime was rendered non-operational by Parliament in March 1998 – but that seems to reflect a Labour government view that such a regime was wrong in principle rather than reflecting progress in the political talks.

The talks survived prominent instances of the use of violence by the UFF and by PIRA, resulting in the short-term exclusion of related political parties, the Ulster Democratic Party and Sinn Fein, respectively. They survived, despite the continuation of violence by extremist splinter groups from militant republicanism and loyalism; however, they looked very much like collapsing in failure as the Maundy Thursday midnight deadline approached. Thanks to immense efforts by all concerned, including the British and Irish prime ministers, on Good Friday an agreement was produced full of compromises in respect of which all parties present declared their support. This agreement[8] is founded firmly on the principle that there can be no change in the status of Northern Ireland as part of the United Kingdom without the consent of a majority of the people of Northern Ireland, something to be em-

bodied in a United Kingdom statute and in changes to the Irish
Constitution. The agreement established a framework for an intri-
cate institutional structure designed to deal with all the relationships
within and between the two islands. There is now a Northern
Ireland Assembly, elected by proportional representation, exercising devolved legislative powers in relation to Northern Ireland,
with the courts having the power to invalidate legislation contrary
to the devolutionary statute or to a bill of rights. Executive power
in relation to devolved matters is now exercised on its behalf by a
power-sharing executive whose cross-community composition reflects that of parties in the Assembly. It has David Trimble, the
Ulster Unionist leader, as first minister and Seamus Mallon, the
leader of the constitutional nationalist party, the SDLP, as his
deputy. There is now also a North–South Ministerial Council,
comprising ministers from the Northern Ireland and Irish governments, to develop consultation, cooperation and action (including
on an all-island, cross-border basis) within the island of Ireland
on matters of mutual interest. A British–Irish Council, made up of
representatives of the United Kingdom and Irish governments and
of devolved institutions in Northern Ireland, Scotland and Wales,
the Isle of Man and the Channel Islands has been established. This
Council will exchange information, consult, discuss and try to
reach agreement on matters of common interest such as agricul-
ture, transport and approaches to EU issues. A new treaty between
the UK and Ireland, replacing the Anglo-Irish Agreement (1985),
set up a new British–Irish conference to discuss matters of mutual
interest, at prime ministerial or other suitable ministerial level,
and to keep under review the workings of the new instut[sic]utional
arrangements. Within Northern Ireland there is now a Human
Rights Commission, an important practical and institutional underpinning of the new bill of rights, and an Equality Commission
to enforce fair employment and other anti-discrimination legislation. An independent Commission was established to make
recommendations for policing in Northern Ireland and there is
ongoing United Kingdom governmental review, involving an independent element, of the criminal justice system in the province.
The United Kingdom and Irish governments set in place mechanisms for the accelerated release of paramilitary prisoners attached
to organizations maintaining ceasefires. This meant that all such
prisoners would be released within two years. Finally, but cru-
cially, the participants in the talks have reaffirmed their commitment
to work with the Independent Commission on Decommissioning,

to total paramilitary disarmament and to try to achieve that within two years of the agreement being endorsed by referendums north and south of the border in May 1998.

Such an agreement founded on compromises did not please everyone. There are indications of significant opposition within Trimble's Ulster Unionist Party. The more extreme Loyalists, repesented by Paisley's Democratic Unionist Party are opposed. Sinn Fein's annual conference endorsed the agreement in April 1998 and it won acceptance in referendums held in Northern Ireland and in the Republic in May 1998. But if PIRA were eventually to reject it and return to violence, possibly producing a comparable violent response from mainstream or extreme Loyalist paramilitaries, the security legislation examined in this chapter will remain largely intact, with adaptations here and there to meet new threats or to be seen to be 'doing something'. If significant violence spread to the mainland, the exclusion order regime could be reintroduced. 'Selective' internment of the organizers and operatives of political violence, on one or both sides of the border in Ireland, is unlikely to be an option for fear of alienating the nationalist community and undercutting support for the SDLP (the constitutional nationalist party) and of opprobrium abroad.

If, however, the agreement is endorsed by the bulk of Republicans, Nationalists and Loyalists, but violently resisted by small, extremist groups on both sides of the sectarian divide, resort to the drastic option of internment might paradoxically have some attraction as a means of producing stability to ensure the success of the agreed scheme. However, widespread agreement on a new mode of government – and this agreement gives greater hope of that than at any time in the last 25 years – might so undermine community support for those inclined to violence as to make them more amenable to policing and the criminal process (the community might assist in giving them up) and render internment unnecessary. But problems of intimidation of witnesses and/or jurors could remain, so that dismantling of the 'Diplock' regime might well not be an immediate prospect. Over time, however, the level of terrorist violence might merely be residual, allowing normal policing using standard powers for combating serious crime with no greater need for military support than elsewhere in the United Kingdom and a criminal justice system with jury trial at its heart. That would open up the prospect of a permanent United Kingdom anti-terrorist statute to deal principally with international terrorism, in particular countering terrorist funding and arms trafficking and preventing the United Kingdom being a safe haven for those who promote or support terrorism. A consultation paper, based in part on recommendations of the review carried out by Lord Lloyd of Berwick on the assumption that the peace process would succeed, was published in December 1998.[9] The removal of political violence connected with Northern Irish affairs as a terrorist threat to the United Kingdom would thus mean the demise of the Northern Ireland emergency provisions, and the end of proscription and exclusion under the PTA and the offences connected with those processes. But the powers of arrest and extended detention without charge and the provisions to deal with the financing of terror are likely to be retained in permanent if modified form to deal with the perceived threat of international terrorism and international cooperation on that matter. However, given that compliance with the ECHR after *Brogan* v. *UK* (1988) and without an emergency situation allows only four days' detention without judicial involvement, reformulation of the arrest/detention provisions will be necessary, inevitably provoking a debate as to the necessity in that sphere for wider powers than those afforded to deal with other species of serious crime (including non-Irish forms of domestic terrorism) which similarly allow up to four days' detention.

Those who thought the best outcome is a united Ireland will remain unhappy with the agreement. Such an outcome would probably reduce the tendency to violence on the Republican side of the divide (their main goal achieved) but, unless overwhelmingly endorsed by the people of Northern Ireland, would be unlikely to produce greater stability than that offered by the agreement. Extreme Loyalists might well violently resist absorption into the new entity, and attacks by them on the Catholic community in the North of Ireland might well provoke 'defensive' military action by PIRA. All such violence would then be met in the new entity by a battery of security laws similar to those examined in the third section of this chapter (Hogan and Walker, 1989). In short, there is the possibility that the nature of the problem would remain the same (the use of violence for political ends centring on the issue of to which state Northern Ireland should belong): all one would have altered is its location and the identity of the government responsible for dealing with it.

Developments Since April 1998

Since 1998 the 'peace process' has stumbled, encountering peaks of hope and troughs of despair. First there came endorsement of the agreement in a referendum in Northern Ireland, although the result manifested a significant degree of opposition amongst Unionists. The Northern Ireland Assembly was put in place and a cross-party, cross-community executive was re-established, following a review of the peace process conducted by former US Senator Mitchell, with the Unionist leader, David Trimble as first minister and two ministers from Sinn Fein. However, the two ministers from Dr Paisley's DUP boycotted the executive. PIRA appointed an unnamed representative to engage in dialogue with General de Chastelain over arms decommissioning. Release of prisoners from organisations maintaining a ceasefire was completed. The problem remains actual decommissioning of paramilitary weapons, the deadline for which is now June 2001. PIRA indicated no decommissioning until the democratic institutions have been tried and tested, a process of years not months. The UK government then suspended the Executive and the devolutionary arrangement. Both were re-instated when PIRA set in motion periodic inspection of its arms dumps by PIRA selected international observers, Cyril Ramaphosa and Martti Ahtisaari. The danger of entire collapse of the structure was averted. But peace remains fragile and the current feuding between loyalist paramilitary groups in Belfast gives cause for concern.

The period since Good Friday 1998 has seen the emergence of a variety of splinter groups opposed to the agreement: the Real IRA, the Continuity IRA, the Loyalist Volunteer Force. The Omagh bombing in August 1998 saw legislation rushed through Parliament to amend the PTA 1989 to attempt to make it easier to convict persons thought to be members of proscribed organizations not maintaining an effective ceasefire, and to forfeit property. An alternative policy of highly selective internment without trial was not pursued. There are real doubts about the effectiveness of the response chosen. There has been little attempt to abandon the security apparatus in terms of legislation, although the exclusion order part of the PTA was put into abeyance in March 1998, and the power of internment removed from the statute book. The RUC is to be renamed and reformed to make it more attractive in recruitment terms to Catholics. So far the plans have evoked a hostile response from police representative bodies covering RUC personnel and from political Unionism, deepening the impasse.

As to the future, the Government, building on Lord Lloyd of Berwick's report[10] and the consultation paper, *Legislation against Terrorism*,[11] has put through Parliament its Terrorism Bill. The Terrorism Act, 2000 renders permanent the central provisions of

the PTAs (other than exclusion orders) and extends them to terrorism generally. To this end, it deploys a very wide definition of
terrorism and terrorist, apt, on broad interpretation, to catch those
engaged in varieties of public protest and those involved in industrial disputes involving key utilities like water, electricity, or the
National Health Service.[12] It continues, as temporary provisions
pending a final peace in Northern Ireland, the central provisions of
NIEPA (e.g. Diplock courts).

For over a quarter of a century, the United Kingdom, its anti-
terrorist laws and policies have been a prime focus of attention for
students of the phenomenon of terrorism, principally in terms of
constructing repressive legal regimes to contain terrorism. The Good
Friday agreement presents an opportunity for the United Kingdom
to be studied instead from a more rewarding perspective: how to
achieve and formulate constitutional and political structures to re-
vitalize a society divided by political violence and the burden of its
sectarian history. It remains to be seen whether that opportunity
will be grasped or missed.

Notes

1   Material in this section comes from Bishop and Mallie (1988: ch.
     2), Coogan (1987: ch. 1; 1995: ch. 9), Toolis (1995) and Bruce
     (1992; 1994).

2   On the concept 'pro-state', as distinct from 'state' terror, see Bruce
     (1992: ch. 11).

3   Contrast Bruce (1992: ch. 8) with Coogan (1995: 262–71).

4   This now happens with immigration powers: see the Special Immi-
     gration Appeals Commission Act 1998.

5   The Human Rights Act 1998 incorporates the Convention from 2
     October 2000. Judges will not be able to use it to invalidate stat-
     utes, but otherwise decisions of public bodies will be unlawful if
     they do not comply with the Convention.

6   1997, c. 68.

7   The information in this section of the chapter is taken from sundry
     newspaper reports and government statements in the House of
     Commons, and the Northern Ireland Office Website (htttp://
     www.nio.gov.uk). A very useful source is an *Irish Times* special
     publication, *The Path to Peace* (April 1998), which is available at
     http://www.irishtimes.com/irishtimes/special/peace/).

8   The text of the agreement, distributed to all homes in Northern Ireland, can be found at http://www.nio.gov.uk/agreement.htm.

9   *Legislation against Terrorism* Cm. 4178 (December 1998).

10   Cm. 3420 (October 1996) (2 vols).

11   Cm. 4178.

12   See clauses 1, 38, 39.

References

Aksoy v. Turkey. 1996. Judgment of the Court, 18 December. 23 *European Human Rights Reports (EHRR)* 553.

Bishop, Patrick and Eamon Mallie. 1988. *The Provisional IRA*. London: Corgi Books.

Bonner, David. 1985. *Emergency Powers in Peacetime*. London: Sweet & Maxwell.

Bonner, David. 1987. 'Combating Terrorism: Supergrass Trials in Northern Ireland'. *Modern Law Review* 51.

Bonner, David. 1989. 'Combating Terrorism in the 1990s: the Role of the Prevention of Terrorism (Temporary Provisions) Act 1989'. *Public Law* 440.

Brannigan and McBride v. UK. 1993. Series A, Vd. 258–B, Judgment of the Court, 26 May.

Brind and McLaughlin v. UK. 1994. Nos 18714/91 and 18759/91, 77A DR 42.

Brogan v. UK. 1988. Series A, Vol. 145, Judgment of the Court, 24 November.

Bruce, Steve. 1992. *The Red Hand: Protestant Paramilitaries in Northern Ireland*. Oxford: Oxford University Press.

Bruce, Steve. 1994. *The Edge of the Union: The Ulster Loyalist Political Vision*. Oxford: Oxford University Press.

Chahal v. UK. 1996. Judgment of the Court, 15 November. 23 *EHRR* 413.

Ciulla v. Italy. 1989. Series A, Vol. 148, Judgment of the Court, 22 February.

Coogan, Tim. 1987. *The IRA*. London: Fontana.

Coogan, Tim. 1995. *The Troubles: Ireland's Ordeal 1966–1995 and the Search for Peace*. London: Hutchinson.

Donnelly v. UK. 1975. Nos 5577–5583/72, 4 DR 64.

Douglas-Scott, S. and J. Kimble. 1994. 'The Adams Exclusion Case: New Enforceable Rights in the post Maastricht European Union'. *Public Law* 516.

European Court of Human Rights. 1996. *Press Release* 57 (8 February).

Farrell v. *UK*. 1982. No. 9013/80, 30 DR 96.

Farrell v. *UK*. 1984. 38 DR 44.

Finnie, W. 1989. 'The Prevention of Terrorism Act and the European Convention on Human Rights'. *Modern Law Review* 52.

Finnie, W. 1991. 'Anti-Terrorist Legislation and the European Convention on Human Rights'. *Modern Law Review* 54.

Fox, Campbell and Hartley v. *UK*. 1990. Series A, Vol. 182, Judgment of the Court, 30 August.

The Greek Case. 1969. 12 *Yearbook of the European Convention on Human Rights: The Greek Case*. Opinion of the Commission.

Greer, Steven. 1986. 'Supergrasses and the Legal System in Britain and Northern Ireland'. *Law Quarterly Review* 102.

Greer, Steven. 1995. *Supergrasses: A Study in Anti-Terrorist Law Enforcement in Northern Ireland*. Oxford: Clarendon Press.

Greer, Steven and Antony White. 1986. *Abolishing the Diplock Courts: The Case for Restoring Jury Trial to Scheduled Offences in Northern Ireland*. London: Cobden Trust.

Harris, D.J., M. O'Boyle and Clive Warbrick. 1995. *Law of the European Convention on Human Rights*. London: Butterworths.

Hogan, Gerard and Clive Walker. 1989. *Political Violence and the Law in Ireland*. Manchester: Manchester University Press.

Ireland v. *United Kingdom*. 1978. 2 EHRR 25, 98–100.

Jones, T. 1995. 'The Devaluation of Human Rights under the European Convention'. *Public Law* 430.

Kelly v. *UK*. 1993. No. 17579/90, unreported decision.

Lawless v. *Ireland*. 1961. 1 *EHRR* 15.

M. v. *UK and Ireland*. 1986. 9387/82, 47 DR 27.

Marks, Susan. 1993. 52 *Cambridge Law Journal* 360.

Marks, Susan. 1995. 15 *Oxford Journal of Legal Studies* 69.

McCann and Others v. *UK*. 1995. Judgment of the Court, Series A, Vol. 324, 27 September.

McFeeley v. *UK*. 1980. No. 8317/78, 20 DR 44.

McVeigh v. *UK*. 1981. 5 *EHRR* 71.

Murray v. *UK*. 1994. Judgment of the Court, Series A, Vol. 300, 28 October.

Murray v. *UK*. 1996. Judgment of the Court, 8 February. 22 *EHRR* 29.

Nelson, Sarah. 1984. *Ulster's Uncertain Defenders*. Belfast: Appletree Press.

R. v. *Secretary of State for the Home Department, ex parte Adams* (Divisional Court, QBD). 1995. All ER (EC) 177.

R. v. *Secretary of State for the Home Department, ex parte Brind*. 1991. 1 All ER 720.

R. v. Secretary of State for the Home Department, ex parte McQuillen. 1995. 4 All ER 400.

Raimondo v. Italy. 1994. Judgment of the Court, Series A, Vol. 281–A, 22 February.

Re McLaughlin's Application. 1991. 1 *BNIL* 36.

SACHR. 1986–7. *Annual Report for 1985–86*, H.C. 151.

Stewart v. UK. 1984. No. 10044/82, 39 DR 162.

Taylor, P. 1980. *Beating the Terrorists.* Harmondsworth: Penguin.

Toolis, Kevin. 1995. *Rebel Hearts: Journeys within the IRA's soul.* London: Picador.

W v. UK. 1983. No. 9348/81, DR 190.

Walker, Clive. 1992. *The Prevention of Terrorism in British Law.* Manchester: Manchester University Press.

Wilkinson, Paul. 1986. *Terrorism and the Liberal State.* London: Macmillan.

The Author

David Bonner is Senior Lecturer in Law at the University of Leicester, England.

3 Les Politiques de Lutte contre le Terrorisme: Enjeux Français

DANIEL HERMANT AND DIDIER BIGO

Introduction: l'Antiterrorisme comme Stratégie, l'Antiterrorisme comme Politique

L'accusation

Il existe un impensé quant à la constitution de la catégorie d'analyse du terrorisme qui mérite réflexion car il conditionne en amont quasiment toutes les 'évidences' et tous les discours des acteurs sur le sujet des politiques antiterroristes. La quasi totalité des analyses confondent les attentats, faits matériels assortis de violence directe et produisant souvent des victimes, et le terrorisme, dénomination donnée par certains acteurs (les acteurs en position dominante) à ces phénomènes. Cet impensé fait croire à une naturalité de la catégorie de terrorisme, au fait qu'il a toujours existé et qu'il est un signe de la barbarie de certains être humains. Le terrorisme existe donc et quelque part il a toujours existé à travers toutes les époques sous des formes diverses. Le terrorisme est un fait. Oser mettre en question cette affirmation, c'est immédiatement, aux yeux de certains, insulter les victimes des attentats ou chercher à justifier les actes de ceux qui commettent les attentats. Au contraire, il est indispensable de faire cette distinction entre d'une part les attentats, les assassinats qui sont les marqueurs d'une forme de la violence collective qui dans une société a toujours des causes relationnelles et dont les actes pour être compris doivent être réinsérés au sein du tissu sociétal et d'autres part des interactions politiques au sein desquelles le terrorisme est un moyen d'accuser l'autre d'être le seul responsable, le seul fauteur de trouble. On comprend alors mieux ce qu'est le terrorisme et l'antiterrorisme car, bien plus qu'une lutte armée, c'est déjà sur le terrain du conflit de légitimité (et donc des usages sémantiques) que se déroule les combats, même s'ils ne s'y cantonnent pas.

La particularité de la notion de terrorisme tient en effet à ce qu'elle se définit comme une notion totalement et pleinement négative, dévalorisante, dont aucun acteur violent ne se réclame spontanément, mais qu'on assène à un adversaire pour le délégitimer. Personne n'accepte l'étiquette de terroriste contrairement à celle de guérillero ou de révolutionnaire. En effet, les organisations clandestines se disent révolutionnaire, armée de libération, mouvement nationaliste de décolonisation ou bras armé d'une révolution et refusent d'être dites terroristes. Qualifier quelqu'un de terroriste c'est le disqualifier, c'est mobiliser la légitimité à son détriment. La violence terroriste est toujours celle de l'autre, de l'adversaire, mieux de l'ennemi, de celui dont l'altérité est maximale et qui se met à l'écart de la communauté politique (Bigo, 1994; Bigo et Hermant, 1984). L'usage du terme terrorisme renvoie ainsi à un mécanisme accusatoire dont la finalité est de disqualifier l'adversaire, et symétriquement de légitimer sa propre violence, sentie comme une réponse à une agression inqualifiable. L'originalité du terrorisme ne tient donc pas simplement à ce qu'il s'agisse d'un terme inapproprié, repris du langage commun, ou administratif et inapte à devenir un concept; ceci est vrai de nombreux termes en science politique. On pourrait en dire presque autant du terme de violence lui-même, ou du terme nationalisme. L'originalité tient à ce qu'à la différence d'autres termes, il est directement une arme dans un combat symbolique, il est un moyen d'accuser l'adversaire. Le mécanisme accusatoire, lorsqu'il fonctionne bien, non seulement délégitime l'usage de la violence de l'adversaire mais purifie, sanctifie la 'réponse'. La cause de l'antiterrorisme permet de justifier aux yeux d'acteurs gouvernementaux, une violence peu légitime comme le montre l'action de certains responsables espagnols à travers le GAL (Grupos Antiterroristas de Liberación). Mais François Tricaud et René Girard ont montré que les sociétés contemporaines ont bien compris le mécanisme du bouc émissaire et que ceux qui sont accusés n'acceptent pas le verdict (Tricaud, 1977; Girard, 1978; 1982). Ils mettent en cause leurs accusateurs. Les accusations sont réciproques: le terroriste des uns est le vengeur des autres, l'antiterroriste est le terroriste. La lutte symbolique et politique sur le sens de la violence est alors au cœur du combat entre les adversaires. Elle importe même souvent plus que la lutte 'militaire' entre les adversaires lorsqu'il y a une asymétrie manifeste dans le rapport de force. Mais il n'est pas simple de renverser les rapports de force symbolique lorsqu'ils ont une légitimité historique forte et c'est ce qui sauve depuis longtemps les sociétés démocratiques de longue date, car il ne suffit pas de se proclamer porte-parole du peuple révolutionnaire ou nationaliste pour l'être. Ce sont les situations duelles de polarisation de double illégitimité (Colombie, Pérou, Algérie...) qui sont les plus difficiles à gérer car il y est nécessaire, pour bénéficier d'une mobilisation du tiers, de le convaincre au moins de l'illégitimité de l'adversaire. Cela permet aux autorités en cas de succès de figer définitivement à leur avantage le rapport de force avec les organisations clandestines ou leurs parrains. Le conflit porte bien sur la légitimité des deux adversaires et celle-ci départage souvent les catégories honorables de la guérilla révolutionnaire et de l'État de Droit, de celles infamantes de terroristes, de criminels et de régime totalitaire.

L'Objectivation du Terme ne signifie pas son Objectivité

Croire après cela à une définition objective du phénomène qui pourrait éviter de prendre parti (et de prendre parti pour le vainqueur du combat sur la légitimité, mais est-ce forcément le plus juste ou simplement celui qui dispose des ressources les plus efficaces en matière de propagande et plus généralement de discours et de symboles à forte efficacité symbolique?) relève d'une certaine naïveté, utilisée par certains en fonction d'intérêts politiques. Il faut donc admettre que le terme de terrorisme oscillera en fonction des options éthiques et politiques, non par mauvaise volonté, absence dommageable de consensus sur des valeurs, mais avant tout parce que son usage, à la différence de termes comme combattant, est une arme dans le combat politique et symbolique entre les adversaires.

Le terrorisme n'est pas le fait d'un acteur indépendamment du contexte ou n'est pas le fait d'une idéologie particulière. C'est une labellisation administrative lestée d'un poids judiciaire lorsqu'elle apparaît comme incrimination dans les différents codes pénaux. Mais ce n'est pas pour autant une conceptualisation opératoire pour rendre compte de la violence d'organisations clandestines frappant des États.

Cette violence des organisations clandestines a certes des caractéristiques communes que nous avons établies. Imprévisibilité de l'action, secret, petit groupe se prétendant (souvent à tort) représentant d'une communauté plus large, utilisation d'une technologie de la violence souvent assez rudimentaire mais qui permet de se tenir à distance du moment de l'attaque et qui n'est suivie par aucune autre opération d'accompagnement militaire, présence parfois de revendications. Et si l'on compare ces critères

avec ceux donnés par Holsti à propos des guerres de troisième
génération qu'il situe exclusivement dans les États faibles, on retrouve
à peu près les mêmes. Les modalités d'actions de la violence, attentats,
assassinats ne permettent pas vraiment de caractériser ce qu'est le
terrorisme. C'est donc à travers une approche relationnelle prenant
en compte l'organisation clandestine, le gouvernement et le rapport
aux tiers que sont les citoyens qu'il faut analyser les phénomènes.

L'Unification par l'Accusation empêche d'appréhender la Diversité des Actions

La diversité des contextes, des acteurs, des relations entretenues
par les organisations avec la clandestinité et l'action violente empêchent
en effet de les fondre dans une seule et même catégorie. Rien ne relie,
sinon une commune 'accusation' et une même mise en série statistique,
les actes commis par une organisation clandestine comme le Front de
libération national corse (FLNC), les assassinats d'opposants iraniens
sur le territoire français, et les attentats du groupe islamique armée
(GIA) qui prolongent sur le territoire français la guerre civile algérienne.
La conceptualisation de ces différents actes de violence passe alors
par d'autres ressorts que nous avons longuement développés ailleurs
(Bigo et Hermant, 1983; 1984; 1986a; 1989). Analyser les phénomènes
de violence politique sur le territoire d'un État suppose en effet de
repérer les différentes logiques d'actions impliquant des organisations
clandestines et les gouvernements en montrant leur diversité, diversité
selon leurs motivations, selon la nature de l'organisation, selon la
taille de l'organisation, selon le degré de clandestinité, selon la nature
du gouvernement, selon la cohésion des pouvoirs publics, selon les
processus démocratiques, selon l'existence d'une médiatisation
importante, selon le degré de professionnalisme des journalistes et
plus important encore selon les types de relations entretenus entre les
acteurs: mimétisme dans les discours et l'action masqué par la rivalité
qui les opposent, coupure, voire inversion entre les projets de départ
et les résultats de l'action, confusion entre notoriété médiatique et
légitimité sociale, distanciation créée par la médiatisation, la
théâtralisation de la violence et la fictionalisation (Bigo et Hermant,
1986a; 1986b; 1989).

L'Antiterrorisme: une Politique sans 'Objet'?

On voit toute la difficulté de la tâche d'analyse des politiques
antiterroristes puisque celles-ci ne reposent pas sur un 'objet' cohérent
et constitué. Le sens commun a beau faire du terrorisme une forme
de violence s'attaquant à des individus innocents, le plus souvent

par le biais d'attentats spectaculaires, afin de paralyser, d'intimider tous les autres membres de la société ou de la communauté visée, le problème tient au caractère très partiel d'une telle 'définition', au fait qu'elle n'a de sens qu'en fonction d'une certaine conception de la 'responsabilité', et à son instrumentalisation fréquente, à des fins de politique intérieure ou de politique étrangère, par les États (non démocratiques). Certes, certaines organisations clandestines luttant dans des États de droit par le moyen d'attentats dits aveugles (Ordine Nero en Italie avec la piazza Fontana ou la gare de Bologne par exemple, en France les comité de solidarité avec les prisonniers politiques arabes et du proche-orient (CSPPA) avec les attentats de 1985 et 1986, les groupes du GIA en 1995 et 1996...) semblent être l'incarnation d'une telle définition, mais qu'en est-il des autres organisations clandestines qui frappent des individus symbolisant leur adversaire direct (la PIRA frappant les soldats anglais en Irlande du Nord, ETA contre la guardia civile au pays basque espagnol, Action Directe s'en prenant à l'ingénieur général Audran ou à Georges Besse ou le Congrès national africain (l'ANC) s'en prenant à des responsables de l'apartheid il y a peu)? Comment séparer les innocents des autres? Faut-il les dire terroristes à certains moments et pas à d'autres? Tout le monde est-il innocent ou personne? L'anonymat et l'absence d'exercice de responsabilités peuvent-ils être des critères de différenciation? Qu'est-ce que la notion de non combattant et comment lui trouver une définition indépendante des contextes locaux? L'innocence des victimes est un critère pour le moins délicat à l'utilisation, au moins en terme de réflexion de sciences sociales, même s'il est celui sur lequel se fonde l'opinion lorsqu'elle pense spontanément au terrorisme.

L'idée que le terrorisme terroriserait, intimiderait, outre son caractère tautologique, est quant à elle aussi douteuse. Les attentats, loin de terroriser, ont plutôt tendance à révolter, scandaliser, raffermir les solidarités avec les garants de l'ordre public ou à lasser des spectateurs blasés de violence télévisuelle. Le terrorisme ne terrorise pas. Il faut se méfier des étymologies faciles et de ce que l'on veut leur faire dire. En revanche, il fascine sans doute comme d'autres formes spectaculaires de violence, provoquant ainsi des angoisses pouvant générer un imaginaire de l'insécurité qui placera le terrorisme parfois en tête des angoisses des français devant la guerre nucléaire ou les conflits conventionnels. Mais il s'agit plus d'un imaginaire que d'une appréhension rationnelle d'un risque, le terrorisme ne représentant, même dans son acception la plus large, que 0,2 pour cent de la criminalité.[1]

A tous ces titres le terme de terrorisme appartient au langage des
acteurs mais ne peut appartenir à celui du sociologue, sinon pour
constater les usages des acteurs et les stratégies symboliques qu'ils
emploient. Dès nos premiers travaux, nous avons insisté sur la
portée symbolique de l'accusation et sur les jeux de stigmatisation
qui l'accompagnent. Ils sont partie intégrante de l'analyse des
stratégies des acteurs et ne sont pas simple précaution
épistémologique. En ce sens, malgré tous les efforts de leurs
promoteurs, les politiques antiterroristes ne peuvent être des
politiques publiques au même titre que celles prises en matière de
sécurité routière, d'aménagement du territoire... Elles jouent sur les
croyances, les émotions, les valeurs. Les prendre pour de simples
réponses à une diversité d'actes de violence qui, peu ou prou, se
ressembleraient, c'est déjà admettre un certain point de vue selon
lequel la catégorie nominaliste de terrorisme recouvrerait
effectivement une classe spécifique de violence politique comparables
entre elles. Or, selon nous, ceci n'est pas possible, d'où une réflexion
préalable à tenir sur le rapport entre les événements tels qu'ils se
produisent (attentats, assassinats) et leur labellisation comme
terrorisme afin de repérer le travail de construction opéré par les
journalistes, par les hommes politiques lorsqu'ils nomment ou ne
nomment pas tel ou tel phénomène terroriste. Non pas pour nier la
réalité des attentats, bien évidemment, mais pour discuter la perti-
nence des rapprochements entre attentats, entre organisations
clandestines sur lesquels est fondée une politique qui se dit
antiterroriste et qui se veut une politique homogène répondant à un
même phénomène (Bigo et Hermant, s.f.).

L'Antiterrorisme ne répond pas au Terrorisme, il le définit 'officiellement'

Si l'on devait donc donner une définition du terrorisme,
celle-ci serait quelque peu paradoxale et tiendrait en une phrase: à
l'échelle internationale tout comme nationale, ce sont les
gouvernements qui désignent qui est terroriste et qui ne l'est pas
(Quadruppani, 1989; Bigo, Hermant et Leveau, 1991).[2] Ils opèrent
un tri au milieu des actes de violence armée qui ont lieu sur leur
territoire ou contre leurs citoyens et leur confèrent ce 'label'.[3] Ainsi
on ne prend pas en compte tous les attentats commis mais
uniquement ceux qui contreviennent à une certaine conception de
l'action politique tant sur le plan intérieur où elle est établie par
consensus entre les partis politiques sur ce qui est tolérable, que sur
le plan international où elle renvoie à des discussions ou à des

marchandages entre les Etats. Les terroristes sont ceux qui sont 'hors jeux', qui 'transgressent les règles posées par les autres'. Ainsi, l'unité de la labellisation terroriste ne tiendrait pas tant aux formes de violence qu'elle décrirait, à une liste d'actes matériels (attentats, assassinats...) ou à une intention de terreur de la part des auteurs de ces actes comme les diverses incriminations juridiques tendent à nous le faire croire, elle reposerait en fait sur la collaboration antiterroriste des partis et des États, sur les jugements de valeurs qu'ils ont les uns par rapport aux autres (degré de démocratie...) et sur les critères qu'ils mettent au point dans leur législation pour décider de ce qu'est le terrorisme (et de ce qu'il n'est pas).[4]

Nous devons comprendre, à partir de cette élargissement du point de vue, qu'il existe une dynamique d'interaction entre les acteurs usant de violence et les gouvernants. Dynamique que l'on doit appréhender à travers une approche relationnelle en se refusant à focaliser son attention sur un seul acteur, que ce soit l'organisation ou le gouvernement. Nous devons comprendre l'impact du pouvoir de définition des gouvernants et la capacité de surprise et d'agression générant l'incertitude des organisations clandestines. Nous devons analyser les attentats pour ce qu'ils sont, des répertoires d'actions au sein d'une lutte politique et nous pouvons apprécier leur légitimité ou leur illégitimité en fonction de chaque cas concret. Nous devons dans le même temps analyser les politiques de lutte antiterroriste comme des moyens d'ordonner, de classer la réalité, premier temps du travail symbolique permettant de rassurer éventuellement la population. Ce qui est en jeu est en effet autant de l'ordre du symbolique, de l'émotion politique, que de la rationalité et de l'instrumentalité d'une politique publique.

Classer et ordonner la Réalité: Usage stratégique de la Notion de Terrorisme comme Délégitimation des Actes de violence dans les Démocraties

Si, à toute époque, le pouvoir a certes pris des mesures pour contrôler la violence politique et plus spécifiquement pour empêcher les attentats et punir leurs auteurs, la notion de terrorisme n'apparaît véritablement dans le langage politique que dans les années 1960. Non pas que des usages occasionnels n'aient pas existé auparavant, mais ils n'ont rien de systématique. Comme le souligne Yves Michaud, les perceptions de la violence varient dans le temps et l'espace. Des phénomènes considérés comme normaux sont jugés violents dans d'autres époques et d'autres lieux. On peut certes toujours refabriquer une histoire du terrorisme à partir des Assassins, du vieux de la Montagne ou de Judas le zélote, cette histoire est une récollection approximative de faits détachés de leurs contextes et qui même subjectivement ne fait pas sens pour les acteurs (Laqueur, 1978). Les histoires générales du terrorisme ne font qu'objectiver une accusation en la 'naturalisant', en l'inscrivant comme fait transhistorique, à partir d'une vision rétrodictive, là où au contraire il faut comprendre la genèse du mécanisme et du terme. Instrumentalement le terrorisme ne devient une accusation efficace que lorsqu'elle est mise en branle par des gouvernements occidentaux pour délégitimer des formes d'action violente à motivations déclarées politiques dès que celles-ci s'inspirent des modèles révolutionnaires ou indépendantistes mais en demandent l'application sur le territoire des démocraties occidentales. On considère en effet que l'usage de la violence dans une démocratie représentative lorsqu'il ne repose pas sur un mouvement de masse est une forme d'action criminelle et que les motivations politiques ne justifient pas les actes d'assassinats, d'attentats qui sont perpétrés. La notion de subversion révolutionnaire, jusque là très en vogue pour labelliser les phénomènes de violence politique, s'efface alors au profit de celle de terrorisme qui introduit l'idée d'illégitimité par nature de tels actes de violence. En ce sens la notion de terrorisme est bien liée à celle de la démocratie. Elle a sur celle de subversion cet avantage que l'acte violent lui-même, indépendamment de ses motivations, devient intolérable. C'est la violence qui est condamnée.

Violence politique, Violence révolutionnaire et Démocratie en France

Il se trouve que la France marquée par son passé révolutionnaire, est quelque peu en retard sur ce plan. L'idée de proscrire la violence comme répertoire d'action du politique est malmenée. Le mythe révolutionnaire est toujours là, des groupes s'en servent pour mobiliser. Malgré tout, le travail de fond de forclusion de la violence dans l'espace démocratique se poursuit et l'immense majorité de la population est en accord avec l'idée que le droit de vote est un substitut normal à la violence et que l'on doit s'exprimer par le bulletin et non par les armes. Dès la troisième République et l'écrasement dans le sang de la commune de Paris, la construction d'une démocratie représentative se fait sur cette nécessaire substitution des moyens d'arriver au pouvoir: oubli de la violence et usage du bulletin de vote (Deloye et Ihl, 1993).

Au moment où des groupes révolutionnaires réclament les armes à la main le droit d'exercer la violence à des fins de transformations sociales et politiques, on fait tout pour les inclure dans la catégorie terroriste. Au départ, on agira au cas par cas côté gouvernemental, et on les reconnaîtra parfois comme interlocuteur pour les criminaliser le lendemain, mais avec les années 1970 et surtout les années 1980 et 1990, une véritable stratégie gouvernementale va s'élaborer. Les terroristes ne sont pas simplement les alliés du camp d'en face. Ils ne sont pas simplement des ennemis, des subversifs, ils sont hors l'humanité, au delà même des barbares. Ils ne sont plus dans la sphère du politique mais dans celle du Mal. Les combattre c'est combattre le Mal lui-même. L'accusation purifie la lutte 'contre' l'adversaire. Rien d'idéologique dans le combat, juste un sens de défense de l'humanité. Avec l'antiterrorisme, il s'agira de constituer une mobilisation des moyens symboliques et matériels pour délégitimer définitivement le recours à la violence sur le territoire français, d'abord de la part de tous les nationaux, ensuite de tous ceux qui y vivent ou le traversent. A ce titre nous voudrions montrer le formidable travail symbolique de construction d'une évidence, non pas pour renverser simplement la polarité de l'accusation (ce qui serait naïf et sans doute injuste quand on partage l'idée que le droit de vote est une arme politique à privilégier sur la violence quand on peut en faire usage), mais pour montrer comment s'est créée, au coup par coup, puis avec de plus en plus de croyances partagées l'idée que le terrorisme était une catégorie particulière de violence suscitant des réponses exceptionnelles.

Archéologie de l'Antiterrorisme

Nous nous proposons dans la suite de ce texte de décrire les grandes dispositions et les logiques constitutives de cette nouvelle stratégie de délégitimation de la violence politique de certaines organisations clandestines. La situation de la France, État de Droit de vieille date, dote son gouvernement dans le conflit de légitimité qui l'oppose à des organisations clandestines, d'un fort capital symbolique qui lui permet de remettre en cause la prétention de ces organisations à le concurrencer. Cette situation diffère fondamentale-ment de celle qui pouvait exister dans l'Afrique du Sud de l'apartheid ou même de ce que connaît le Pérou de Fujimori. Évoquer le conflit de légitimité et le faire resurgir comme problème n'équivaut donc pas, comme des lectures rapides ou idéologiques pourraient le supposer, à légitimer de ce fait l'action violente des organisations clandestines. Le but est de montrer sur quoi reposent les politiques de lutte antiterroriste et d'analyser comment elles se sont construites. Notre travail s'apparente alors à celui permettant de redécouvrir

par un travail de genèse comment la notion d'antiterrorisme et celle
de terrorisme se sont objectivées jusqu'à devenir des évidences, des
'faits'. Cette démarche génétique nous semble un des moyens
d'échapper à ce que Pierre Bourdieu a désigné comme une des plus
grandes difficultés lorsqu'on cherche à penser l'État, celui de ne pas
être prisonnier d'une pensée d'État, en méconnaissant ce qui en fait
d'abord un État, à savoir sa capacité 'à produire et imposer les
catégories de pensée que nous appliquons spontanément à toute
chose du monde, et à l'Etat lui-même' (Bourdieu, 1994).

L'antiterrorisme est une de ces catégories construites par l'État
que nous appliquons maintenant spontanément sans même prendre
conscience de ce qu'elle implique, et nous le faisons d'autant plus
facilement que nous croyons qu'elle répond plus ou moins bien à un
phénomène que l'on pourrait appeler légitimement terrorisme.
Pourtant l'histoire des trente dernières années nous montre un
véritable processus de construction sociale d'une 'évidence'. Le
schéma général reste, au premier abord, celui d'une politique
construite par touches successives, plus en prise directe avec la
conjoncture quand des attentats interviennent à l'improviste qu'avec
un projet défini. Le passage de la notion de subversion à celle de
terrorisme n'est pas machiavélique, elle ressort d'émotions politiques
partagées par les hommes politiques et une large majorité de la
population. Néanmoins des instrumentalisations des effets positifs
pour le gouvernement de l'accusation de terrorisme vont le pousser
à employer la notion de plus en plus fréquemment et pour des faits
très différents. Puis à transformer la législation pour donner un
critère juridique. Moyens policiers, moyens juridiques vont
s'ordonner autour de cette représentation qu'il existe un phénomène
terroriste, et si débat initial il y a en, peu à peu les routines ont
organisé les représentations du social. Le débat gauche–droite a
existé. Mais il y eu incrémentation des années 1970 et 1980 a qui
va permettre de faire refluer le débat sur la notion de terrorisme.
Celle-ci va se constituer en catégorie d'évidence, jusqu'à parfois
gêner le gouvernement lui-même dans ses tractations avec certaines
organisations qu'il a qualifiées de terroristes mais qu'il ne veut pas
totalement traiter comme telles (cf. en Corse). On constatera ce que
les économistes appellent un effet de cliquet des législations, à peine
remis en cause en 1981, qui permettra de constituer 'une' politique
antiterroriste faite de multiples services, de moyens… objectivée
sous la catégorie de politique publique ce qui lui permettra d'acquérir
une consistance symbolique renforçant toujours plus les moyens
humains et matériels spécifiques. A partir de là, il ne deviendra plus

possible de s'interroger sur la légitimité politique des actions conduites par des organisations recourant à la violence, en particulier lorsqu'il y a mort d'hommes. L'antiterrorisme va y gagner ses lettres de noblesse, il est 'le dernier rempart de la démocratie', ce qui l'empêche de succomber devant tous ses ennemis, qu'ils viennent de gauche, de droite ou/et de l'étranger. Il est ce qui protège par excellence tant par la prévention que par les actions des commandos d'élites. Il est l'instrument particulier de ces périodes qui ne sont ni paix, ni guerre mais crises quasi permanente.

De manière interne, les organisations clandestines radicalisées et souvent coupées de bases populaires selon un processus d'inversion ne pourront justifier leurs actions aux yeux de la population. Elles seront assimilées à des terroristes, c'est à dire à des combattants sans légitimité. Le gouvernement gagnera tous les combats symboliques (sauf peut-être en Corse auprès de certains insulaires). En revanche, le découplage créé par cette notion de terrorisme et d'antiterrorisme va brouiller les liens entre la politique étrangère de la France et ses retombées sur notre propre territoire. La réflexion sur le GIA, tout comme celle sur le Hezbollah, a pâti de ce découplage qui les présente différemment selon qu'ils agissent sur leur territoire ou en France. Compréhensible ailleurs, leurs actions seraient celles de fanatiques dangereux, de fous plus ou moins manipulés lorsqu'elles auraient lieu chez nous. Les enjeux transnationaux vont être ignorés ou instrumentalisés et les logiques sociales qui les commandent vont être tellement mal perçues que des contradictions permanentes vont être générées, car, si le gouvernement n'a aucun mal à gagner le combat symbolique auprès des citoyen français, il se pose lui même la question de l'allégeance des citoyens français d'origine étrangère et des immigrés et il a bien du mal à convaincre de sa bonne foi ceux qui vivent les effets de sa politique étrangère qui est parfois, en particulier sur la scène du Proche Orient, une réalpolitik bien éloignée de ce qui est annoncé et perçu par les citoyens français. Or, comprendre les derniers événements qui ont frappé la France suppose de reconstituer tous ces liens.

Les Années soixante-dix: Constitution ad hoc de l'Antiterrorisme et du Terrorisme

Subversion et Terrorisme

Après la vague d'attentats et d'opérations clandestines liés à la guerre d'Algérie (Font de libération nationale, FLN et Organisa-

tion armée secrète, OAS) et culminant avec l'attentat du Petit
Clamart, pour lequel on emploie la notion de terrorisme, il faut
attendre une dizaine d'années pour voir réapparaître une telle notion (Delarue, 1981). Pourtant les violences ne manquent pas, mais
elles semblent liées aux mouvements sociaux, à l'apparition d'une
nouvelle classe ouvrière moins intégrée, plus paysanne, plus féminine
et plus immigrée. Dès lors, même si l'on parle, côté sociologue, de
violence anomique, ou de résurgence de l'anarchisme, on évoque
peu le terrorisme (Klein, 1977: 139–68; Labin, 1978; Lakos, s.f.;
Laqueur, 1977; Laqueur, 1976: 99–105; Lehning, 1976; Marenssin,
1972). Les termes de violences nationalistes et de subversion ou
d'atteintes à la sûreté de l'État sont eux bien plus utilisés par les
autorités que celui de terrorisme (Kitson, 1971; Mucchielli, 1973;
Hamilton, 1979). Un changement de registre se produit après 1970.
La peur révolutionnaire du post 1968 a quelque peu disparu mais
les exemples allemands et italiens sont présents à l'esprit des
dirigeants français. Certes, les organisations à vocation
révolutionnaire de l'après 68 restées embryonnaires ne constituent
pas à l'époque en France une réelle menace. Elles ne réussissent pas,
malgré un discours militant, à s'implanter dans le milieu ouvrier et,
après quelques opérations spectaculaires (enlèvements de Tramoni)
elles finiront par s'autodissoudre Nouvelle Résistance Populaire
(NRP) refusant une évolution à l'allemande (Marcellin, 1969; Liniers,
1985).

Mais on est inquiet des connexions possibles entre ces mouvements
régionalistes et l'idéologie révolutionnaire estudiantine. On y voit
les prolégomènes d'une déstabilisation du pouvoir en place, malgré
montrer l'inanité d'un certain nombre d'actions destructrices et leur
peu de rapport avec les situations sociales. Les plasticages de relais
de télévision en Bretagne (1974, 1977), l'attentat du Font de
libération de la Bretagne (FLB) contre le château de Versailles, et
dans une moindre mesure les défis aux forces de l'ordre, et l'affaire
de la cave d'Aléria en Corse, seront des prétextes. On reparle de
terrorisme et d'atteintes à la sûreté de l'État, on réactive la Cour de
Sûreté de l'État dont les magistrats diront après, leur malaise de
juger des actes aussi insignifiants. Le FLB déjà démantelé deux fois
(1968/69, 1972) et largement infiltré est montré du doigt comme la
menace principale touchant la France. Ainsi, le pli est pris. Les
violences nationalistes et sociales seront dites terroristes (anonyme,
s.f.; Nicolas, 1987; Landorf, s.f.; Roi, 1986). Les professions de foi
internationalistes de certains groupuscules seront brusquement prises
au sérieux pour justifier d'une éventuelle connexion avec l'étranger

et tout particulièrement l'URSS. Par ailleurs les bilans dressés par la police ne manquent pas d'impressionner, mais l'aspect massif que produit toujours une mise en série ne doit pas faire oublier que ces violences se produisent sur une durée assez longue, restent discontinues et renvoient à un factuel assez divers derrière lequel se trouvent des acteurs multiples et des violences diverses puisqu'on y inclut, outre les violences nationalistes et dégradations de bâtiments publics (y compris lors de manifestations), les quelques détournements d'avions, les prises d'otages dans les ambassades étrangères à Paris ou françaises à l'étranger (1973, 1974, 1977), les règlements de compte et fusillades (rue Touviers, 1975) et bien sûr les quelques attentats dits 'aveugles' (rue Copernic, jet de grenade de Carlos au drugstore Saint Germain, 1974) (Betancourt, 1981; Dobson et Payne, 1976; Dobson, 1977; González, 1976; Smith, s.f.; Soto, 1976; Tobon, 1978).

Le gouvernement réagit sous deux angles, d'abord en utilisant la notion de terrorisme pour tous ces événements, aussi divers soient-ils et en mettant l'accent sur les plus spectaculaires. Renforçant le sentiment d'horreur provoqué dans la population par certains de ces actes, toutes les actions sont finalement rejetées de la même manière. Ensuite il est important de mettre l'accent sur le caractère criminel de ces actes qui les délégitime. Les discours dépolitisent les groupes mais on maintient malgré tout la Cour de Sûreté de l'État et ses procédures d'exception. Pendant les années Marcellin (ministre de l'intérieur de 1968 à 1974) les autorités utilisent pour mener une répression ponctuelle, mais ferme, les techniques policières traditionnelles à base d'infiltration et de surveillance des milieux 'à risque' qui avaient montré leur efficacité pendant la guerre d'Algérie, mais on met en place aussi les réflexions sur les lois anticasseurs et le Ministre ne cache pas sa croyance dans le fait que ces organisations subversives auraient des relais à l'étranger (Marcellin, 1978; 1985). En 1973 les militants bretons sont déférés devant la Cour de Sûreté de l'État mais celle-ci prononce des peines bien légères, déconnectées des discours sur le danger terroriste de l'exécutif. Sans doute la proximité des élections législatives et certains sondages exagérant peut-être l'attachement nationaliste des bretons expliquent-ils aussi ce 'retournement' qui, pour être un des premiers, ne sera pas le dernier lorsqu'il faudra, en Bretagne comme en Corse, penser non seulement à la violence mais aux votes nationalistes.

Sous le septennat de Valery Giscard d'Estaing, les condamnés bénéficieront de l'amnistie présidentielle, ce qui suscitera des protestations. Aussi, devant la montée de la violence en Corse, la police durcit ses méthodes et tâche de décourager les sympathisants en pratiquant, selon une expression imagée, la 'pêche au chalut', c'est à dire en augmentant le nombre d'arrestations et de condamnations dans les milieux de sympathisants. Il s'agit de renforcer les méthodes de surveillance et de dissuader le passage à l'acte en visant toutes les personnes qui fournissent de l'aide. Artisanalement, la France se met à l'heure allemande et élargit la sphère des personnes surveillées. Seulement, cette politique ne donnera pas les résultats escomptés; si elle décourage effectivement quelques militants elle donne par la dimension politique qu'a nécessairement un procès devant la Cour de Sûreté de l'État, un label politique aux prévenus, légitime ainsi ses auteurs, devenu des victimes du pouvoir et enracine les organisation dans le paysage ordinaire de l'île. La contradiction entre Cour de Sûreté de l'État issue d'une vision en terme de subversion révolutionnaire et action de l'étranger, et criminalisation via le terrorisme, n'est pas résolue. Il faudra attendre 1981 pour voir un choix fait avec l'abolition de la Cour de Sûreté et le retour à des tribunaux ordinaires. Sans qu'aucune directive officielle n'ait vu le jour une sorte de répartition des compétences se met en place: à l'égard des attentats commis par les organisations clandestines à vocation nationalistes comme le FLB et le FLNC, la gendarmerie nationale sera maître d'oeuvre malgré quelques tiraillements avec le services régionaux de police judiciaire (SRPJ) d'Ajaccio; à l'égard d'Action Directe, c'est plus directement la police nationale et la brigade de répression du banditisme qui se charge de ces questions. Concernant les pratiques violentes dans les squats on charge la Direction centrale des Renseignements généraux (DCRG) de surveiller les milieux à risque, dans ces années-là les réfugiés gauchistes de Turquie.

Les Palestiniens: des Terroristes internationaux?

En ce qui concerne la menace des organisations palestiniennes, le gouvernement est gêné. Il pourrait certes, comme le demandent les israéliens, considérer les palestiniens comme des criminels. Mais la 'politique arabe de la France' empêche d'appliquer vers l'étranger les raisonnements tenus à l'égard des groupes internes. Les palestiniens ne sont pas 'aussi' illégitimes dans leur combat, même ceux qui usent de violence. Le gouvernement français se donne donc les moyens de réagir techniquement avec efficacité aux prises d'otages en créant des unités spécialisées (création du groupe d'intervention de la gendarmerie nationale (GIGN) en 1974) et pense que sa position générale lui permet de compléter le traitement policier par des méthodes diplomatiques. Dès lors, à chaque fois les autorités françaises réagissent aux attentats comme s'il s'agissait d'un accident, d'une méprise des organisations clandestines palestiniennes qui se tromperaient d'adversaires. Cette attitude suppose des contacts directs – ou par intermédiaire – avec les organisations; et le secret absolu autour de ces contacts, ainsi que de bons rapports avec les gouvernements de la région. Jouant sur les liens avec le fatah d'Arafat, on pense qu'il peut et qu'il doit mettre de l'ordre dans 'ses' rangs, alors même que le Front populaire de la libération de la Palestine (FPLP) et le groupe Abou Nidal qui échappent largement à son influence sont disposés à attaquer le territoire français. Ce qui pourrait apparaître comme des erreurs de jugements durera longtemps mais la Direction de la surveillance du territoire (DST) qui ne créera que tardivement un département antiterroriste est persuadée que seule cette méthode visant à ne pas changer d'allié au sein des fluctuations des mouvements palestiniens est efficace. Sur le plan interne ses conséquences, expulsion plus que jugement, impunité pour les activités de certains groupes, négation des solidarités européennes et occidentales, seront diversement appréciées, on s'en doute (Nicolas, 1987; Bigo et Hermant, s.f.).

L'Exception française?

Mais, peu importe, dans les années 70 pour le gouvernement, comme pour l'opinion, il y a bien finalement une exception française. La presse oppose volontiers cette situation enviable à celle existant dans les autres pays. Certes, il existe en France des mouvements nationalistes violents à l'image de l'IRA ou de l'ETA basque, mais ni les bretons du FLB, ni les mouvements corses, ne peuvent rivaliser avec leur modèle; contrairement à l'irrédentisme irlandais, l'identité corse n'est pas immédiatement synonyme d'indépendance et la violence politique est plutôt destinée à attirer l'attention des autorités. Les basques d'Ipartarrak gênent les projets d'ETA qui sont avant tout de faire de la France une base de repli pour ses militants, projet excluant des provocations à l'égard des autorités françaises. Dès lors on leur conseille le calme. Sur la scène idéologique Action Directe (AD) apparaît également comme une pale imitation de la RAF allemande. Ne l'oublions pas, à cette époque en France, les grands débats sur le terrorisme concernent l'attitude du gouvernement allemand à l'égard de la bande à Baader, spectacularisé par le voyage de J.P. Sartre à la prison de Stammheim puis un peu plus tard par l'extradition de l'avocat de la RAF Klaus Croissant. L'enlèvement puis l'assassinat d'Aldo Moro par les brigades rouges semble impensable en France. Quand aux attentats de groupes provenant du Proche Orient, malgré leur dimension spectaculaire ils n'ont pas le côté dramatique de ceux qui se déroulent à l'extérieur (drame de Munich en 1972, otages de l'Organisation des pays exportateurs de pétrole (l'OPEP) à Vienne en 1975). Les observateurs notent avec satisfaction que la France reste relativement épargnée.

A la fin des années 70 le terrorisme, simple qualificatif donnant un air de famille à des violences au contexte très divers, n'est en aucun cas considéré en France comme un défi global que le gouvernement doit relever. Dispersée, superficielle, la violence dite terroriste relève moins d'une politique au sens où cela supposerait une réponse construite et cohérente à un défi, puisque celui-ci n'existe pas, que d'une suite de décisions sur des questions assez différentes: aménagement du territoire, répression policière, tractations internationales. Elle est redevable d'un antiterrorisme ad hoc, pourrait-on dire. L'antiterrorisme est avant tout une stratégie et non une politique. Il relève de la politique des différents services, des différents adversaires qu'ils se donnent. Il s'agit, pour ces derniers, soit de criminaliser leur adversaire en lui niant un statut politique, soit de le valoriser jusqu'à en faire un quasi-égal avec qui une guerre qui ne dit pas son nom a commencé. Le rapport au terrorisme oscille ainsi toujours entre une conception purement interne et judiciaire tendant à le ramener à la criminalité ordinaire (conception de la police judiciaire (PJ), d'une partie des Renseignements Généraux (RG), de la gendarmerie, des juges) et une conception plutôt externe et militaire tendant à le traiter comme les prolégomènes d'une guerre, comme un conflit de basse intensité (conceptions de la DST, de la Direction Générale de la Sécurité Extérieure (DGSE), de certains membres des RG) (Burdan, 1990; Bigo et Hermant, 1986d). Le droit enregistre souvent des moments particuliers au sein de cette oscillation et dépend à cette époque des figures concrètes prises par l'adversaire. Il s'impose ensuite comme norme jusqu'à ce qu'un contexte particulier vienne de nouveau modifier l'image de la menace. Les gouvernements ne sont donc pas entièrement libres dans leur choix, même si, selon les organisations, leur répertoire de classification est plus ou moins ouvert. Les contextes mènent autant les hommes politiques qu'ils ne tentent de les anticiper.

Par ailleurs ce qui est inadmissible d'un côté des Pyrénées est peut-être justifiable de l'autre. Entre résistant ou terroriste on peut choisir, quitte à dénoncer le moyen utilisé pour défendre une cause juste. L'attentat contre l'amiral Carrero Blanco en 1972 est exemplaire de ce point de vue de l'attitude ambiguë du gouvernement français: réprouvé du bout des lèvres par les autorités françaises, il n'est pas admissible de faire sauter la voiture d'un premier ministre, fut-il franquiste, il a tout de même été accueilli avec satisfaction par une large partie de l'opinion, qui y voyait une sorte de réplique posthume à Guernica portant un coup fatal à une dictature moribonde. Ce mélange de condamnation et de compréhension se retrouve également dans le regard de la France sur les années de plomb allemande et italienne. La thèse en vogue fait donc des organisations clandestines des enfants naturels du fascisme et du nazisme, des groupes totalitaires prêts à s'allier au totalitarisme soviétique, toute chose impossible en France, imagine-t-on. La critique est donc double. Elle porte sur les organisations clandestines mais aussi sur les gouvernements. On reproche au gouvernement allemand sa politique qui dit-on déploie des moyens quasi fasciste pour sauver la démocratie menacée par la bande Baader–Meinhof alors qu'en même temps on se gausse de l'inefficacité italienne. Cette marge d'appréciation politique amène le gouvernement et les juges français à être très regardant sur les extraditions et à en refuser certaines. Le changement apparaît tardivement: la convention de Strasbourg de 1977 proposée par le gouvernement français comme un des éléments de l'espace judiciaire européen n'est ratifiée qu' avec la clause de sauvegarde qui permet de ne pas faire jouer l'automaticité de l'extradition. Les juges sont donc toujours libres de juger sur le fond. Leur sévérité existera. Avec l'affaire Klaus Croissant, par exemple, où la chambre d'accusation de Paris dans son avis du 16 novembre 1977, puis le conseil d'État dans son arrêt du 7 juillet 1978, considèrent que si le but poursuivi par Croissant était bien politique, cela ne suffit pas à regarder les faits qui lui ont été reprochés, 'compte tenu de leur gravité, comme ayant un caractère politique' et que dès lors il peut être extradé. C'est dans le même esprit que la cour d'appel d'Aix en Provence émet un avis favorable à l'extradition du neo-fasciste italien Affatigato, après l'attentat de Bologne, ou la chambre d'accusation de Paris et le conseil d'État autorise l'extradition vers la RFA de Jean Salati, de G. Winter et de F. Piperno vers l'Italie. Seulement, en refusant l'automaticité de l'extradition, et en jugeant au cas par cas la France se pose en juge de la légitimité du combat des organisations clandestines et de la politique des gouvernements. Nul doute que vue d'Allemagne, d'Italie ou d'Espagne cette attitude ait fortement déplu.

Changement de Majorité Politique en France: un Tournant?

La Réforme Badinter

Dans la prolongation de cette politique, le ministre de l'intérieur Gaston Deferre fait des déclarations sur la 'jeunesse' de la démocratie espagnole et sur les pratiques de tortures qui se prolongent dans les commissariats espagnols. Les juges français refusent d'extrader vers l'Italie, l'Allemagne ou l'Espagne, et encore plus d'expulser les personnes. La collaboration politique entre États, y compris européens, doit être subordonnée à l'examen individuel des situations. Cela ne signifie pas protéger les membres des organisations clandestines puisque ceux-ci sont plus des criminels que des combattants de la liberté, mais le principe d'une étude au cas par cas est nécessaire (Labayle, 1981).

Pour les socialistes, il faut donc continuer à criminaliser le terrorisme mais en étant cohérent jusqu'au bout, en le renvoyant devant des tribunaux ordinaires et en abolissant la Cour de Sûreté de l'État. Robert Badinter mettra tout son prestige dans la balance pour pousser François Mitterrand à cette réforme. Les socialistes pensaient qu'il fallait par cette réforme judiciaire éviter de transformer la violence/moyen publicitaire; d'avertissement, en violence/fin pour elle-même par une répression trop forte. La Cour de Sûreté de l'État utilisée pour punir les régionalistes leur paraissait disproportionnée avec les violences réelles; de surcroît, elle confirait, par l'effet médiatique, une dimension politique, non au problème corse, mais aux poseurs de bombes. Elle transformait ce qui peut être considéré comme le symptôme d'un malaise ou comme le révélateur d'un vrai problème en défi de groupuscules violents à l'égard de l'Etat. Seulement, quand les affaires arrivent devant les tribunaux ordinaires, les autorités exécutives doivent gérer le couple criminalisation/politisation inhérent à ce genre d'affaires et ne peuvent éviter de faire des commentaires devant les médias. Or, soit le gouvernement fait jouer la logique d'appel à la condamnation morale de l'opinion, soit il est obligé de se taire pour ne pas trop interférer avec la justice. Soit il nie la dimension politique, non pas du problème, mais des auteurs, soit au contraire il la souligne.

Le choix de la normalisation juridique par la suppression de la Cour de Sûreté de l'État et de l'amnistie montre clairement la nouvelle direction qu'entendait prendre le gouvernement, mais elle sera fortement critiquée et dès le départ, y compris au sein du Parti socialiste (PS) lui-même. La criminalisation ne porte ses fruits que face à des organisations incapables de prolonger leurs actions et face à des organisations acceptant d'autolimiter leur violence. Or, les organisations clandestines, loin d'être prêtes à faire la paix avec un pouvoir de gauche, le considèrent comme un 'traître' et renforcent leurs actions violentes. Ceci prend à contre-pied les socialistes convaincus que le terrorisme régionaliste, c'est à dire l'ensemble de violences que l'on mettait sous ce qualificatif, est le symptôme de difficultés réelles et que dès qu'ils verraient les bienfaits de la politique de décentralisation, les autonomistes arrêteraient la violence. Sans être faux, ce raisonnement ne prévoit pas la radicalisation d'une frange des nationalistes (ou des membres d'Action Directe). La politique menée fait certainement tomber drastiquement le nombre de personnes prêtes à passer à la violence, comme le montre d'anciens témoignages, mais la politique structurelle régionale et la mise en place d'une assemblée régionale corse n'arrêtent pas la violence; au contraire moins d'hommes, mais plus soudés, font plus d'actions d'éclats. Ce que les socialistes, mais aussi certains sociologues, ont du mal à comprendre, c'est qu'agir sur les grandes causes ne modifie pas forcément la fréquence des attentats car les décisions individuelles sont ici d'ordre microsociologique (prestige interne, carrière dans la clandestinité...) (Crenshaw, 1987). Sur le terrain l'organisation d'une répression sélective visant à n'arrêter que les irréductibles n'a pas que des supporters parmi les policiers qui ont l'impression que l'on relâche la surveillance et que l'on libère des coupables.

La France, Cible privilégiée?

Par ailleurs, à partir de 1982 devant la nouvelle série d'attentats en provenance du Moyen Orient, rue Marbeuf, rue des Rosiers, gare St Charles à Marseille, on a l'impression que les organisations testent le nouveau pouvoir politique français. Engagée dans les affaires du Liban où la France participe au maintien de la paix, ce qui lui vaudra sur place de connaître de sanglants revers (assassinat de l'ambassadeur Delamarre, et conjointement aux américains, attentat contre Drakkar en 1983), on apprécie mal les capacités d'action, à la fois de la Syrie et du Hezbollah. En France même, Armée Secrète Arménienne pour la Libération de l'Arménie (l'ASALA) va commettre des attentats dont le plus grave est l'attentat d'Orly en 1983. La même année, l'apparition du terrorisme du GAL, plus ou moins commandité par les plus hautes autorités espagnoles, inquiète encore plus que tous les autres attentats le gouvernement français. Le GAL assassine sur le territoire français

des demandeurs d'asile suspectés d'appartenir à l'ETA et toute une
série de personnes sans relation aucune avec ETA afin de faire plier
par la force le gouvernement français et l'obliger à coopérer en
matière d'extradition. Le gouvernement soupçonne certains membres
de la police française d'être impliqué dans ces affaires, mais le
reconnaître serait créer une crise majeure.[5] Ces méthodes font croire
que décidément tout converge et que le terrorisme existe bien, y
compris en terme de terrorisme d'État.

La France n'est plus épargnée, elle est devenue la cible privilégiée
de diverses organisations, toutes pour des raisons différentes mais
toutes en même temps. On est alors persuadé qu'il faut une seule et
même politique pour traiter tous ces phénomènes. François
Mitterrand, inquiet des critiques sur le laxisme, renforce les pouvoirs
d'une cellule présidentielle dont il avait confié la direction à un
gendarme dès 1981 et qui répondra dès ce moment là directement à
Gilles Ménage, son conseiller en sécurité à l'Élysée.[6] La cellule
antiterroriste aura des activités qui iront bien plus loin que la lutte
antiterroriste, montrant les dérives possibles d'une organisation
secrète et protégée au plus haut niveau. Elle jouera néanmoins un
rôle pour établir des contacts au Moyen Orient où la France cherche
à se maintenir coûte que coûte. Mitterrand demande aussi à Pierre
Mauroy de créer un secrétariat d'État à la sécurité qui est confié le
17 août 1982 à Joseph Francesci et on envoie en Corse comme
préfet Robert Broussard, le célèbre policier de l'antigang. Les rivalités
gendarmerie/police nationale sont très vives et ne facilitent pas la
tâche des hommes qui, sur le terrain, sont pourtant plus enclins à
collaborer. Mais les attentats continuent et le contexte de tensions
internationales Est/Ouest avec la crise des Euromissiles porte les
questions de sécurité au premier plan. Pour montrer combien le
problème était pris au sérieux, le terrorisme devient l'affaire du chef
de l'État, on évoque avec la cellule la version française du National
Security Council (NSC) américain. Celui-ci se met en première ligne
et François Mitterrand, souvent avare de discours, intervient presque
systématiquement. L'opposition de droite y voit une opportunité et
redouble de critiques en demandant le rétablissement de la Cour de
Sûreté de l'État, des mesures pénales d'exception et la création d'un
service antiterroriste. Le rapport sur le terrorisme publié par le
sénateur Masson en 1983 apparaît comme une critique de la politique
du gouvernement et comme une plate forme des propositions de
l'opposition (Masson, 1984). Il sera un point de césure important
car, à partir de sa publication, les socialistes se sentiront toujours
pris en défaut sur le dossier de la violence politique et, dans leur

recomposition idéologique globale de 1984, ils voudront montrer leur 'culture de gouvernement' en reprenant les thèses de la droite sur ce point du terrorisme (Bigo et Hermant, 1990).

Cette politique de 1981 a pourtant eu des effets importants à long terme. Elle a réussi à dissocier les organisations clandestines de nombre de leurs soutiens, en particulier en Corse, en tout cas de ceux pour qui le terrorisme était bien un signal d'alarme. Elle a sans doute aussi limité les soutiens d'Action Directe et permis que des moyens judiciaires traditionnels mettent fin à l'existence de ce groupe bien plus tard. Mais il ne fallait pas être pressé et croire au miracle. Or, les hommes politiques sont liés par la vitesse des temps électoraux. Par ailleurs si cette politique avait un sens concernant la Corse ou même Action Directe, en croyant à la notion de terrorisme et en croyant qu'on pouvait l'appliquer aussi aux organisations venant de l'extérieur du territoire français, les socialistes se sont exposés à des revers importants.

Le Virage des Années 1984/86: Objectivation du Terrorisme via le Terrorisme International ou la France face aux Guerres de troisième type

Guerre et Terrorisme, les Guerres de troisième type

Dès 1982 pour les attentats provenant de l'étranger et à partir de 1984 pour les autres, le gouvernement change de stratégie. Il est impossible de criminaliser le terrorisme en en faisant un acte ordinaire et banal. Devant leur nombre impressionnant, une fois qu'ils sont mis en série, les journalistes accusent le gouvernement d'impuissance. Celui-ci tend alors à inverser la tendance et à chercher au contraire à désigner un adversaire puissant comme dans une guerre, pour expliquer au moins son échec momentané mais pour aussi rassurer en désignant un adversaire connu. Thème que les journalistes et les relais d'opinion reprennent à loisir (Francis, 1983: 54–8; Hamon et Marchand, 1986; Jacquard, 1987; Villeneuve et Péret, 1987; Collectif, 1990). Cette guerre à deux visages: les organisations clandestines internes sont finalement reliées entre elles à l'échelle européenne. C'est l'euroterrorisme qui sert de justification à la coopération européenne des polices. Tous les 'partis communistes combattants' sont les relais d'une stratégie de Moscou. Concernant les organisations clandestines provenant du Moyen Orient, toutes sont plus ou moins reliées, dit-on, aux mêmes sponsors. La révolution iranienne et le Hezbollah d'une part, la Syrie d'autre part sont désignés comme les responsables, les commanditaires des attentats. Un fil vert se substitue ou complète le fil rouge (Parat, 1989). Pierre Mauroy définit le terrorisme comme un crime qui dispose de moyens de guerre, avec parfois l'appui des États dès 1982, prenant ainsi le contre-pied de la politique de son ministre de la justice, Badinter.

Mais c'est à partir de 1984 que les retournements sont les plus sensibles. Dans un contexte où les missiles sont à l'Est et les pacifistes à l'Ouest, on invoque un nouveau danger: l'euroterrorisme regroupant la fraction armée rouge (RAF), Action Directe, les Cellules Communistes Combattantes, les débris des Communistes Organisés pour la Liberation Prolétarienne (COLP) et des Brigades Rouges, les FP 25, le 17 Novembre... et s'attaquant à des cibles militaires de l'OTAN en s'alignant sur les thèses de Moscou.[7] Des groupes au sein du PS veulent donner une image de fermeté et critiquent eux aussi la 'communication du gouvernement' en matière de lutte contre le terrorisme et l'insécurité. Bien que les enquêtes menées dans les différents pays par les moyens les plus traditionnels de la police judiciaire montreront que ces organisations ne se regroupaient au contraire qu'en raison de leur isolement grandissant sur le plan national qui bloquait les recrutements et obligeait chacune des organisations clandestines à faire appel aux spécialistes des autres organisations (Bigo et Hermant, 1985) et que la réalité des connexions se limitait à des individus isolés, recherchés par les polices nationales, qui se donnaient mutuellement des adresses de 'planque' et, à l'occasion, envisageaient une action ponctuelle contre le seul dénominateur commun qui puisse leur fournir une cible – l'armée américaine en Europe – nombre d'hommes politiques et de responsables de services seront intimement persuadés du danger de l'euroterrorisme.[8] Bien qu'existant ponctuellement, il fut largement surévalué, à la fois pour des raisons structurelles qui poussent à prévoir le pire, et pour des raisons conjoncturelles qui favorisaient les sujets de réflexions pour les groupes européens qui venaient de se constituer ou du moins d'être présentés à la presse plus officiellement (Bigo, 1996).

Création de l'UCLAT

Phénomène très important, pour la première fois, on pousse les services à collaborer parce qu'ils auraient à faire à une même menace, le terrorisme. Malgré la réticence très forte des services de renseignements d'ouvrir certains dossiers à leur collègue de la PJ et

de la gendarmerie, on crée le 8 octobre 1984 l'Unité de Coordination et de Liaison Anti-Terroriste (UCLAT) dont le but est de faciliter
les échanges d'informations entre services français. Placée directement
à l'échelle du Directeur général de la Police nationale, l'UCLAT
représente une petite dizaine de fonctionnaires et n'est pas en mesure
de concurrencer les services existants, mais sa haute place dans la
hiérarchie et la qualité des policiers qui en seront les dirigeants font
que l'UCLAT va s'imposer comme un lieu d'échange des
renseignements ponctuels d'abord, plus stratégiques ensuite. Y
participent Direction de la Surveillance du Territoire (DST), Direction centrale des renseignements généraux (DCRG), Renseignements
généraux de la préfecture de police (RGPP), Direction centrale de la
police judiciaire (DCPJ), Police de l'air et des frontières (PAF) et
même par la suite gendarmes et magistrats.

L'UCLAT ne réussira pas en un jour, les tensions avec les
magistrats et même entre services se prolongeront. Son
opérationnalité sera discutée en 1986, mais son existence
institutionnalisera un lieu et des personnes chargées de se réunir en
cas de crise et de faire des suivis de dossiers. Par ailleurs
l'européanisation passant par les offices centraux, l'UCLAT apportera
une plus value aux services qui la composent, ce qui les amènera à
être plus disposés à collaborer. L'UCLAT n'arrivera pas forcément
aux mêmes résultats selon les formes diversifiées d'attentats. Policiers
et gendarmes délivrent peu d'informations sur la Corse, chacun
doutant de l'autre, infiltration d'un côté, inefficacité de l'autre. Sur
Action Directe, on sait aussi le transit complexe des informations
qui permirent certes l'arrestation de Rouillan et Ménigon, mais bien
plus tard que si les informations avaient été délivrées normalement.
En revanche sur le Proche Orient, les services policiers lisent
quasiment tous (à l'exception de quelques personnes qui insistent
au contraire sur la diversité de la scène orientale) les événements du
Proche Orient comme un seul et même phénomène et voient dans
les attaques libyennes contre le Royaume-Uni, syriennes contre
l'Allemagne, du Hezbollah contre la France une sorte de lutte entre
les extrémistes proche-orientaux et les démocraties européennes.
Mais cette fois ce seront les autres gouvernements européens qui
seront réticents à collaborer avec la France dans ce milieu des
années 80, car la France est plus touchée que les autres pays et
n'arrive pas à imposer sa politique étrangère comme la politique
étrangère des autres européens. L'Europe ne se sent pas 'responsable'
du Liban. Beaucoup y voient de vieux rêves de gloire français ou au
mieux des amitiés légitimes mais que le rapport de force interna-

tional ne permet plus de maintenir à tout prix. Tout cela culminera
avec la crise des otages du Liban en 1985 et la grande vague
d'attentats de 1985/86 dominée dans la mémoire par l'explosion de
la rue de Rennes en Septembre 1986 mais initiée par le réseau Ali
Fouad Saleh dès l'attentat contre les Galeries Lafayette de décembre
1985 puis les attentats de février et mars 1986 (Bigo, 1991).
Allemagne et Espagne géreront très différemment de la France leur
propre crise des otages, tout comme les attentats qui commencent
(Lemasson, 1992). La France va alors, pour de nombreuses années,
être le lieu privilégié des attentats provenant des groupes en lutte au
Liban. L'arrivée au pouvoir de la droite en mars 1986 ne change
quasiment rien aux pratiques mais les rhétoriques sont comme
libérées des ambiguïtés restantes sur le caractère parfois politique
(et légitime?) des combats des organisations clandestines.

Guerre, Terrorisme et Gestion de l'Opinion

En 1986, Jacques Chirac déclare, 'le terrorisme, c'est la
guerre'. Le terrorisme est désormais défini comme une menace qui
attaque l'État à son sommet, comme un défi au chef d'État. Le chef
de l'État, le chef du gouvernement se trouvent personnellement
impliqués dans la lutte contre le terrorisme. Les auteurs des attentats
jouent d'ailleurs volontiers sur ce lien.[9] En 1986, Jacques Chirac se
sent personnellement visé comme maire de Paris. Cette politisation
au sommet, sensible depuis la prise en main du dossier terroriste
par François Mitterrand, ne se démentira plus. Mais elle a de
redoutables effets (Bigo et Hermant, 1986d). En effet, secteur
particulièrement visible de l'action du gouvernement, ou d'ailleurs
des autres acteurs publics, l'antiterrorisme implique une
personnalisation au plus haut niveau avec toutes les conséquences
que cela suppose: dramatisation et médiatisation. Le moindre attentat fait la une des journaux. En période de crise, la rubrique
terrorisme devient quasi quotidienne, même pour répéter jusqu'à
plus soif les mêmes informations ou le même manque d'information.
Il faut absolument parler, le pouvoir doit s'exprimer, condamner,
communiquer, rassurer. La politique symbolique devient prioritaire.
Les commentaires journalistiques et de certains experts ne délivrent
pas d'informations mais s'apparentent assez bien à ce travail de
deuil des pleureuses dans les sociétés méditerranéennes. Travail de
deuil peut-être nécessaire à la société mais qui insécurise autant
qu'il rassure, étant donné la désacralisation de ce travail de deuil où
le commercial joue autant que le respect des victimes. Le côté
spectaculaire de ces attentats, l'effet de télescopage des explosions

de diverses origines frappent bien sûr le gouvernement dans ce qui constitue sa tâche première: assurer la sécurité des personnes; on comprend donc cette nécessité de 'communiquer' mais, à trop paraître sur la scène, la répétition des images brise l'émotion, surtout lorsqu'on met du temps à reconnaître aux victimes du terrorisme les mêmes droits que ceux des victimes de guerre.

Sous la cohabitation le terrorisme restera une pomme de discorde entre Chirac et Mitterrand; le sommet étant atteint lors du face à face lors de la campagne électorale de 1988 à propos du dossier Gordgi où chacun accusera l'autre de mentir. Mais, en réalité, ces querelles politiciennes se déroulent sur un fond consensuel. L'opposition entre droite et gauche paraît largement un jeu de faux semblants sur fond de compétition électorale. Car, d'une certaine manière après le dissensus, le consensus s'impose parce que l'image du terrorisme s'est définitivement fixée dans le pôle de l'horreur après les attentats de 1986. Qui oserait discuter la légitimité d'un gouvernement s'attaquant à des terroristes tuant des citoyens français? Qui oserait rappeler la connexion avec la politique étrangère de la France au Proche Orient, le prêt de ses avions (et de ses pilotes?) militaires à l'Irak et la destruction de villages iraniens ou les actions de formation contre les membres du Front Islamique du Salut (FIS) en Algérie, si ce n'est des avocats comme Jacques Verges ou Ali Fouad Saleh lui-même?

Face à un terrorisme, symbole de la barbarie et de l'inattendu, on se protège en parlant encore et toujours. En témoigne la multiplication d'ouvrages sur le terrorisme en France qui paraissent quasiment 'en direct', quelques mois après les faits, et l'indifférence parfois choquante des média pour les moments des procès où l'on juge les coupables. Mais les journalistes ne sont pas les seuls. Ministères et Parlement se penchent sur la question et font rapport sur rapport en des termes apocalyptiques. La longue crise des otages au Liban qui s'achève en 1988 après deux ans achève de médiatiser la question. Après 1986, il n'est plus possible d'analyser le terrorisme en France de la même manière, les implications sociétales ont changé. La politique antiterroriste est définitivement centrée sur la gestion de l'opinion et elle est quasiment unifiée.

Décentrement du Terrorisme et Objectivation française

En dix ans la conception du terrorisme et de l'antiterrorisme a changé. Si le terrorisme pouvait dans les années 70 dépasser les frontières et devenir international, il ne l'était que superficiellement,

ou minoritairement. Le cœur de l'anti-terrorisme était la délégitimation des combats à vocation révolutionnaires ou nationalistes. Il
s'agissait de punir sévèrement, comme des criminels, les organisations clandestines continuant à user de violence au lieu de rentrer
dans les règles du jeu démocratique et du bulletin de vote. La notion
de terrorisme était plus prédicative que substantive, elle soulignait
la violence plus qu'elle ne la constituait, elle renvoyait à la manipulation (des services secrets de l'Est), à la simple bavure, ou encore,
comme moyen violent de communication, elle pouvait être considérée
comme un éclat arraché à une violence traditionnelle (nationale,
sociale ou les deux), dont le sens profond était de rendre visible
pour l'opinion occidentale un conflit local. A l'échelle internationale,
le terrorisme ne faisait que souligner le rôle prééminent des puissances
occidentales. Sur le fond les analyses du terrorisme de l'époque
s'inspirent de la querelle sur la nature – et l'efficacité – de la
violence politique qui se déroula à la fin du XIXème siècle au sein
des organisations ouvrières dans laquelle on distinguait
soigneusement entre violence révolutionnaire, expression d'un
mouvement social, et violence anarchiste, on dira plus tard terroriste,
maniée, elle, par des petits groupes qui espéraient par ce moyen
réveiller les consciences et mobiliser. La problématique de
l'enracinement était déjà placée au centre de ces réflexions, ce qui
permet d'ailleurs de comprendre pourquoi le terme – politiquement
injurieux depuis Lénine – est encore refusé par les militants
révolutionnaire marxistes des années 70: succès donc, selon cette
grille de lecture, des Brigades Rouge qui pendant peu de temps,
auront une véritable base sociale, échec de la RAF qui ne réussira
pas à enclencher un mouvement social à partir du climat de révolte
des années 1968, échec encore, mais échec responsable, en France
quand la Gauche prolétarienne refusera la 'militarisation' de la
protestation et s'autodissoudra. Un peu plus tard, échec, après une
courte trajectoire, d'Action directe.

   Quand au terrorisme à base régionale ou locale, il suit le modèle
du mouvement de libération nationale qui avait sous-tendu la
décolonisation. Ce qui, là encore, sous-entend une résonance directe
entre une population et l'organisation clandestine, résonance faite
de sympathie sur les objectifs, l'indépendance ou la souffrance d'un
peuple, et de passivité sur le moyen employé (la violence). Vainqueur,
ou en expansion, le terrorisme gagne ses lettres de noblesses
révolutionnaires; vaincu, il qualifie les organisations révolutionnaires
ou indépendantistes qui n'arrivent pas à s'enraciner et restent des
groupuscules. Elles s'isolent alors de la société, s'enferment sur

elles-mêmes et certains désignent là une pathologie sociale, hors de la morale humaine. En conséquence pour l'observateur l'usage de la notion de terrorisme se confond avec la coupure entre les problèmes réels dont les auteurs des attentats se réclament, et les attentats eux-mêmes. Michel Wieviorka (1989) dans son ouvrage 'Sociétés et terrorisme' a sans doute été l'auteur qui a analysé le plus finement les divers cas de violence politique en mettant en avant l'idée d'inversion[10] caractérisant le parcours de ces groupes par rapport à leur communauté d'origine, tout en ayant assez de lucidité pour refuser, surtout à l'époque, d'y inclure absolument tous les groupes ayant des revendications communautaires et agissant sur territoire étranger.[11] En distinguant le terrorisme comme logique d'action et moyen d'action, il faisait des premiers l'archétype du terrorisme au moment où la communauté n'avait d'yeux que pour les seconds, ceux qui, délocalisant la violence, la rendait intolérable parce qu'elle frappait des sociétés en paix.

Le terrorisme devenait alors un terme signifiant ce décalage: il permettait de coupler légitimité d'une syntaxe politique violente au Moyen Orient et illégitimité de son transfert en Europe, tout en soulignant l'importance et quelquefois la dimension désespérée de l'appel aux gouvernements occidentaux.

Ces analyses subtiles sont en définitive rassurantes pour le gouvernement français puisque structurellement le terrorisme ne peut qu'échouer. Les autorités n'ont plus qu'à gérer l'urgence, et peuvent se contenter d'un traitement purement policier de la vio-lence. Les problèmes de fond seront traités sur le moyen terme dans le cadre traditionnel de la politique intérieure ou étrangère (et régionale) du gouvernement. Il n'était pas prévu qu'ils deviennent aussi fréquents et que ce que l'on appelait les conflits de troisième génération dans les pays du Tiers-Monde puisse devenir une pra-tique, certes très rare, mais pensable dans les démocraties occidentales.

Dans le milieu des années 80, surtout après 1986 et encore plus après la fin de la bipolarité, le terrorisme n'est plus simplement un label englobant; on retourne la perspective en faisant du terrorisme international l'élément structurant de l'analyse. On n'analyse plus les attentats des organisations pour voir si tactiquement on a intérêt à les classer sous le vocable de terrorisme, avec forcément toutes les luttes que cela suppose entre services et Ministères (voir le rôle du Ministère des Affaires Étrangères prévenant Gordgi qu'il sera arrêté par les policiers s'il sort de l'ambassade iranienne de Paris). On insère tout acte violent dans une grille de lecture prédéfinie et suffisamment large pour qu'on puisse appliquer les mêmes méthodes.[12] Le terrorisme n'est plus une simple projection momentanée de violence venue d'ailleurs, il est une 'guerre qui ne dit pas son nom', proclame les officiels. Les menaces ne sont plus celles de l'invasion militaire par l'URSS mais l'agitation interne par la manipulation des milieux immigrés via des arguments religieux ou jouant sur les difficultés du travail (trafiquants de drogue...). Les menaces sont celles du terrorisme venus de l'intégrisme et de l'anti-occidentalisme.

La France a des ennemis dans le monde qui ont nom euroterrorisme, radicalisme islamique, fanatisme religieux. Instrument de politique étrangère et de déstabilisation, ce terrorisme new-look ou de troisième type est adossé à des États hostiles, ou à des idéologies, des mouvements d'opinion plus vaste comme l'intégrisme islamiste. Si dans son modus operandi il renvoie toujours à de petits groupes isolés et fanatiques, ces derniers, situés au bout d'une chaîne d'acteurs, ne jouent pas un rôle central dans cette relation violente animé par des acteurs permanents que sont les États. Il y a désormais stabilité et continuité de la menace. Pourvu aux yeux de ceux qui s'y réfèrent de cohérence interne, doté d'une sorte d'encaisse de légitimité, le terrorisme existe préalablement à ses futures manifestations, il sert désormais de matrice d'explication surplombant la violence et la vectorisant. Analyser le terrorisme c'est démonter alors un système de violence pourvu d'acteurs spécifiques, de méthodes et de buts. Nous ne sommes plus en face d'une simple collection de violences insérées dans des contextes différents, et superficiellement reliées par des similitudes formelles, nous sommes en face d'un système dont les éclats (attentats, procès...) cachent la continuité. Le terrorisme augmente sa masse molaire si l'on peut dire, il devient un objet politique à forte attraction entraînant des actes qui monopolisent l'espace politique un peu comme un corps lourd s'impose à des éléments plus légers. A l'antiterrorisme ponctuel, souvent doublé de compréhension sur les causes qu'il défend, – malgré les moyens utilisés pour les défendre, elles ont droit de cité dans le débat démocratique – succède un antiterrorisme sans concession, justifié par l'extraordinaire capacité de nuisance de leur projet déstabilisateur – ce qui n'est pas difficile à faire croire au moment où les bombes explosent et qu'on ne sait pas si elles vont s'arrêter...

Antiterrorisme en France, Influence américaine et Contexte du désordre international

Fortement adossée aux discours venus des États-Unis à propos du terrorisme international et du rôle du radicalisme iranien, cette rhétorique n'interroge plus la diversité des acteurs, des actions, des contextes, elle vise au contraire à tout intégrer. Régis Debray, qui ne peut être soupçonné ni d'être de droite, ni d'être pro-américain, tient lui aussi dès 1989 un tel discours:

> Subordonnée aux priorités atlantiques et entraînée par elle, l'Europe Otanisée a durci son flanc allemand et dégarni son flanc méridional. A tous points de vue, et pas simplement militaire, nous sommes durs face au mou et mous face au dur. Si grossièrement parlant, le vert a remplacé le rouge comme force mondiale montante, nous centrons notre attention sur un front devenu secondaire... et nous les économisons face à des adversaires potentiels offensifs... Chaque identité s'aiguise contre sa voisine. L'Europe, et non l'Amérique ou l'Asie est l'Autre de l'Islam... Islam qui risque de combiner l'archaïsme religieux ou tribal et la technologie ultramoderne. (Debray, 1989: 192)

Samuel Huntington (1993) remettra au goût du jour et popularisera encore plus ce thème du clash civilisationnel mais dès ce moment il est la grille de lecture qui conduit l'analyse de la violence politique touchant la France (Huntington, 1993; a contrario Bigo, 1995). On suppose alors que les types de solidarité religieuse ou nationaliste avec le pays d'origine priment sur les types de solidarité citoyenne dans le pays d'accueil, ce qui expliquerait le passage à l'acte de groupes d'immigrés, mal intégrés dans une société, ou celui de leurs enfants. Olivier Roy (s.f.), parmi d'autres a plusieurs fois insisté sur cette possibilité d'inversion des allégeances. A un niveau plus général Bertrand Badie (1994) a évoqué cette possibilité de solidarités transnationales remettant en cause les allégeances citoyennes. Gilles Kepel et Rémy Leveau (1992), après enquête, ont montré que justement il n'en était rien aussi bien en 1985/1986 où lors des attentats la communauté musulmane vivant en France était la première à s'en émouvoir, qu'au moment de la guerre du Golfe où elle répondit à 'l'exigence de loyauté'. Il y a néanmoins là une question véritable qui alimente les spéculations sur les attitudes des jeunes issus de l'immigration. Seulement il s'agit de spéculations non confirmées, de plausibilité d'un discours qui se nourrit de sa cohérence logique mais guère d'éléments concrets.

Les Attentats de 1995 et 1996: les Interprétations qui en sont faites

Le débat autour des attentats de 1995 et 1996 est à cet égard significatif. La France médiatique s'est tournée vers ses immigrés, vers ses étrangers de l'intérieur, a fait des reportages sur les banlieues, le mal vivre, le radicalisme religieux des mosquées françaises, sur de nouveau le foulard islamique et a finalement peu analysé les raisons de la guerre civile en Algérie et la participation de la France à ce conflit. Plutôt qu'une équipe de professionnels venant de l'étranger (des spécialistes du GIA), on s'orientait alors vers plusieurs équipes d'amateurs venant de 'l'étranger intérieur': les banlieues. Mais, et ceci est fondamental, la structure du continuum sécuritaire permit une transition 'en douceur' entre ces deux hypothèses comme si elles ne faisaient qu'une, comme si les islamistes radicaux des GIA algériens, les immigrés algériens en France et leurs enfants étaient les 'mêmes'.

Le malaise des banlieues était la soi-disant explication de l'endoctrinement des jeunes. On présentait quelques jeunes barbus pour 'prouver' leur 'fanatisme religieux'. Ne pouvant les montrer en train de poser des bombes, on les montrait en train de prier à la mosquée. Les effets d'amalgame permettaient à une société française de croiser à tous les coins de rue un terroriste potentiel. La 'visibilisation' avait à ce point réussi que le terroriste était partout! Vigipirate était nécessaire. On pourrait détailler bien plus que nous ne le faisons ici et reprendre ces rhétoriques sur l'ennemi intérieur. Michel Wieviorka (1995) dans *Libération*, Jocelyne Cesari (1995) dans *le Monde* ont déjà insisté sur les dangereux glissements de sens qui conduisent à amalgamer islam, intégrisme, terrorisme et banlieues. Cette dernière rappelait que l'islamisation révèle une recherche d'identité et qu'il n'y aura véritable reconnaissance de l'islam dans la société française qu'à partir du moment où l'on comprendra qu'il s'agit d'hommes et de femmes aussi divers par leurs pratiques religieuses que par leurs origines sociales et ethniques. On pourrait se demander pourquoi le nom de Khaled Kelkal est aussi médiatique alors que les noms des principaux organisateurs du réseau, venant de l'étranger ou y vivant sont quasi inconnus. Des études sont en cours. Pour l'instant admettons au moins que cela suppose de revenir sur le sens politique de nos relations avec l'Algérie et d'en finir avec les processus de construction d'un ennemi qui hantent les forces de sécurité depuis la fin de la bipolarité.

Quiconque remet en cause l'existence d'un phénomène terroriste et son homogénéité se voit renvoyer à la 'longue liste d'attentats subis par la France'. La diversité des acteurs, le fait que la France est parfois champ clos entre adversaires tout autant que cible d'une alliance de groupes contre elle, disparaît. On adapte, un peu comme au temps de la guerre froide, une grille de lecture a priori où le terrorisme est le produit du clash civilisationnel et de la présence des immigrés sur le territoire des démocraties occidentales. On généralise à l'excès, prenant la France pour l'ensemble de l'Europe alors qu'elle est cette fois-ci en première ligne, et en disant que toutes les formes de terrorisme la frappe simultanément (Raufer, 1982) alors même que le calme complet règne dans les organisations clandestines à vocation révolutionnaire après le démantèlement d'Action Directe et que le conflit nationaliste corse suit des règles bien différentes d'autolimitation tactique de la violence (Lefebvre, 1992).[13]

Ce retournement met la France sur le même registre que les Américains pour qui la lutte contre le terrorisme était dans les années 80 essentiellement externe mais va devenir aussi interne dans le début des années 90. En plus de l'interne, il faudra donc aux deux pays penser l'interface interne/externe et le rapport au terrorisme. Cela se fera par une extension des concepts de sécurité qui ne s'impose pas du jour au lendemain. Elle se construit à la fois dans les discours des experts et dans ceux de la classe politique en donnant lieu à une consécration juridique de la notion de terrorisme dans le droit français. Elle se construit aussi et surtout par la mise en place du plan Vigipirate qui finit par instituer cette étrange 'crise permanente'.

Les Politiques Antiterroristes en Place: Crise Intermittente ou Permanente? La République en Danger?

Faire une Infraction spécifique?

Le changement de majorité aux législatives de 1986 et la fin de la série d'attentats du réseau Ali Fouad Saleh (qui sont les plus meurtriers) accélérèrent le processus de simulation guerrière. Arrivé avec un programme accusant de laxisme la gauche, le gouvernement Chirac crée un conseil de sécurité intérieure avec le Ministre de l'intérieur et celui des affaires étrangères mais sans coordination présidentielle, et reprenant l'ancienne Cellule Interministérielle du Lutte Antiterroriste (CILAT). Le ministère de l'intérieur se voit donner beaucoup de latitude. Il joue un rôle de plus en plus important dans les affaires extérieures, ce qui remet en cause les rapports internes/ externes traditionnels (par exemple, entre DST et DGSE). Mais, soucieux aussi de ne pas se faire censurer par le président Mitterrand, et peut-être de prendre des distances avec les déclarations qu'il avait faites dans l'opposition, Jacques Chirac va s'autolimiter et proposera un arsenal législatif en deçà des désirs de beaucoup des membres du Rassemblement pour la République (RPR). Il veut renforcer encore plus les effectifs, renforcer les dispositions pénales, mais ceci avait déjà été commencé avec la période de Pierre Joxe à l'Intérieur et la sévérité des juges français est connue, la mesure de peine incompressible à trente ans étant plus symbolique qu'autre chose.

Si l'on n'ose donc pas remettre en cause l'UCLAT et lui substituer un service antiterroriste comme le souhaitaient les cercles proches de Charles Pasqua, et si l'on n'ose revenir à la Cour de Sûreté de l'État, on centralise en revanche la procédure judiciaire par la loi du 9 septembre 1986 complétée par celle du 30 décembre 1986 sur la spécialisation de la 8ème section du parquet de Paris dans les affaires de terrorisme (qui deviendra 14ème section).[14] Cette mesure tient à un compromis entre la définition d'une infraction de terrorisme voulu par certains membres de la commission Justice du RPR et les membres de la chancellerie, encore mitterrandistes et qui préparaient un texte sur une centralisation éventuelle de procédure.[15] Le juge Marsaud, qui deviendra par la suite député RPR, jouera un rôle non négligeable dans ces lois et dans la suite des propositions de la droite en ce domaine. Il sera, avec d'autres personnes de la chancellerie, à la base de cette réforme fondamentale qui, en permettant la centralisation, permettra sur des enquêtes jusque-là sectorisées de renouer des fils disjoints (mettant fin ainsi à la réforme Badinter à partir d'un critère d'efficacité des recherches et non d'une nouvelle querelle idéologique) et Gilles Boulouque sera un des premiers juges d'instruction spécialisés à pouvoir en profiter pour comprendre les réseaux de financements et d'acheminement des armes des attentes de 1986 par le groupe Ali Fouad Saleh. Mais la spécialisation montrera aussi ses limites en braquant les projecteurs des media sur les juges, ce que certains supporteront moins que d'autres, ou ce qui poussera d'autres encore à convoquer la presse pour évoquer leurs hypothèses, et même jouer des coups politiques à l'égard de certains gouvernants. En même temps, la spécialisation atteindra ses limites quand il n'y aura guère de nouveaux attentats entre 1990 et 1994.

Néanmoins cette loi de 1986 fut jugée cohérente d'autant qu'elle permit effectivement aux juges locaux de décider par eux-mêmes s'ils devaient se dessaisir ou non, et dans le procès Ali Fouad Saleh elle montra son efficacité. La loi du 9 Septembre 1986 introduira aussi, et ceci est plus discutable, la possibilité de prolonger la garde à vue au delà de quarante-huit heures pour une nouvelle période de quarante-huit heures; si les 'nécessités de l'enquête en matière de terrorisme l'exigent', et le fait que les perquisitions, visites domiciliaires et les saisies de pièces à conviction peuvent avoir lieu 'sans l'assentiment des personnes chez qui elles ont lieu'. Pour éviter que les jurés populaires tirés au sort ne se trouvent être l'objet de pression lors des audiences de jugement, la loi instituera une cour d'assise spécialement composée de magistrats professionnels. Enfin la loi prévoira une disposition spéciale sur les repentis, auteur ou complice d'un acte de terrorisme, ayant 'averti l'autorité administrative ou judiciaire' et permis ainsi 'que l'infraction ne se réalise et d'identifier, le cas échéant, les autres coupables'.

En même temps, subtilement, Marsaud proposait à Chirac de se refuser à définir le terrorisme comme une infraction, mais plutôt de le définir comme une circonstance aggravante à des infractions criminelles. Il n'introduisait ainsi la notion que par le biais de la procédure pénale (articles 706–16 de ce code), sans en faire une incrimination spécifique, et permettait une plasticité très grande selon les cas d'espèces tout en donnant l'impression au public que la notion de terrorisme était bien juridiquement définie. La loi précisait que les infractions étaient terroristes 'quand elles sont en relation avec une entreprise individuelle ou collective ayant pour but de troubler gravement l'ordre public par l'intimidation ou la terreur' mais donnait une liste d'infractions criminelles limitatives. C'est donc par le biais de l'intention de l'auteur qu'un acte peut être qualifié de terroriste et non par l'acte lui-même, nous dit le commentaire, mais en fait l'intention de l'auteur est toujours de le dire politique. C'est donc en fait la manière dont le gouvernement analyse l'intention de l'auteur plus que intention elle-même qui comptera. Donc s'il utilise la violence à des fins politiques en France, il est terroriste dès que sa forme de violence a été prévue comme une infraction. Nous frisons ces moments où dans un État de Droit la démocratie se défend avec des armes à double tranchants. En effet, les actes de terrorisme échappent ainsi à la définition classique des infractions politiques par nature et redeviennent des infractions de droit commun bien que le but recherché soit politique car elles usent de moyens criminels. La subtilité juridique réussit donc à exclure du politique en démocratie tout acte violent sans pourtant s'attaquer de front au changement de norme qui avait conduit au contraire à admettre l'usage légitime de celle-ci dans les situations révolutionnaires françaises. Cette stratégie est d'ailleurs reprise dans le nouveau code pénal de 1992 qui fait des actes de terrorisme des infractions punies en vertu d'une échelle de peines propres, impliquant une aggravation des peines par rapport aux mêmes délits ou crimes quand ils ne revêtent pas un caractère terroriste. L'article 421-1 du code qui définit les actes de terrorisme est complété par l'article 421-2 définissant le crime de terrorisme écologique. Malgré la volonté de ne pas introduire un droit d'exception, la volonté d'efficacité des autorités, que personne, dans la classe politique, ne conteste, produit un effet d'expansion qui menace l'équilibre répression/liberté individuelle en attirant dans son orbite des pans entiers de législation.

A cet égard, la loi du 22 juillet 1996, présentée au Parlement le 25 octobre 1995 donc, pendant la vague d'attentats de la même année, élargit la liste des infractions pouvant être qualifiées de terroristes en y rattachant par exemple les délits en matière de groupes de combat ou de reconstitution de ligues dissoutes, ou de recel de criminel. Mais l'élargissement sans fin de la liste des infractions pose un problème surtout lorsqu'elle suppose par exemple qu'accueillir chez soi des personnes sans-papiers peut être associé à une infraction connexe à du terrorisme, s'il est prouvé a posteriori que celles-ci ont commis ou ont été complices d'actes de terrorisme sur le territoire français. Loi de circonstance, destinée à renforcer la lutte contre le terrorisme, elle a été censurée par le Conseil constitutionnel sur l'extension des perquisitions pendant la nuit, qui sont de nature à entraîner des atteintes excessives à la liberté individuelle. Ces perquisitions seront autorisées uniquement en cas de 'flagrance', c'est à dire si l'acte terroriste est en train de se commettre ou vient de se commettre. Plus important, le Conseil constitutionnel a censuré l'assimilation faite par la loi de l'aide à un étranger en situation irrégulière et de la présomption d'assistance à une entreprise terroriste. Il entendait ainsi écarter tout risque d'extension de l'incrimination de terrorisme à des comportements périphériques et empêcher la création d'un véritable 'continuum sécuritaire' qui brouille les frontières entre législation sur les étrangers et loi antiterroriste, continuum dont nous avons expliqué la constitution ailleurs mais qui, résumé, peut s'expliquer à travers le fait que le travail policier a mis l'accent sur les interconnexions entre crime et drogue, drogue et terrorisme, filière de drogue et filière d'immigration clandestine, immigration clandestine et jeunes issus de l'immigration, terrorisme et jeunes issus de l'immigration... d'où la tentation d'user des arguments de la lutte anti-terroriste jugés légitimes (ou comme un mal nécessaire mais qu'il faut accepter contre la violence ouverte), pour traiter d'autres problèmes de sociétés comme la place des étrangers en France avec les visas de tourisme, le fichage de ceux qui les reçoivent, la place des jeunes des cités dans la vie quotidienne...

Seulement, malgré les limites posées par le Conseil constitutionnel, violemment critiqué par certains députés au point qu'on dut les rappeler à la décence de leur fonction, cette extension sans fin du terrorisme par les multiples infractions auquel il correspondrait et son insertion dans le code modifient les équilibres sécurité/liberté et ce, d'autant qu'on a été tenté de lui faire jouer un rôle dans le débat sur l'immigration et les expulsions en disant que les mesures antiterroristes étaient dissuasives pour l'immigration clandestine. L'instauration en France des visas pour la majorité des étrangers non-européens fut justifiée par les attentats de 1986 alors même qu'elle était planifiée avec les autres membres de Schengen pour lutter contre l'immigration illégale. Les expulsions des sans papiers par charters n'ont jamais été si nombreusers que pendant les périodes des attentats en France en profitant d'un climat d'opinion qui les comprehensive. Les surveillances renforcées et les points sensibles désignés par Vigipirate ont aussi une logique dépassant semble-t-il la surveillance des points stratégiques militaires pour renforcer les contrôles migratoires ou les contrôles des cités à problèmes. Mais jusqu'où peut-on aller dans cette voie?

En effet, depuis 1986, la mise en place du plan Vigipirate a transformé assez fortement l'organisation policière en unifiant de facto cette dernière et en adjoignant des forces militaires à la lutte antiterroriste, renouant par là avec la situation proche de l'État d'urgence, mais celle-ci peut-elle être permanente?

Cette question se pose d'autant plus que, moins que la violence, on dit vouloir prévenir la menace de la violence. Or, une menace n'a pas de limite, elle occupe tout l'espace imaginable. Il n'y a pas de limite à la menace, aux acteurs potentiels. Cette virtualisation fait que le terrorisme est à géométrie variable. Il peut occuper n'importe quel créneau. Par définition une menace n'indique pas son actualisation. L'antiterrorisme ne balise pas un domaine précis. Il est extensible à l'infini. Sa prévention devient permanente, mais si elle passe par des moyens militaires, quelles en sont les implications? Ceci est d'autant plus important que l'espace européen se constitue et qu'il faut définir l'espace pertinent de contrôle. Enfin, comme nous l'avons déjà signalé, les discours sur le désordre international post bipolaire et le clash civilisationnel n'encouragent pas une appréciation raisonnée et poussent au contraire à une sorte d'angoisse permanente justifiant le maintien d'outils conçus pour des situations d'exceptions.

Vigipirate: l'Antiterrorisme au permanent?

Dans nos sociétés, dans laquelle la notion d'assurance est fort ancienne, la notion de responsabilité sans faute laisse l'État face à ses devoirs envers les victimes des attentats. Grâce à la reconnaissance du statut de victime de guerre, les victimes du terrorisme ont pu être indemnisées, même si ce ne fut pas sans difficulté et s'il fallut une mobilisation qui ne put compter sur une générosité et une compassion spontanées (Rudelski, 1992). Aussi l'Etat se sent-il le droit et le devoir de prévenir au maximum tout phénomène engageant sa responsabilité. Des plans de crise, de catastrophe, de prise en considération du risque sont courants dans les domaines les plus divers. Cette sensibilité se note par exemple dans les années 70 par la création d'un secrétariat aux risques naturels (et technologiques). Les mesures de prévention des attentats s'inscrivent quelque part dans la même perspective. Les plans de mobilisation des moyens médicaux (plan blanc) ou de coordination des moyens d'urgence sous l'autorité des pompiers de Paris (plan rouge) sont des plans qui s'inscrivent autour des secours d'urgence et pas simplement dans le cadre du terrorisme. Une catastrophe aérienne serait de ce point de vue plus éprouvante qu'un attentat terroriste. Quoi qu'il en soit, ce côté technique de la lutte est maintenant bien rodé. Il a bénéficié de l'expérience accumulée et là il est pertinent de parler d'une politique publique ayant un objet défini et un périmètre cohérent.

En revanche, comme nous l'avons noté tout au long de ce chapitre, la coordination des moyens des services a été tardive parce que leurs objets concrets différaient trop et parce que ne s'imposait que difficilement la notion qu'ils appartenaient tous à une même classe de phénomène: le terrorisme. Il a fallu un long travail d'objectivation, de construction symbolique pour homogénéiser l'espace diversifié des violences politiques en France sous la rubrique de terrorisme. Il a fallu une constante délégitimation du recours à la violence, que ce soit pour des causes intérieures ou extérieures. Mais, pour ces dernières, il est difficile d'annuler les causalités réciproques et de ne produire que celles de l'acteur désigné comme terroriste. Les actions violentes récentes doivent bien s'analyser (et sont analysées d'ailleurs par bien des professionnels) comme les retombées explosives collatérales de la politique étrangère de la France au Moyen Orient et au Maghreb. C'est aussi pourquoi on y a progressivement engagé l'armée, même si le terrorisme est considéré comme une menace non militaire.

Le plan Vigipirate existait dans les cartons depuis la fin des années 70 mais il s'agissait au départ, dit-on, d'un plan s'appliquant à une menace de type terrorisme BCN bactériologique, chimique ou nucléaire, et il ne fut pas considéré comme pertinent par les socialistes dans les années 80. Il a néanmoins été utilisé par le gouvernement Chirac dès le 15 septembre 1986 pour faire face au défi de guerre lancé pensait-on, par les frères Abdallah et la Syrie, à moins que ce ne fût le Hezbollah et l'Iran de Khomeyni. Ceci correspondait à la fois à une mesure visant à rassurer la population par la présence physique de l'armée et à donner un signal qu'une escalade armée était toujours possible, surtout après la rupture des relations diplomatiques avec l'Iran. Ce plan durera jusqu'au mois d'octobre 1987 et mobilisera près de deux mille militaires assistant les forces de polices, de gendarmerie et de douanes surveillant les frontières, les aérogares, les gares et les points névralgiques de communication.

Décidé par le premier ministre, ce plan d'alerte et de prévention en cas de menace d'actions terroristes associe les ministres agissant dans le cadre de leur responsabilité de défense. Le ministre de l'Intérieur y joue au départ un rôle clef puisque c'est lui qui assure la centralisation et le traitement du renseignement concernant le terrorisme sur le territoire national et les départements et territoires d'outre-mer (DOM-TOM). Ce plan a pour objectif d'accentuer la vigilance des fonctionnaires civils et militaires et de renforcer les mesures de protection des points et réseaux sensibles du pays. Il comprend une gamme de dispositions adaptée à des formes particulières de menaces.[16] Divisé en deux phases de vigilance, Vigipirate simple (forces de sécurité intérieure seules) et Vigipirate renforcé (appel aux armées, mise en œuvre des plans de crise), il prévoit l'utilisation de l'armée pour participer aux tâches de surveillance à partir du moment où l'on dépasse le stade des mesures policières discrètes et celui de la mise en place des forces de CRS (compagnies républicaines de sécurité) et d'escadrons mobiles de gendarmerie.

Ce plan général précise la répartition des responsabilités centrales et territoriales. Il précise aussi les volumes d'engagement des forces en fonction de leur catégories, du stade auquel elles entreront en action et de leurs responsabilités propres, le plus délicat tenant à connaître précisément ce que peuvent et ce que ne peuvent pas faire les forces militaires lorsqu'elles appuient des contrôles d'identités et participent au maintien de l'ordre.

Au niveau local, les préfets de départements peuvent élaborer des plans Vigipirates locaux. Il a été utilisé pour la première fois de décembre 1985 à décembre 1986, puis de janvier à avril 1991; les bâtiments surveillés étant, dans le contexte de la guerre du Golfe, les ministères et les entreprises travaillant pour la défense nationale. En 1995, il entre à nouveau en vigueur le 7 septembre après l'attentat de Villeurbanne contre une école juive, les établissements scolaires et les transports étant cette fois-ci particulièrement surveillés. Le stationnement auprès des établissements et des sorties scolaires furent interdits. De son côté la RATP (Régie autonome des transports parisiens) a considérablement renforcé son dispositif de sécurité. Après l'attentat du 17 octobre 1995 commis sur la ligne C du Réseau Express Régional (RER), Vigipirate entra dans sa phase renforcée, ce qui permettait d'utiliser l'armée alors que dans la première phase seuls les moyens classiques de sécurité intérieure, police, gendarmerie, douanes, avaient été utilisés. Pendant cette période, 32 000 fonctionnaires ont été mobilisés par le plan Vigipirate.

Malgré son retour 15 janvier 1996 à la phase simple, le plan Vigipirate avait continué d'utiliser des militaires pour assurer la surveillance des gares parisiennes et des interconnexions avec le RER ou le métro. Enfin le plan a été réactivé le 3 décembre 1996, juste après l'attentat du RER, Port Royal. La surveillance portera plus spécialement sur les lieux publics (notamment en cette fin d'année dans les grands magasins et les salles de spectacle) et bien sûr les transports. Un communiqué daté du 1 janvier 1997 de l'armée islamique du salut, organisation armée du FIS, tout en prenant ses distances avec le GIA, 'conseille' à l'Occident de 'se tenir à l'écart' du conflit algérien. Ce communiqué prévient 'avec insistance' contre les dangers d'une politique d'aide au gouvernement algérien, et souligne 'les conséquences de cette aide qui génèrent du tort et non du bien pour le peuple algérien'. C'est dire clairement qu'une politique étrangère peut avoir un 'coût' intérieur humain.

Modifié le 26 juillet 1995 par un document du Secrétariat Général de la Défense Nationale (SGDN) classé confidentiel défense, rédigé à partir d'une directive du premier ministre signée le 15 juin précédent, le plan Vigipirate renvoie à une situation de crise. Il est à comparer avec les situations intermédiaires entre la paix et la guerre que sont l'état de siège, qui substitue l'autorité militaire à l'autorité civile et l'état d'urgence proclamé en cas de 'péril imminent résultant d'atteinte grave à l'ordre public' qui étend considérablement les pouvoirs de police. Il peut bien sûr se concevoir comme une extension logique des missions de défense dans le cadre de la défense civile mais il ne précise pas suffisamment si les armées sont en soutien aux forces civiles et pour quelles missions précises. Doit-on demander leur concours, les réquisitionner? Que doivent-elles faire si les policiers, mais aussi parfois les agents de la RATP qu'elles accompagnent, sont face à un phénomène de petite délinquance: refus de payer les billets, destruction de matériel...?

Pourtant, ni la presse ni les partis d'opposition n'ont jamais véritablement discuté de la légalité des différentes mesures concrètes d'intervention des militaires; on s'est contenté de sondages d'opinions faits souvent à chaud, quelques jours après les attentats, mais si les missions se prolongent et si elles se concentrent sur les quartiers difficiles aura-t-on une même perspective positive de la part des gens qui vivent dans ces quartiers et dont une radio locale disait qu'un groupe de jeunes avait ajouté dans la liste des villes auxquelles il se compare après Gaza, Hébron, pour ne pas dire Bagdad, Belfast: symbole d'une présence militaire encerclant les 'fauteurs de troubles'.

Le plan Vigipirate a donc eu pour l'instant des effets de consensus, comme si, à travers lui, se manifestait concrètement la solidarité nationale, et face aux agressions venues de l'étranger, on ne peut que s'en féliciter. Pourtant les ambiguïtés internes ne manquent pas. Plan de crise, répondant à une situation exceptionnelle, Vigipirate a été maintenu pendant plus d'un an. Il s'est transformé par le biais de la multiplication des contrôles d'identité en une sorte de complément non officiel du dispositif de lutte contre l'immigration. L'utilisation du plan Vigipirate dans des missions sans rapport avec le terrorisme a provoqué à Strasbourg une polémique, les média locaux affirmant que les militaires affectés à la surveillance des bus étaient intervenus dans la lutte contre la délinquance urbaine sans être accompagnés de policiers, ce que démentaient les ministères incriminés et ce qui avait obligé in fine le préfet du haut Rhin à intervenir en suspendant ces opérations. La commission nationale consultative des droits de l'homme placée auprès du premier ministre a regretté le 19 décembre 1995 que 'dans plusieurs communiqués du ministère de l'intérieur relatifs aux résultats du plan Vigipirate, aient été mis en relief les constats d'infractions à la législation sur les étrangers, alors même que ces infractions étaient sans aucun lien avec les menaces terroristes que ce plan a pour objectif de prévenir'. Une fois de plus, les discours de certains hommes politiques n'hésitent pas alors à faire des amalgames que les administrations pourtant se refusent à faire, et il n'est pas certain qu'une France sous perfusion sécuritaire avec un plan Vigipirate permanent soit une France sauvegardée des attentats.

Notes

1   Voir les travaux du CEVIPOF commandé par l'IHESI, 1991, *Les cahiers de la sécurité intérieure*, 1.

2   La thèse de Quadrupanni pose de réelles questions mais se contente d'inverser le propos et tend à diaboliser les policiers. Au contraire, pour nous les processus de construction de définition du terrorisme et de l'antiterrorisme ne sont pas le reflet d'un complot entre les polices contre les libertés mais le produit des structures des luttes entre ces mêmes policiers et entre eux et les hommes politiques.

3   Pour l'économie des luttes autour de ce label dans les enceintes internationales voire Bettati (1975), Lejeune (1993).

4   Un exemple frappant du fait que définir le terrorisme c'est définir qui est démocratique et qui ne l'est pas peut être trouvé dans le document du Conseil de l'Europe, 'La défense de la démocratie contre le terrorisme en Europe', 1978. Les interventions espagnoles et turques sont à cet égard très intéressantes dans leur maximalisme concernant la coopération automatique des États. Les relire à 20 ans de distance montre quelle a été la tendance globale suivie.

5   Les tensions avec l'Espagne seront maximales jusqu'à ce que Pierre Joxe remplace Gaston Defferre et inverse la politique suivie, en consacrant le principe de la collaboration politique entre démocraties qui n'ont pas à se juger entre elles.

6   Les controverses sur les activités de la cellule présidentielle et les écoutes illégales auxquelles elle procéda sont nombreuses. Tous les acteurs se sont exprimés dans des livres justificateurs: Prouteau, Barril, Baud côté gendarmes, Plenel côté victime des écoutes...

7   Sans doute sous l'influence des analyses plus discrètes mais plus fines du groupe de travail sur le terrorisme de l'OTAN: rapport rendu public en février 1987. (Document de l'Assemblée de l'Atlantique Nord.)

8   Des entretiens avec des policiers et certains membres de ces organisations montrent que ces derniers étaient surpris et fiers d'être pris aussi au sérieux et que cela leur redonnait confiance dans leur projet révolutionnaire puisqu'ils réussissaient à affoler l'État.

9   Ce sera le cas avec la diatribe des frères Abdallah contre la bande
     de Chirac, le clan Chirac, en 1986. Et dix ans après: 'Sachez,
     Jacques Chirac et vous tous qui êtes avec lui, que durant le combat
     que nous menons contre vous, nous vous avons contactés à plusieurs
     reprises (…) Mon frère Abu-Abdallah, que Dieu ait son âme, s'est
     adressé à vous, mais vous vous êtes entêté. Abu-Abdurrahman
     vous a invité à vous convertir à l'islam, mais vous avez choisi
     l'impiété' (*AFP*, 1996).

10   Inversion: les pratiques de l'organisation vont finir par prendre le
     contre-pied du discours idéologique autour duquel elles se sont
     constituées.

11   Son explication cohérente pour les mouvements sociaux italiens,
     allemands et plus ou moins basques, perdait en revanche de sa
     cohérence dès qu'il y incluait le Pérou sans mettre l'accent sur la
     différence d'État et donc de légitimité des combats. Citons aussi
     l'ouvrage de Donatella Della Porta (1995) qui en prenant au sérieux
     les hypothèses les plus solides de l'action collective cherche à rendre
     compte des formes de violence dite terroriste en Italie et en
     Allemagne. Succès certain du livre sur ces deux exemples mais sans
     doute parce qu'ils sont atypiques et ont été de réels mouvements
     sociaux disqualifiés à l'époque par les pouvoirs en place. En
     revanche, sur le terrorisme noir italien d'Ordine Nero, ou sur
     nombre d'organisations clandestines aux pratiques plus erratiques,
     les modèles explicatifs de l'action collective, même revus par Sidney
     Tarrow, semblent bien limités.

12   En parallèle avec ce que Michel Wieviorka (1989) a analysé à
     propos des idéologies des groupes clandestins, à savoir le travail
     idéologique de justification de la violence comme moyen pratique
     de fusionner des exigences inconciliables (sociales, politiques,
     nationales), on pourrait émettre l'hypothèse un peu provocante
     que les politiques antiterroristes ont alors quasiment la même
     fonction de justification (légitimation de la violence coercitive) tout
     en maintenant des exigences contradictoires qu'elles tentent de
     fusionner (autonomie des politiques étrangères, jeu sur les opinion
     publiques nationales, compétition politique interne, rôle du droit et
     de la raison d'État) et parfois quasiment le même résultat (augmen-
     tation du sentiment d'insécurité chez les tiers autant que sécurité
     renforcée)!

13   La violence reste bien sûr endémique en Corse, malgré un reflux
     après les nuits bleues des années 1987, 1988 mais il est significatif
     qu'après avoir été jusqu'à interdire aux journalistes et hommes

politiques d'utiliser le terme de FLNC et de les obliger à parler d'ex-FLNC puisque celui-ci était officiellement dissous, on va essayer de gérer la violence nationaliste par des moyens plus discrets et plus patrimonialisés. On s'intéressera de plus près à leurs sources de revenus. En les révélant cela mettra en cause leur différence avec les autres clans, leur image se ternira à coup de révélation et de scission interne avec mort d'hommes. L'actualité corse est marquée en priorité depuis 1989 par les scissions du mouvement nationaliste qui s'accompagnent d'une lutte d'influence accrue entre les organisations, ponctuées d'assassinats. L'affaire n'est quasiment plus terroriste, elle devient 'culturelle': on revient sur le vieux stéréotype de la nature exaltée des corses et de la vendetta. Le gouvernement pense alors opportun d'ouvrir une voie de sortie à quelques nationalistes isolés, mais les tractations sont rendues publiques par ces derniers, et dès lors, il faut au moins en apparence donner tous les signes de l'autorité même si l'on ne tient pas à appliquer un plan vigipirate en Corse.

14   Loi n°86-1020 du 9 septembre 1986 relative à la lutte contre le terrorisme et aux atteintes à la sûreté de l'État; Loi n°86-1322 du 30 décembre 1986 modifiant le code de procédure pénale et complétant la Loi 86-1020 du 9 septembre.

15   La commission Justice du RPR suggérait une refonte de l'article 93 du Code pénal dans les termes suivants: 'ceux qui auront commis un attentat ou un acte de terrorisme ayant pour but ou pour effet de porter le massacre ou la dévastation sur le territoire national seront punis' afin de créer une incrimination spécifique de crime terroriste.

16   Piratair: détournement d'avions ou prise d'otages au sol à bord d'avions. Piratome: attentat commis à l'aide de substance nucléaires, ou touchant à des installations nucléaires. Piratox: attentat avec des matières toxiques.

References

Anonyme. s.f. *Terrorisme corse et action de la gendarmerie.* Nice: Mémoire de dess. Faculté de droit de Nice.

AFP. 1996. 'Extrait du message au président de la France, Jacques Chirac, signé par l'Emir du GIA, Antar Zouari'. *AFP* 24 December.

Badie, Bertrand. 1994. *L'Etat importé.* Paris: Fayard.

Betancourt, L.A. 1981. *¿Por qué Carlos?* New York: Ediciones Vitral.

Bettati. A. 1975. 'La lutte internationale contre le terrorisme'. *La documentation française, problèmes politiques et sociaux* 25.

Bigo, Didier. 1991. 'Les attentats en France en 1986: un cas de violence transnationale et ses implications'. *Cultures & Conflicts* 4.

Bigo, Didier. 1994. 'Terrorisme (le terrorisme n'existe pas)', *Encyclopédie Hachette*. Paris: Hachette.

Bigo, Didier. 1996. *Polices en réseaux, l'expérience européenne*. Paris: Presses de Sciences-Po.

Bigo, Didier and Jean-Yves Haine. 1995. 'Troubler et inquiéter: les discours du désordre international'. *Cultures & Conflicts* 19/20.

Bigo, Didier and Daniel Hermant. s.f. 'Analyse comparative des politiques de lutte contre le terrorisme'. Rapport établi pour le compte du CNEF.

Bigo, Didier and Daniel Hermant. 1983. 'Terrorisme: approches françaises'. Rapport pour le compte du GROUPES.

Bigo, Didier and Daniel Hermant. 1984. 'La relation terroriste'. *Etudes Polémologiques* 30–31.

Bigo, Didier and Daniel Hermant. 1985. 'Résurgence du terrorisme en Europe?' *Esprit* Avril.

Bigo, Didier and Daniel Hermant. 1986a. 'Un terrorisme ou des terrorismes?' *Esprit* 94/95.

Bigo, Didier and Daniel Hermant. 1986b. 'Guerre et terrorisme'. *Revue Science et Vie* 157.

Bigo, Didier and Daniel Hermant. 1986c. 'Les différentes formes de terrorisme en France'. *Etudes Polémologiques* 37.

Bigo, Didier and Daniel Hermant. 1986d. 'Simulation et dissimulation. Les politiques de lutte contre le terrorisme en France'. *Revue Sociologie du Travail*. October.

Bigo, Didier and Daniel Hermant. 1988. 'La relation terroriste'. *Etudes Polémologiques* 47.

Bigo, Didier and Daniel Hermant. 1989. 'Tiers, médiateurs et parasites'. *Etudes Polémologiques* 49.

Bigo, Didier and Daniel Hermant. 1990. 'Terrorisme et antiterrorisme en France'. *Cahiers de la Sécurité Intérieure* 1.

Bigo, Didier, Daniel Hermant and Rémy Leveau. 1991. *L'Europe et les problèmes de sécurité intérieure à l'horizon 1992*. 2 vols. Paris: Contrat de recherche du CERI avec l'IHESI et le MRT.

Bourdieu, Pierre. 1994. 'Esprit d'Etat'. *Raisons pratiques*. Paris: Seuil.

Burdan, Daniel. 1990. *DST, neuf ans... la division antiterroriste*. Paris: Robert Laffont.

Cesari, Jocelyne. 1995. 'Vigilance civique contre vigipirate'. *Le Monde*, 20 September.

Collectif. 1990. *Paroles directes: autour d'action directe*.

Crenshaw, Martha. 1987. 'Theories of terrorism: instrumental and organizational approaches'. *Journal of Strategic Studies*. Frank Cass: UK.

Debray, Régis. 1989. *Tous azimuts*. Paris: Odile Jacob.

Delarue, Jacques. 1981. *L'OAS contre De Gaulle*. Paris: Fayard.

Della Porta, Donatella. 1995. 'Social movements, political violence and the state, a comparative analysis of Italy and Germany'. *Studies in comparative politics*. Cambridge: Cambridge University Press.

Deloye, Yves and Olivier Ihl. 1993. 'La civilité électorale: vote et forclusion de la violence en France'. *Cultures & Conflicts* 9/10.

Dobson, Christopher. 1977. *The Carlos complex: a pattern of violence*. London: Hodder & Stoughton.

Dobson, Christopher and Ronald Payne. 1976. *Carlos l'insaisissable*. Paris: Albin Michel.

Francis, Samuel. 1983. 'Terrorist renaissance: France 1980–1983'. *World Affairs*.

Girard, René. 1978. *Des choses cachées depuis la fondation du monde*. Paris: Grasset.

Girard, René. 1982. *Le bouc émissaire*. Paris: Grasset.

González, P. 1976. *Carlos, la internacional del terrorismo*. Madrid: A.Q. Ediciones.

Hamilton, P. 1979. *Espionage, terrorism and subversion*. Surrey: Peter A. Helms.

Hamon, Alain and Jean-Charles Marchand. 1986. *Action directe: du terrorisme français à l'euro-terrorisme*. Paris: Seuil.

Huntington, Samuel P. 1993. *The clash of civilizations? The debate; with responses by Fouad Ajami*. New York: Foreign Affairs.

Jacquard, Roland. 1987. *La longue traque d'Action directe*. Paris: Albin Michel.

Kepel, Gilles and Rémy Leveau. 1992. *Enquête IFOP*.

Kitson, Franck. 1971. *Low intensity operations: subversion, insurgency and peacekeeping*. London: Faber & Faber.

Klein, J.K. 1977. *Der deutsche terrorismus in den perspektiven der konfliktforschung, beitage zur konfliktforschung*.

Labayle, Henri. 1981. 'La collaboration entre états dans la lutte contre la violence'. Thèse, Université de Toulouse.

Labin, Suzanne. 1978. *La violence politique*. Paris: France Empire.

Lakos, A. s.f. *Terrorism, 1970–1978: a bibliography*. Boulder Co.: Westview Press, University of Waterloo.

Landorf, S. s.f. 'Légalisme et violence dans le mouvement autonomiste corse: l'année 1976'. *Les temps modernes*.

Laqueur, Walter. 1976. *The futility of terrorism*. 3, Harper's, pp. 99–105.

Laqueur, Walter. 1977. 'Interpretations of terrorism: fact, fiction and political science'. *Journal of Contemporary History*, pp. 1–41. UK: Sage.

Laqueur, Walter. 1978. *The terrorism reader: a historical anthology*. New York: Meridian.

Lefebvre, Christian. 1992. 'Nationalismes corses et perspectives européennes'. *Cultures & Conflicts 7*.

Lehning, Arthur. 1976. *Michel Bakounine et les autres*. Paris: Gallimard.

Lejeune, Pierrick. 1993. *La lutte européenne contre le terrorisme, problèmes politiques et sociaux*. Paris: documentation française.

Lemasson, Sylvie. 1992. 'La libération des otages allemands au Liban: analyse politique et judiciaire'. *Cultures & Conflicts 5*.

Liniers, Antoine. 1985. 'Objections contre une prise d'armes'. In *Terrorisme et démocratie*, edited by F. Furet. Paris: Fayard.

Marcellin, Raymond. 1969. *L'ordre public et les groupes révolutionnaires*. Paris: Plon.

Marcellin, Raymond. 1978. *L'Importune Vérité*. Paris: Plon.

Marcellin, Raymond. 1985. *La guerre politique*. Paris: Plon.

Marenssin, Emile. 1972. *La bande à Baader ou la violence révolutionnaire*. Paris: Ed. Champ libre.

Masson, Paul. 1984. *Rapport au nom de la commission de contrôle des conditions de fonctionnement d'intervention et de coordination des services de police et de sécurité engagés dans la lutte contre le terrorisme...* Annexe au procès verbal du 17 mai, rapport n° 322. Paris: Sénat.

Mucchielli, R. 1973. *La subversion*. Paris: Bordas.

Nelson, Daniel Nicolas. 1987. *La coopération juridique internationale des démocraties occidentales en matière de lutte contre le terrorisme*. Paris: L'Harmattan.

Nicolas, Michel. 1987. *Histoire du mouvement breton*. Paris: Syros.

Parat, L. 1989. *L'Europe de l'antiterrorisme en 1988, utopie ou réalité?* Université de Grenoble.

Quadruppani, Serge. 1989. *L'antiterrorisme en France ou la terreur intégrée*. Paris: La Découverte.

Raufer, Xavier. 1982. *Terrorisme, maintenant la France?* Paris: Garnier.

Roi, Jacques. 1986. *Violence ou dissuasion, l'exemple de la Corse*. Paris: Beauchesne.

Roy, Oliver. s.f. *Esprit*.

Rudelski, Françoise. 1992. *L'indemnisation des victimes du terrorisme*. Paris: Pédone.

Smith, Colin. s.f. *Carlos, portrait d'un terroriste*. Paris: Gallimard.

Soto Guerrero, A. 1976. *El chacal venezolano: Carlos*. Caracas: El Cid Editor.

Tobon. 1978. *¿Carlos: terrorista o guerrillero?* Barcelona: Grijalbo.

Tricaud, François. 1977. *L'accusation, recherche sur les figures de l'agression éthique*. Paris: Philosophie Du Droit-Dalloz.

Villeneuve, Charles and Jean-Pierre Péret. 1987. *Histoire secrète du terrorisme*. Paris: Plon.
Wieviorka, Michel. 1989. *Societé et terrorisme*. Paris: Le Seuil.
Wieviorka, Michel. 1995. 'Terrorisme et fantasmes'. *Libération*, 6 September.

The Authors

Daniel Hermant is the editor of the journal, *Cultures & Conflicts*.
Didier Bigo is Professor of Political Science at the Institut d'Etudes Politiques in Paris, France.

4 Countering Terrorism in a New Democracy: the Case of Spain

FERNANDO REINARES AND
OSCAR JAIME-JIMÉNEZ

Introduction

Spain underwent during the second half of the 1970s a successful democratization of its political system. Nevertheless, this process was severely affected both by the threat of a military reaction and by the violent activity of some terrorist organizations. Indeed, these two factors seriously disrupted the transition from authoritarian rule, the latter of them becoming a major problem for democratic consolidation even when the former ceased. As the preceding dictatorship, which lasted for nearly 40 years, crumbled away, the transition from one regime to another developed throughout an initial period of uncertainty, subsequently culminating in the establishment of a new democracy. Political change was in this case gradual and incremental, thanks to a series of both domestic and international circumstances (Carr and Fusi, 1979; Tezanos *et al.*, 1989; Cotarelo, 1992; Pérez Díaz, 1993). First of all, there was a series of pragmatic negotiations involving figures of the outgoing authoritarian regime, namely Francoism, and moderate leaders of the democratic opposition to the dictatorship. The active role as mediator and arbitrator played by King Juan Carlos made the monarchy much more relevant an institution than the continuative one which authoritarian rulers had intended it to be. Also contributing to the political change were the pressures arising from an increasingly articulated civil society and the approval of traditional actors in unique positions of influence, such as the Catholic Church. The weight of public opinion overwhelmingly in favour of national reconciliation and democratization, as well as the favourable international context at the time, helped move this process along, despite its coincidence with a period of harsh economic crisis.

Francisco Franco, the army general who personified the mentioned dictatorship, died in November 1975. As early as March

1976, a referendum on political reform called for the dissolution of the legislative assembly existing under the authoritarian regime. In June 1977, the first free general elections were held. They resulted in a mandate for a moderate party, the *Unión de Centro Democrático* (UCD, Democratic Centre Union) to form a government after securing a relative majority of parliamentary seats. This rather brief legislature prepared the draft of a democratic constitution which was subsequently approved in a December 1978 referendum. Once that foundational document was ratified and proclaimed, the Parliament underwent a second renovation in the general elections of March 1979, when UCD again obtained a relative majority and retained control over the Cabinet. All these events marked the beginning of a new democracy. Regarding peripheral territorial demands, particularly intense in the Basque Country and Catalonia, the constitution of 1978 recognizes the existence of the nationalities and regions within Spain, and allows ample degrees of autonomy for those desiring it. On this basis, three northern Basque provinces (Álava, Guipúzcoa and Vizcaya) opted in 1979 to establish an autonomous community through a referendum in which the proposed statute was sanctioned by a large majority of the voters. As a result, since 1980, *Euskadi* or *País Vasco*, as the Basque autonomous community styles itself in the vernacular tongue and Castilian language, respectively, has had its own executive and legislature. Much the same occurred in the northeastern territory of Catalonia. Although it is certainly true that the transition to democracy was substantially complete by the end of 1978, when voters approved the constitution, it would perhaps be more accurate to consider that this process did not properly culminate until two years later, when the autonomy statutes for the Basque Country and Catalonia came into force. At the very least, it could be argued that the period in between constitutes a transitory phase, and the precise point at which the transition leaves off and a new democracy begins to consolidate itself is blurred.

From a comparative perspective, this process of regime change evolved rather peacefully. Between 1976 and 1980, however, almost 400 people died as a result of terrorist incidents; that is, around 75 fatalities every year during the political transition period. Since 1981, well over 500 fatalities have been registered: close to 30 deaths caused by terrorism every year. However, most of the terrorist organizations active during the democratic transition and immediately afterwards were formed during the late 1960s and early 1970s, as the dictatorship entered a stage of crisis and liberalization – a context which facilitated the mobilization of political dissent but also its eventual radicalization as a result of both unfulfilled expectations and regime repressiveness (Maravall, 1978; Reinares, 1990). Actually, it could be said that most Spaniards were convinced that insurgent terrorism would disappear once the authoritarian regime was replaced by a new, democratic one. This generalized belief persisted even during 1976 and 1977, a period of uncertainty when the frequency of terrorist actions resulting in fatalities was slightly lower than in 1975, the last year under the dictatorship. But events would not be long in demonstrating that such widely shared conviction was, at least in the short term, wishful thinking. Actually, a dramatic terrorist escalation took place between 1978 and 1980, precisely the most critical period of the regime change. In the 1980s, terrorism remained at significantly lower but nevertheless quite alarming levels, declining even more sharply during the 1990s (see Table 4.1 and Figure 4.1).

The two factions into which the small Basque secessionist organization ETA (*Euskadi ta Askatasuna*: Basque Homeland and Freedom) was divided from 1974 were mainly responsible for the terrorist escalation during the political transition period and for the persistence of such violence throughout the following two decades. Together, the so-called 'political military faction', ETA(político militar) or ETA(pm), and the faction known as the 'military wing', ETA(militar) or ETA(m), were blamed for more than 70 per cent of the attacks in which blood was spilt between 1976 and 1980, as well as for 90 per cent of those which have taken place since that time. The left-wing terrorist organization known as GRAPO (*Grupos de Resistencia Antifascista Primero de Octubre*: First of October Anti-fascist Resistance Groups), claimed responsibility for 13 and 6 per cent, respectively, of the deaths registered during these same periods. Reactive terrorist activity by diverse, often overlapping extreme right-wing groups was particularly notorious during the political transition years and fell off sharply as the new democracy was consolidated. However, during the late 1970s there was an even greater number of political assassinations perpetrated by neo-fascist agitators who were not members of underground terrorist organizations even if they belonged to legal or tolerated groups included in the same extremist ideological sector. Between the middle of that decade and the late 1990s, the remaining terrorist events resulting in fatalities were carried out by some reduced groups emerging from the radical left and other peripheral nationalist movements, or were actually acts of international terrorism. In addition,

Table 4.1:   Annual Distribution of Terrorist Actions Resulting in Fatalities, According to Different Organizations or Sectors of Organizations, Spain, 1968–98

Year	ETA		GRAPO		Right-wing		Others		Total	
1968	2	(2)							2	(2)
1969	1	(1)							1	(1)
1970									0	(0)
1971							1	(1)	1	(1)
1972	1	(1)					1	(1)	2	(2)
1973	2	(6)					2	(2)	4	(8)
1974	6	(17)							6	(17)
1975	16	(16)	5	(5)			5	(5)	26	(26)
1976	11	(17)	1	(1)	3	(3)			15	(21)
1977	10	(12)	5	(7)	4	(8)	1	(1)	20	(28)
1978	58	(65)	6	(6)	1	(1)	6	(13)	71	(85)
1979	63	(78)	23	(31)	5	(6)	3	(3)	94	(118)
1980	72	(96)	4	(6)	13	(20)	2	(2)	91	(124)
1981	27	(30)	4	(5)	1	(1)	2	(2)	34	(38)
1982	31	(40)	2	(2)			2	(2)	35	(44)
1983	35	(40)	2	(2)			2	(2)	39	(44)
1984	26	(33)	4	(5)			3	(3)	33	(41)
1985	31	(37)					3	(21)	34	(58)
1986	19	(41)					1	(1)	20	(42)
1987	17	(52)					3	(3)	20	(55)
1988	14	(18)	2	(2)					16	(20)
1989	15	(18)	3	(5)	1	(1)	2	(2)	21	(26)
1990	17	(25)	2	(2)			1	(1)	20	(28)
1991	28	(45)							28	(45)
1992	17	(26)							17	(26)
1993	8	(14)	1	(1)					9	(15)
1994	13	(14)							13	(14)
1995	10	(15)							10	(15)
1996	5	(5)							5	(5)
1997	13	(13)							13	(13)
1998	5	(6)							5	(6)
Total	573	(783)	64	(80)	28	(40)	40	(65)	705	(968)

Source: Data gathered from the Spanish Ministry of the Interior and contemporary press reports. Elaboration by the authors.

Note: Figures in parentheses indicate number of fatalities.

Figure 4.1:   Terrorist Actions Resulting in Fatalities, Spain,
1968–98

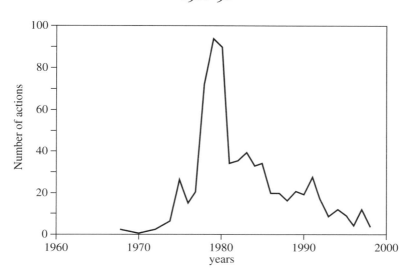

the vigilante GAL (*Grupos Antiterroristas de Liberación*: Anti-
terrorist Liberation Groups), a clandestine organization active for
five years around the middle of the 1980s, linked to some state
authorities and members of security agencies, caused 27 fatalities,
most of them in the French Basque Country.

Transition from Authoritarian Rule and State Responses to Terrorism

In order for a terrorist organization to carry out a sustained
campaign of violence, a certain amount of human and material
resources is needed, as well as a shared definition of the situation
among its leaders more in terms of opportunities than of constraints (Reinares, 1998a: 84–90). But mobilized resources and
perceived opportunities for armed action, taken alone, would only
in part account for the dramatic upsurge in terrorist attacks that
Spain witnessed between 1978 and 1980. The exceptional pattern
of this escalation and the way in which it evolved suggests that it
was more than just a case of there being the requisite number of
groups with the goals and the means for carrying them out, as
indeed had been the case before. That is to say, a special set of
circumstances had to exist for such a phenomenon to happen. First

of all, the intensification of armed insurgency tends to become a likely alternative when proponents of more or less maximalist political stances see their very high expectations frustrated, especially among sectors of society that might have been politically socialized in a sub-culture of violence. In this case, what seems to have been especially influential was the initial reluctance of the first governments under the restored monarchy to grant an amnesty to over 600 Basques, most of them ETA militants or collaborators, who had been imprisoned under the Franco regime. True, those governments were not the only ones to blame. In 1977, for instance, the central government opened talks with ETA(pm) aiming for a deal under which prisoners could be released prior to the first free general elections. But the other terrorist organization, ETA(m), refused to take part because, as later became apparent, it would rely on the issue of the prisoners as a fundamental resource for mobilizing a significant amount of popular support based on affective and family ties with those jailed. To this contributory factor were added the mistakes and delays in heeding the more symbolic demands of resurgent nationalism, as well as law and order measures that were scarcely to be differentiated from those of the previous dictatorship. For instance, between 1977 and 1979, 39 people died in the whole of Spain as a consequence of police behaviour in street clashes with demonstrators.

Furthermore, the prevailing economic crisis during the second half of the 1970s generated a sense of unease in considerable segments of Basque society which took a long time to dissipate, providing fertile ground for the politicization of discontent through radical Basque nationalism and its induced violence. Finally, as a consequence of the first free general elections held in 1977, various small and marginalized political groups turned to violence as a more effective means to advance some common goals and thus continue to take part in the power contest. Actually, election results in the Basque Country showed greater support not only for nonnationalist than for nationalist formations, but also for the more moderate options within the latter sector, to the extent that they were considered a failure among radical independentists. These somehow electorally marginalized groups gathered around ETA(m), creating in 1979 a rather heterogeneous political coalition known as *Herri Batasuna* (HB: People's Unity). This disloyal opposition based its main collective arguments on the fact that the 1978 Spanish constitution does not recognize the right to national self-determination, thus capitalizing on the difficulties which arose during the implementation of the autonomy arrangements. The fact that the adjoining province of Navarre, which has a considerable though clearly minoritarian number of inhabitants who consider themselves to be Basques, was not included in the Basque autonomous community created in 1979 also contributed to the formulation of an anti-system frame of reference, as did perceived official negligence towards the Basque language and still frequently abusive behaviour by the police. Above all, it was a time in which an entire generation of Basques that had politically come of age during the first half of the 1970s, just when the Franco regime was in crisis and nationalism dominated the Basque public sphere, resisted or rejected the democratic institutions being created and thus found no sufficient grounds for opposing ETA violence (Llera, 1987: 176).

But apart from the uneven progress of the democratic transition, another set of circumstances facilitated the astonishing escalation of violence between 1978 and 1980. The faster the country moved towards democracy, the more terrorism increased. This was so mainly because a favourable political opportunity structure existed for such a remarkable development to happen (Reinares, 1996). First of all, the change from a repressive regime to another, tolerant and pluralistic one is bound to lead to a certain relaxation of state control mechanisms which in turn tends to reinforce the likelihood of mobilization for any type of collective action attempting to achieve direct influence over the distribution of power. Indeed, terrorism and other serious internal security issues did not enjoy a privileged place on the political agenda during the very first years of post-Francoism, since the emerging political elites tended to rely upon the alleged regulatory capabilities of democratization itself substantially to solve these kinds of problems. In addition, these elites shared certain mistrust towards the existing, still unreformed, security forces (Jaime-Jiménez, 1997). In this initial and uncertain period of the transition from authoritarian rule, political initiatives aimed at peaceful conflict regulation, particularly with respect to the Basque nationalist demands, were dissociated from police activity. Efforts at countering terrorism were not being efficiently coordinated and a coherent political consensus as to how the problem should be addressed was yet to emerge. These circumstances meant that all legislative measures attempting to deal with the phenomenon of terrorism in general, and that perpetrated by ETA factions in particular, ended up quite limited in their effectiveness, and in a good number of cases were merely counterproductive. As for external factors, one may refer to the role of other countries or foreign-based groups in providing logistical support or cover to the domestic terrorists.

Until the later months of 1980, anti-terrorist policies implemented by successive governments of the UCD were particularly inconsistent. This was precisely the period when the terrorists escalated their campaigns. Those with responsibility over public order issues at that time proved to be incapable of establishing a coherent and effective series of measures to replace the repertory of responses, predominantly inspired by military assumptions, that the Franco regime applied to all internal security matters. The policing apparatus left in place by the former dictatorship was only partially amenable to reforming pressures from the main opposition parties and the informal arrangements that facilitated the democratic transition. True, some veteran specialists were reclassified or given new duties, the hierarchy was shuffled here and there, but it was not until 1979 that a formal adaptation of those state security agencies to the new political situation was initiated. Meanwhile, incumbent politicians were afraid of provoking a rebellion of the then militarized security forces, as evidenced by the eloquent testimony of Rodolfo Martín (1984: 150–58), who was Minister of the Interior from July 1976 to April 1979. Likewise, leaders of the then main opposition parties did not insist on introducing significant changes concerning the police agencies, since they also shared the impression that these transformations could disrupt internal security structures at a critical moment, thus endangering the democratization process, particularly if the terrorist threat was not faced with enough determination.

As a result, a dysfunctional situation within the internal security structures became generalized. Information-gathering mechanisms for intelligence purposes, which are of critical importance in the fight against terrorism, were not only inadequate but frequently fairly crude, and operated with few if any governmental controls. There was a notorious lack of coordination between this intelligence function and the various state security agencies. At the end of 1975, a number of different secret intelligence services were operating in competition with one another, instead of pooling and coordinating their efforts. Under such circumstances, it is scarcely to be wondered at that most successful results in counterterrorist operations were obtained at the local or provincial level, though these were, of course, necessarily limited in their impact. Given such an outlook, the Spanish government had no choice but to turn to neighbouring countries for intelligence and direct help in dealing with a mounting terrorist problem. Following a visit made by the Minister of the Interior to West Germany in September 1978, seeking advice on counterterrorism matters, a selected group of 60 experienced policemen were sent to the Basque Country with the main objective of carrying out an extensive search and updating the available information on the two factions of ETA. In February 1979, that unit was joined by 120 men belonging to the special *Policía Nacional* (National Police) task force known as *Grupo Especial de Operaciones* (GEO, Special Operations Group) and 450 men of the *Grupos Antiterroristas Rurales* (GAR: Rural Anti-terrorist Groups) belonging to the *Guardia Civil* (Civil Guard), both created the previous year on the advice of foreign experts. In addition, as many as 6000 national policemen and 12 000 civil guards were deployed during this period in the Basque provinces. However, the knowledge of this personnel, largely socialized under the dictatorship, was at that time rather unprofessional and its operational practices frequently far from those which security functionaries are expected to perform in an emerging tolerant, pluralist context.

Often officials whose personal convictions were far from democratic meant that the problems arising from the institutional incompetence of the security agencies were compounded by the inhibited or insubordinate attitude of some of the people in charge of them. The police force inherited from the dictatorship was replete with attitudes that were not only hostile to the current process of democratization but particularly hostile to the Basques in general and to Basque nationalists in particular. During the crisis of Francoism, the most obstinately reactionary partisans of the authoritarian regime made the security agencies, along with the armed forces, their last redoubt. Cases of insubordination within the police were fairly frequent during the democratic transition years. When the time came to control neo-fascist agitators, however, these forces proved to be singularly inhibited, and few arrests were ever made in connection with terrorist attacks by right-wing extremists. On top of that, those who eventually were convicted of reactionary-inspired crimes had no difficulty in receiving coveted furloughs from prison. That these furloughed prisoners later dropped out of sight, only to resurface in some South American country with which Spain had no extradition treaty at the time, came as a surprise to nobody. Finally, the meagre results obtained caused many of the most competent and dedicated personnel to leave the state security agencies, a fact which only served to exacerbate their structural and other shortcomings. The escalation of violent acts perpetrated since

1978 by the two factions of ETA, as well as other small clandestine groups, worsened to the point where pressures coming from the military and other conservative political sectors led in April 1979 to the appointment of an army general as Minister of the Interior. But he was, in turn, replaced by a civilian less than one year later, as a result not only of the abnormality of such designation but also of its notorious lack of success in the fight against terrorism.

For a long while, the terrorists of all kinds benefited from the flagrant lack of political determination that should have been broad, coherent and cohesive enough to contain and gradually eliminate the phenomenon of terrorism. The diverse terrorist organizations derived substantial direct support from groups and minority parties located in their same ideological sector. In addition, they thrived on the calculated ambiguity shown by influential social and political actors when the time came to address directly the question of the legitimacy of insurgent violence in a context of democratic transition. On the left of the political spectrum, there was some tendency to consider insurgent terrorism as merely an inconvenient but predictable collateral product of a capitalist system that, according to this perspective, was thrashing about in its death agonies. These reduced sectors would therefore condemn terrorism, not as a matter of principle, but because they considered it was delaying the mobilization of the masses and the development of class struggle. But the pernicious effects of this ambiguity became especially relevant in the case of ETA, particularly after the Basque electorate was called on to take part in the constitutional referendum of 1978. Contrary to what happened in other parts of Spain, including Navarre, only half the eligible voters in the *vascongadas* provinces (Álava, Guipúzcoa and Vizcaya) turned out to participate, and of this number, fully 20 per cent voted against the constitution. The result of the election cast a pall of ambivalence over all subsequent efforts to assert that the new democratic regime had been duly legitimized. Since politically inspired violence is inseparably linked to the dissonances that appear in the legitimation of emerging political structures and institutions, this ambiguity in itself amounted to a position of implicit support for the terrorists or passivity towards their activities.

Shortly afterwards, however, the moderate Basque nationalist parties accepted the draft of the autonomy statute which they negotiated with the central government and, together with Basque non-nationalist parties, urged Basque citizens to vote in favour. This they did, in 1979, but as long as the constitutional framework in which the referendum was conducted could be called into question, the terrorists and their supporters had grounds for discrediting the results. Once again, this represented the triumph of ambivalence, an attitude which terrorists knew how to exploit (Waldmann, 1991). ETA also derived no small advantage from the attitudes manifested by individuals occupying positions of local authority in the Catholic Church, which was and is still an extremely influential entity in Basque society. Far too much blood had to be shed before Basque Catholicism finally scrapped the attitude of tolerance with which it tempered its condemnation of violence. Since the late 1980s, however, with some recurring exceptions, Basque Catholicism has taken a firmer stance against terrorism (García de Cortázar and Fusi, 1988). In light of the above situation, it has been estimated that, between 1977 and 1980, no more than half of Basque society expressed attitudes that were openly critical of ETA terrorism. Tacit approval or absence of disapproval were more prevalent among the young, among males and, as is only to be expected, among those who supported the basic political postulates of radical independentism (Linz, 1986). All of which describes how a minority outlook may give rise to a predominant climate of opinion in which both fear and ambiguity serve as essential components.

   This, then, was the situation during the years of democratic transition: police forces that were incapable of containing terrorism through effective investigation and pursuit, lack of political consensus to isolate the terrorists socially, and deficient state legitimacy as perceived by many people in the Basque Country. These circumstances had a limiting or diminishing effect on anti-terrorist legislation passed during the democratization period and subsequently toughened. These laws were for the most part improvised, heterogeneous as to content, technically imprecise and transitory. Their aim was to develop constitutional provisions allowing for fundamental civil rights to be suspended in certain exceptional circumstances. These rights included the maximum period of preventative detention, guarantees against unjustified search and seizure, and the inviolability of private communications during investigations into armed groups or terrorist activities (Lamarca, 1985; López Garrido, 1987a; Vercher, 1992). Even though, in cases where these rights were in fact suspended, provision was made for judicial intervention and parliamentary oversight, in practice these safeguards turned out to be no more than relative in their effectiveness and inadequate on the whole. Offering police the legal possibility of maintaining suspects incommunicado for a period of several days was, given the still unreformed nature of security agencies existing in Spain during the democratic transition period, together with the lack of effective political supervision, a propitious occasion for mistreatment and even torture of detainees. And that, inevitably, provided the radicals with a new rallying cry. In the volatile context of Basque nationalism, such actions only backfired on those who were perceived as responsible.

Therefore, in the case of Spain, severe legislative measures did not contribute to a decrease in the frequency of terrorist violence, whereas the inadequacy of security agencies to efficiently counter terrorism in accordance with the rule of law made those legal provisions simply counterproductive (Jaime-Jiménez, 1996). The situation was indeed aggravated by the behaviour of certain members of the security services deployed in the Basque country, whose own hostility towards the new democracy and Basque nationalism made them all too prone to employ unreasonable force and engage in gratuitous provocation. During the transition years, for instance, particularly between 1977 and 1979, some Basque localities suffered looting and pillaging perpetrated by policemen or civil guards. Furthermore, some of these functionaries may have directly encouraged or concealed right-wing terrorist violence against radical nationalists perpetrated by secret, overlapping groups such as the *Batallón Vasco Español* (BVE: Basque Spanish Battalion). The result of all this was a spontaneous additional outpouring of support for ETA in certain sectors of the society affected. 'ETA herria zurekin' ('ETA, the people are with you') read in a vernacular expression the graffiti that defaced many walls across the Basque provinces. The same medium was used to send a short and simple message to the state security forces, though this time in their own Castilian language: 'Que se vayan' ('Get out'). Negative social perception of the role of the police forces increased markedly. That is borne out by public opinion surveys (Centro de Investigaciones Sociológicas, 1982) and other qualitative studies (Pérez Agote, 1987: 63–6). Not surprisingly, the number of Basque citizens enlisting in the state security agencies was proportionally very low compared to those extracted from other regions and nationalities of Spain (López Garrido, 1987b: 75–87).

On the basis of the foregoing considerations, a number of tentative conclusions may already be drawn. First, the two factions of ETA built up support on an underpinning that drew heavily on the empathy they gained through their activities during the terminal stages of Francoism, and from the wellsprings of the Basque national sentiment so harshly persecuted by the dictatorship. To that was added, particularly with respect to the constituency of ETA(m), the frustration felt by a significant segment of mainly young Basques when they perceived that the ensuing political change fell short of their high and rising expectations. Finally, terrorists benefited from the resentments triggered by the excessive behaviour attributed to police forces that were long overdue for purge and reform. In that regard, one might note that the most significant spurt in membership growth of the two factions of ETA was registered precisely during 1978 and 1979 (Clark, 1984: 222; Reinares, 1998b), although this was due in part to the fact that many of the militants who had benefited from the 1977 amnesty immediately returned to the underground, swelling the ranks of the organization. *Herri Batasuna*, the heterogeneous coalition that articulated popular support for the insurgent terrorists, was not formed until 1979. Observing the aesthetics of radical Basque nationalism, especially in its adolescent offshoots, one cannot but be struck by the preponderance of attitudes that manifest extreme exasperation and defiance as expressed by clenched fists, hair standing on end and the shouting masses: precisely the outward signs of hatred and resentment.

In taking up the question of international factors that have contributed to the persistence of terrorism in Spain after 1976 and its abrupt escalation from 1978 to 1980, we must distinguish, first of all, between the active and passive support that ETA factions received from a number of countries, non-governmental entities and similarly minded armed insurgent groups. On the passive side, it is no secret that the French authorities reacted only reluctantly and within narrowly circumscribed limits to the fact that the leadership of ETA was using French territory as a sanctuary from which they could organize their terrorist activities in Spain. Seeking sanctuary on the French side of the border had been an essential component of ETA strategy from its very beginnings, when France was granting political asylum to violent Basque nationalists without asking too many questions. This was not surprising while Francoist rule lasted, but French authorities continued with this practice throughout the Spanish democratic transition. Successive French governments and public opinion in general were reluctant to admit that Spain had, in fact, become a new democracy. Instead, they insisted stubbornly that ETA terrorism was a domestic Spanish problem and restricted their efforts, until well into the 1980s, to imposing residence restrictions on some of the leaders, possibly no more than a precautionary measure to avoid the spread of radical Basque separatism across the border on its own territory, thus following the sanctuary doctrine whenever possible in dealings with transnational or international terrorism (Wieviorka, 1991: 160–62).

Apart from providing the underground leadership with a secure operational base, it was in France that the activists of ETA were formally recruited, received their training in the use of arms and explosives, and underwent ideological indoctrination. Propaganda was published and distributed from there, and all the information which the collaborators of the terrorist group on the other side of the border meticulously gathered prior to an attack was studied and sifted at leisure. France was, in short, the permanent place of refuge, redeployment and reorganization for ETA. On the other hand, for reasons both ideological and pragmatic, from 1976 onwards, ETA(pm) and especially ETA(m) received logistical and material support from various leftist regimes and guerrilla groups in Latin America, communist governments of Eastern Europe and some radicalized Arab states. International terrorist organizations, mainly Palestinian, also contributed with armament and paramilitary training in their Middle Eastern camps. There is some evidence suggesting that the former Soviet Union was the origin of a great many resources which ended up in the hands of ETA terrorists (Goren, 1984). That could also explain why the GRAPO abruptly stopped drawing its ideological inspiration from Maoist China and shifted during this period to stances more favourable to the Soviet Union. As for the right-wing terrorist groups active in Spain, these also maintained transnational links with dictatorial regimes in Latin America and neo-fascist networks across Western Europe. The one thing that can safely be claimed in all this is that, without assistance from abroad, either direct or indirect, active or passive, endogenous terrorist activity in general and ETA terrorism in particular would have declined much sooner than it did, or possibly even vanished. And to be sure, the terrorists would not have had the facilities for orchestrating the dramatic escalation of bloody violence in Spain between 1978 and 1980.

Democratic Consolidation, Internal Security Policy and Decline of Terrorism

The impact which a favourable political opportunity structure, as described above, had on the terrorist escalation during the transition from authoritarian rule would appear to be confirmed by the fact that, when the democracy began to be consolidated, the factors that once had facilitated it began to have negative repercussions on the dynamics of terrorist violence. The average number of yearly deaths from terrorism was down by 70 per cent between 1981 and 1985, compared to the figures for the period between 1978 and 1980, and after 1986 they slumped even further. GRAPO, the main left-wing terrorist group, virtually vanished, despite some recent attempts at reorganization. Extreme right-wing organizations found their operational capacity drastically reduced once its political sector faded away after the failed military coup in February 1981, and as officials sympathetic to their aims were rooted out of the state security agencies (Jabardo and Reinares, 1998). ETA(pm) decided to dissolve itself late that same year, once the Basque statute of autonomy had been approved by a large majority of the *vascongadas* provinces' inhabitants and autonomous institutions were already functioning. ETA(m) thus remained the main source of terrorist activity in Spain during the last two decades. Same as the escalation of terrorism in the late 1970s has been explained in terms of inadequate, even counterproductive, state response, its overall decline throughout the 1980s, and particularly since the late 1980s, can also be interpreted in terms of a more satisfactory and consistent internal security policy, despite some unacceptable decisions that were not taken in accordance with the rule of law, a fact which undoubtedly hampered the overall efficacy of measures adopted.

Anti-terrorist policy began to attain the consistency hitherto so conspicuously lacking and thus to achieve the results it had so desperately needed when Juan José Rosón was appointed as Minister of the Interior in May 1980. At that time, terrorism was at its most bloody and feverish height and the government was still unable to get a grip on the police forces. The new minister lost no time in bringing order to his department and did not hesitate to use his authority to bring into line and coordinate the efforts of the various policing bodies, including those that had been conspicuous for their reluctance to pursue violent right-wing groups that were all but flaunting their impunity. Rosón, for instance, made long overdue efforts to create a professional apparatus devoted to the gathering and analysis of information relevant for counterterrorism purposes. In March 1981, a single centralized command for the fight against terrorism, known as *Mando Unico para la Lucha Contraterrorrista*, was created for the first time since the democratic transition began. Soon afterwards, a significant number of ETA militants were arrested and a good portion of the terrorist structures dismantled, to the point that both factions of this clandestine organization evidenced, perhaps for the first time in at least three years, signs of relative decline. Other passive security initiatives adopted at this time contributed to a reduction in the levels of terrorist lethality; these included the generalized use of self-protection devices among public order personnel, better surveillance systems to prevent incidents, and even the shielding of official vehicles. All these technical efforts aimed at obtaining adequate levels of police efficiency and protecting potential targets paled, however, alongside the audacity Rosón showed in pushing for the introduction of legal and administrative initiatives that would lower the costs of exit from terrorism and allow convicted members of armed clandestine groups who laid down their arms to reclaim a place in society. The most visible result of these reinsertion measures was the self-dissolution of ETA(pm) late in 1981.

Following the victory of the leftist but reformist *Partido Socialista Obrero Español* (PSOE: Spanish Socialist Workers Party) in the October 1982 general elections, efforts were initially made to continue and develop the existing anti-terrorist agenda. A broad anti-terrorist programme, innovative in its comprehensive approach and known as the *Plan Zona Especial Norte* (North Special Zone Plan) was already being implemented in 1983 and its outcomes became evident throughout the decade. This programme, as well as subsequent policies on the same problem, were designed following a few primary guidelines. First of all, emphasis was placed on more effective police work and on channelling resources to this end. New security provisions were drawn up for most contingencies, and considerable progress was made in developing infrastructure for a coordinating authority in the intelligence sector, regardless of some remaining confrontations occasionally observed between the National Police and the Civil Guard. Soon, however, the socialist government showed a notorious, though not exclusive, preference for the latter body, at least in issues concerning the fight against terrorism. This was most probably due to the Civil Guard's more disciplined command structure and the lack of trade union associations within such a militarized state security agency. In any case, authorities also became concerned with improving the public opinion perception of police forces in the Basque Country and elsewhere, looking forward to more and better citizen collaboration.

Secondly, the programme strongly emphasized the need to build a broad political consensus on anti-terrorism among those parties

present in both national and autonomous parliamentary institutions, a goal which was substantially attained despite initial negative
reactions to the plan voiced by moderate nationalists. Then, over a
period of time, it became possible, though not always easy, to bring
legislation gradually into line so as to favour a more effective
policing action. Nevertheless, measures allowing for terrorist suspects to be held incommunicado for a certain time remained in
force, so the allegations of mistreatment persisted. Next, as Spain
adopted an increasingly high profile on the international scene, the
central government finessed a number of diplomatic initiatives aimed
at producing specific bilateral agreements on issues related to terrorism. The last important factor in the context of this plan was the
standing offer allowing the social reinsertion of terrorists in exchange for their renunciation of violence. To date, well over 300
militants and collaborators of different terrorist organizations,
though most of them formerly linked to ETA(pm), have accepted
the terms of this proposal.

As a result, ETA(m) was left to dominate the violent stage in
Spain, claiming responsibility for well over 90 per cent of the
terrorist attacks that have been carried out since 1981 and nearly
100 per cent of those occurring during the 1990s. But even as they
did so, a number of factors helped buttress the anti-terrorist policies
which the government developed to counter this armed clandestine
organization. Most decisive, in this respect, was the unprecedented
degree of cooperation Spanish authorities received from abroad in
their fight against terrorism. Especially noteworthy was, from the
second half of the 1980s, the change in attitudes and behaviour of
the French authorities, which no longer granted political refugee
status to ETA militants, and instead facilitated the arrest, expulsion
or deportation of many of its ringleaders (Morán, 1997). One series
of arrests followed another until, following a series of major round-
ups since 1992, the organization was deprived of its most experienced
leaders. In addition, the collapse of communism had come to the
countries formerly in the orbit of the Soviet Union, where terrorism
was to a certain extent tolerated as a legitimate way of exerting and
affirming the interests of these totalitarian regimes abroad. At the
same time, Palestinian organizations engaged in a peace process for
the Middle East, drastically reducing their involvement with either
transnational or international terrorism. Furthermore, Spain had
become a member state of the European Community in 1986, a fact
of regional integration which surely brought little comfort to ETA
leaders and activists, who probably anticipated closer police coop-

eration between states. They were also affected somewhat by the criminal attacks of the already mentioned GAL. This shadowy organization emerged in 1983, attempting to complement governmental counterterrorism initiatives with an illegal, violent campaign against suspected members of ETA.

Using the same terrorist methods employed by their defined antagonist armed organization, the GAL killed 27 people between October 1983 and July 1987, when its activities finished. Surprisingly, though, about one-third of their victims had no links whatsoever to ETA and resulted from mistakes in identifying targets or from decidedly arbitrary attacks. Such evidence and the fact that most of these killings took place in Southern France are no doubt associated with the main goal of these acts of violence: pressing the French authorities to put an end to the sanctuary that militants and collaborators of ETA were allowed to enjoy within the territory under their jurisdiction. The GAL was allegedly instigated by some incumbent politicians and high-ranking members of the security forces. Actually, it was composed of security functionaries and mercenary delinquents (García, 1988; Miralles and Arqués, 1989). Two implicated policemen were eventually given long jail terms for their role in recruiting the common criminals and foreigners with links to transnational organized crime that often perpetrated the above-mentioned assassinations. Former top officers in command of counterterrorism units and a prominent Basque politician affiliated in the past to the PSOE confessed afterwards their involvement with the GAL, but only after being prosecuted and imprisoned. Links of this vigilante terrorist group to the highest authorities at the Ministry of the Interior when its killings took place were investigated and subsequently proved by judges of the *Audiencia Nacional* (Spanish National Court). Certainly, the terrorist actions perpetrated by GAL activists, to some extent a continuation of similar violent activities conducted sporadically since the mid-1970s by various secret bands typically formed by neo-fascist agitators and criminal gang members, had the immediate effect of severely disorganizing the collectivity of ETA activists living with impunity in southern France. But the mid- and long-term consequences of such state-sponsored terrorism have been very pernicious. Among other negative effects, the political consensus needed to implement governmental anti-terrorist policies was initially endangered and later on disrupted. In addition, supporters of insurgent violence found new arguments, precisely at a time when ETA(m) was weaker than ever before and increasingly divorced from its population of reference. Indeed, state-sponsored terrorism used to counter insurgent terrorism can be considered a major factor explaining why ETA has persisted beyond the democratic transition.

During the 1980s, nevertheless, support or tolerance for political violence gradually lost ground in the Basque Country, where, by the end of the decade, fewer people than ever before acknowledged that they identified themselves with ETA (Pérez Agote, 1987: 66–77). The relative stability of political arrangements that were worked out in the Basque autonomous government, giving rise to a ruling coalition between the two main political forces, that is, the moderate *Partido Nacionalista Vasco* (Basque Nationalist Party) and the Basque offshoot of the Spanish Socialist Party, helped bring about a broad anti-terrorism accord (Reinares, 1987; Llera, 1989). All these factors contributed to alleviating social and political tensions accumulated over decades and to delegitimizing in political terms ETA(m)'s demands and the postulates out of which they were formulated. Following a decade of political instability, economic decline and moral degradation, the democratic and moderate variant of Basque nationalism evolved over this period towards the integration of its aspirations into the constitutional framework characteristic of a consolidated democracy.

To a large extent, Basque politics then ceased to be a highly polarized contest between adversarial parties. Deals and compromises were made in a way that allowed the autonomous political system to function with a high degree of stability (Llera, 1989). No doubt, a major milestone was the anti-violence accord that, in January 1988, was subscribed to by all the political parties represented in the Basque autonomous Parliament, with the still rather obvious exception of *Herri Batasuna*. This agreement, known as the *Pacto de Ajuria Enea*, incorporated the Basque moderate nationalists into a broad consensus on internal security matters and subsequently influenced the central government's policy in a number of measures, such as the definitive abolition of special anti-terrorist legislation that same year (though some provisions were incorporated in the ordinary criminal code), or the implementation of new penitentiary initiatives in 1989, also facilitating a progressive but significant increase in police efficiency when compared to the previous decade (Domínguez Iribarren, 1998b).

Signed by all Basque democratic parties, the *Ajuria Enea* agreement was also fundamental in further reducing social tolerance or popular passivity towards the terrorists. A survey conducted among inhabitants of the Basque autonomous community in 1989 indicated that ETA(m) was either supported or justified by only 8 per cent of those interviewed, this result being consistent with previous findings throughout the 1980s (Llera, 1993: 92). A particular episode which contributed strongly to the delegitimization of ETA(m) was the massive demonstration held on 18 March 1989 in Bilbao under the slogan 'Por la paz, ahora y para siempre' or, in the Basque vernacular, 'Pakea orain eta betirarte' ('For peace, now and for ever'). The Basque Country had never seen anything as massive, in which all the parties represented in the Basque Parliament took part, again with the exception of *Herri Batasuna*. This demonstrated once again that the desire of the vast majority of Basques was that ETA(m) militants should lay down their arms and put an end to the violence. The impulse for peace has permeated all levels of Spanish public opinion, as well as Basque society. Massive demonstrations against violence and for peace became so continuous and pervasive during the 1990s that radical nationalists reacted fiercely from the middle of the decade, trying to spread turmoil in the streets of Basque localities in order to frighten those who voice their opposition to terrorism (Funes, 1998a; 1998b). Finally, as a result of the deployment, partially initiated in 1982, of a Basque autonomous police force, known as *Ertzaintza*, with extensive policing capabilities and strong links to the moderate nationalists who made a renowned effort at coopting its agents, the terms in which ETA(m) mounted its challenge to the security forces changed progressively. Basque autonomous policemen intervened for the first time in a counterterrorist operation in 1990. Soon afterwards, *Ertzaintza* officers became one of the elements victimized by the terrorists.

Over time, all these developments brought very palpable consequences. ETA(m) progressively lost the ability to bring Basque political life to a standstill or to influence central government policies in regard to autonomous communities as well as other areas. And though that terrorist organization still managed to carry out spectacular attacks or assassinations, its decline was underscored by reports of bitter disputes that have divided the leadership and by the damage which the social reinsertion of former activists has inflicted on the internal cohesion of this clandestine group. A split became evident between those ETA leaders who favoured reaching some kind of deal that would allow a solution to be found over the matter of prisoners and exiles, and those who insist that the armed struggle be waged until the legitimate government of the Spanish state caves in to each and every one of their demands. The ETA directorate has made it clear to its militants, on the other hand, that any one of them who may be considering accepting the social reinsertion offer is regarded as a traitor to the cause and will be dealt with accordingly. Indeed, they did not hesitate to gun down one of their own former leaders, María Dolores González Catarain, also known as Yoyes, a woman who had accepted the terms of that offer in 1985 and was already living in the Spanish Basque Country when she was murdered while walking through the streets of her home town with her four-year-old son.

Maintaining internal cohesion and the submission of the militants became a priority for the terrorist organization, particularly with respect to those serving long prison terms and who are an effective tool for mobilizing popular support. Since the late 1970s and during most of the 1980s, the average yearly number of ETA members or collaborators in jail oscillated between 400 and 500, serving their prison terms in just two large penitentiaries. This concentration facilitated the various mechanisms of social control enforced by terrorist leaders. This is why governmental measures were introduced in May 1989, ordering the dispersal of ETA inmates, obliging them to serve their sentences in as many different prisons as possible. This official initiative was aimed at undermining the internal cohesion of the jailed militants and, by extension, the terrorist organization at large. While these measures were implemented in the context of a broad political consensus on anti-terrorism matters, they proved to be quite effective in stimulating individual dissociation from the terrorist organization, renunciation of violence and the acceptance of reinsertion in society.

During the 1990s, a tendency was also detected among some sectors of *Herri Batasuna* to undertake initiatives in the political arena and give outward indications of attitudes that may not exactly conform to the doctrine being pushed at the moment by the leadership of ETA(m). This was probably a further indication that the terrorist organization was well along the way to a much-reduced political as well as operational capability. ETA(m) relied on a type of collective action which once could mobilize masses but now appeared to be losing its edge as ordinary political exchange becomes the norm instead of the exception. Another possible sign that ETA(m) was in decline could be the changes over time in the pattern of its terror attacks. ETA(m) became much more indiscriminate in whom it sought to kill, relying ever more heavily on car bombs and other devices that scatter death at random (see Figure 4.2). While all this was happening, state security agencies

Figure 4.2:   ETA Terrorism, 1968–98

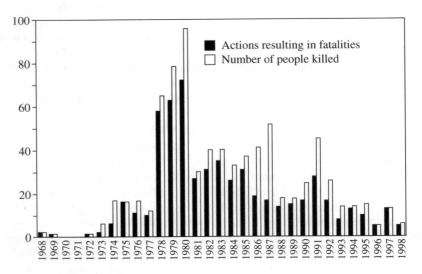

were getting better at their job and public tolerance or passivity in the face of the continuing violence cooled to a quite perceptible degree. Except in a very few places, fear ceased to be the determining factor in the societal reaction to terrorism. Even in the homeland it pretends to be liberating, ETA(m) can no longer count on the infrastructure it requires to carry out its attacks with reasonable assurances of impunity. As a result, since the mid-1980s, ETA(m) has been stepping up the attacks it perpetrates outside the Basque Country, especially in Madrid and Barcelona, where they will bring the organization more of the notoriety it needs, while at the same time they are less likely to cause a groundswell of revulsion among its constituency that might affect negatively the support enjoyed, though less and less, by *Herri Batasuna*.

Finally, the decline of ETA(m) has also been demonstrated by the regularity with which it insists that it wants to negotiate an end to the violence and by the body with whom it insists that it wants to negotiate. In this sense, the terrorist organization presumes the right to negotiate on an equal footing with the Spanish government in hopes of winning at the negotiating table the right to impose its will on the political future of the Basque Country, the victory which it implicitly acknowledges that it will never be able to win through violence. In this, ETA(m) deliberately refuses to recognize that the

Basque people have recourse to all the democratically legitimized institutions of autonomous government required to determine their own political life, and no lack of democrats whom they have chosen to represent them in this endeavour. Even so, it is significant that, whereas in the late 1970s ETA(m) haughtily insisted that it would hold talks only with the Spanish armed forces, from the mid-1980s it tried to get the Spanish government to sit down at the negotiating table (Ibarra, 1987). Implicitly, the terrorists came to admit that elected politicians and not the military are ruling in modern Spain, thus providing a rather uncommon additional indicator of democratic consolidation: the same democratic consolidation which drastically reduced opportunities for carrying out sustained and systematic terrorist activity.

ETA(m) continued and aggravated its organizational decline through the 1990s, mainly due to external factors such as the normalized Basque autonomous polity within a consolidated democracy, the already mentioned growing social reaction against violence, increasing police efficiency in the absence of illegal counterterrorism, unprecedented judicial interventions directed towards the criminal networks created around the armed clandestine group, and rising levels of international cooperation. The latter three of these factors, pertaining to a governmental anti-terrorist programme, intensified notably once the *Partido Popular* (PP, Popular Party) won in the Spanish general elections of 1996 and formed government. Basque elected politicians at national, regional or local level, belonging to that party, soon became priority targets for the terrorist organization. To overcome a very adverse situation, leaders of ETA(m) tried, late in 1998, to implicate leaders of moderate nationalist parties in an initiative aimed at fostering separatist goals in exchange for a possible lasting ceasefire. Though most of the moderate nationalist leaders engaged initially in such a plan, Basque citizens did not support the deal. Actually, subsequent elections held in the Basque Autonomous Community since then resulted not only in votes for non-nationalist parties, also known as constitutionalists, tied with those for nationalist parties, but also in the latter being removed from their previous dominant positions in a number of major cities and territorial entities. Moreover, nationalist voters continue to be a rather small minority in Navarre. Constitutionalist forces aim at preserving and improving the legitimized autonomy arrangements, which they consider accommodated to the cultural and political plurality of Basque society, where the majority of citizens have little or no problem at all in accepting a dual and compatible identity, as both Basques and Spaniards. Some nationalist leaders, on the other hand, remain tempted to create new scenarios, thus trying to advance ethnic goals outside the existing institutional framework. No doubt, the demise of ETA(m) would accelerate provided moderate nationalist parties unambiguously endorse democratic principles and procedures, instead of trying to impose exclusive ethnic propositions by aligning themselves with radical nationalist groups which justify or make use of terrorism.

Conclusions

An analysis of the case of Spain confirms that authoritarian regimes where formal paths to the legal expression of opposition are restricted or blocked, but official repression is inefficient, tend, when compared with totalitarian dictatorships or liberal democracies, to be especially prone to the formation of terrorist groups (see Crenshaw, 1981: 384; Reinares, 1998b: 58–68). In that same country, the demise of terrorism following democratic consolidation is also consistent with those analyses which emphasize how functioning pluralist polities offer better conditions for arrangements likely to regulate social conflicts which have produced violence (Wilkinson, 1986; Reinares, 1998b). However, the relationship between periods of fundamental political change and the evolution of existing terrorist activity by clandestine organizations seems rather ambivalent. On the one side, for instance, democratic transition provides, not only new possibilities for institutional participation and conventional collective action, but also particular opportunities for the disruptive activities of certain kinds of groups, more concretely those which place an extreme value on their objectives, assume the high risks involved in achieving them and even perceive any change in the distribution of power as a threat to their own survival (Tilly, 1978: 135). On the other side, state responses to internal security threats in a context of regime change are expected to have a significant influence on the dynamics of existing terrorism. This chapter has attempted precisely to explain the rise and fall of terrorism in Spain during the consecutive processes of transition from authoritarian rule and democratic consolidation, as a result of the diverse and evolving governmental measures implemented to counter such type of violence.

References

Carr, Raymond and Juan P. Fusi. 1979. *España, de la Dictadura a la Democracia*. Barcelona: Planeta.

Centro de Investigaciones Sociológicas. 1982. 'Opinión Pública Sobre la Policía'. *Revista Española de Investigaciones Sociológicas* 18: 143-69.

Clark, Robert P. 1984. *The Basque Insurgents. ETA, 1952–1980*. Madison: University of Wisconsin Press.

Clark, Robert P. 1990. *Negotiating with ETA. Obstacles to Peace in the Basque Country, 1975–1988*. Reno and Las Vegas: University of Nevada Press.

Cotarelo, Ramón, ed. 1992. *Transición política y consolidación democrática en España (1975–1986)*. Madrid: Centro de Investigaciones Sociológicas.

Crenshaw, Martha. 1981. 'The Causes of Terrorism'. *Comparative Politics* 13: 379–99.

Domínguez Iribarren, Florencio. 1998a. *ETA: Estrategia Organizativa y Actuaciones, 1978–1992*. Bilbao: Servicio Editorial de la Universidad del País Vasco.

Domínguez Iribarren, Florencio. 1998b. *De la Negociación a la Tregua, ¿el Final de ETA?* Madrid: Taurus.

Funes, María J. 1998a. 'Social Responses to Political Violence in the Basque Country: Peace Movements and their Audience'. *Journal of Conflict Resolution* 42: 493–510.

Funes, María J. 1998b. *La salida del silencio. Movilizaciones por la paz en Euskadi 1986–1998*. Madrid: Akal Editor.

García, Javier. 1988. *Los GAL al Descubierto. La Trama de la Guerra Sucia Contra ETA*. Madrid: El País-Aguilar.

García de Cortázar, Fernando and Juan P. Fusi. 1988. *Política, Nacionalidad e Iglesia en el País Vasco*. San Sebastián: Txertoa.

Goren, Roberta. 1984. *The Soviet Union and Terrorism*. London: Allen & Unwin.

Ibarra, Pedro. 1987. *La evolución estratégica de ETA (1963–1987)*. San Sebastián: Kriselu.

Jabardo, Rosario and Fernando Reinares. 1998. 'Démobilisation de l'extrême droite en Espagne'. *Pouvoirs* 87: 115–28.

Jaime-Jiménez, Oscar. 1996. 'Legislación Antiterrorista y Agencias Estatales de Seguridad: un Análisis Preliminar de la Experiencia Española, 1960–1996'. *Revista de Derecho Penal y Criminología* 6: 569–97.

Jaime-Jiménez, Oscar. 1997. 'Avatares Políticos y Organizativos de la Respuesta Policial al Terrorismo en España (1976–1996)'. In *State and Societal Reactions to Terrorism*, edited by Fernando Reinares. Oñati: International Institute for the Sociology of Law.

Jaime-Jiménez, Oscar. 1998. 'Policía y Terrorismo en España (1976–1996)'. *Ciencia Policial* 43: 85–102.

Jaúregui, Gurutz. 1981. *Ideología y Estrategia Política de ETA*. Madrid: Siglo Veintiuno.

Lamarca, Carmen. 1985. *Tratamiento Jurídico del Terrorismo*. Madrid: Ministerio de Justicia.

Linz, Juan J. 1986. *Conflicto en Euskadi*. Madrid: Espasa Calpe.

Llera, Francisco J. 1987. 'Violencia y Sobrevaloración de la Lengua: Conflicto Simbólico en el País Vasco'. In *Comportamiento electoral y nacionalismo en Cataluña, Galicia y País Vasco*, edited by José Vilariño. Santiago de Compostela: Universidad de Santiago de Compostela.

Llera, Francisco J. 1989. 'Continuidad y Cambio en la Política Vasca: Notas Sobre Identidades Sociales y Cultura Política'. *Revista Española de Investigaciones Sociológicas* 47: 107–35.

Llera, Francisco J. 1993. 'Violencia y Opinión Pública en el País Vasco, 1978–1992'. *Revista Internacional de Sociología* 3: 83–111.

Llera, Francisco J. 1994. *Los vascos y la política*. Bilbao: Servicio Editorial de la Universidad del País Vasco.

López Garrido, Diego. 1987a. *Terrorismo, Política y Derecho*. Madrid: Alianza.

López Garrido, Diego. 1987b. *El Aparato Policial en España*. Barcelona: Ariel.

Maravall, José María. 1978. *Dictatorship and Political Dissent. Workers and Students in Franco's Spain*. London: Tavistock.

Maravall, José María and Julián Santamaría. 1985. 'Crisis del Franquismo, Transición Política y Consolidación de la Democracia en España'. *Sistema* 68–9: 79–129.

Martín, Rodolfo. 1984. *Al Servicio del Estado*. Barcelona: Planeta.

Miralles, Melchor and Ricardo Arqués. 1989. *Amedo. El Estado Contra ETA*. Barcelona: Plaza y Janés y Cambio 16.

Morán, Sagrario. 1997. *ETA entre Francia y España*. Madrid: Editorial Complutense.

Pérez Agote, Alfonso. 1984. *La Reproducción del Nacionalismo Vasco*. Madrid: Centro de Investigaciones Sociológicas.

Pérez Agote, Alfonso. 1987. *El Nacionalismo Vasco a la Salida del Franquismo*. Madrid: Centro de Investigaciones Sociológicas.

Pérez Díaz, Víctor. 1993. *La primacía de la sociedad civil. El proceso de formación de la España democrática*. Madrid: Alianza Editorial.

Reinares, Fernando, ed. 1984. *Violencia y Política en Euskadi*. Bilbao: Desclée de Brower.

Reinares, Fernando. 1987. 'The Basque Autonomous Parliament Elections of 1986'. *Electoral Studies* 6: 169–73.

Reinares, Fernando. 1988. 'Nationalism and Violence in Basque Politics'. *Conflict. An International Journal* 8: 141–55.

Reinares, Fernando. 1989. 'Democratización y Terrorismo en el Caso Español'. In *La Transición Democrática Española*, edited by J.F. Tezanos, R. Cotarelo and A. de Blas. Madrid: Sistema.

Reinares, Fernando. 1990. 'Sociogénesis y Evolución del Terrorismo en España'. In *España: Sociedad y Política*, edited by S. Giner. Madrid: Espasa Calpe.

Reinares, Fernando. 1996. 'The Political Conditioning of Collective Violence: Regime Change and Insurgent Terrorism in Spain'. *Research on Democracy and Society* 3: 297–326.

Reinares, Fernando. 1998a. *Terrorismo y antiterrorismo*. Barcelona: Ediciones Paidós.

Reinares, Fernando. 1998b. 'Rasgos sociodemográficos de los integrantes de ETA'. *Ciencia Policial* 43: 103–16.

Sullivan, John. 1988. *El Nacionalismo Vasco Radical, 1959–1986*. Madrid: Alianza Editorial.

Tezanos, José F., Ramón Cotarelo and Andrés de Blas, eds. 1989. *La transición democrática española*. Madrid: Editorial Sistema.

Tilly, Charles. 1978. *From Mobilization to Revolution*. New York: Random House.

Unzueta, Patxo. 1997. *El Terrorismo. ETA y el Problema Vasco*. Barcelona: Ediciones Destino.

Vercher, Antonio. 1992. *Terrorism in Europe. An International Comparative Legal Analysis*. Oxford: Clarendon.

Waldmann, Peter. 1991. 'From the Vindication of Honour to Blackmail: the Impact of the Changing Role of ETA on Society and Politics in the Basque Region of Spain'. In *Tolerating Terrorism in the West*, edited by N. Gal Or. London: Routledge.

Wieviorka, Michel. 1991. 'France Faced with Terrorism'. *Terrorism* 14: 157–70.

Wilkinson, Paul. 1986. *Terrorism and the Liberal State*. London: Macmillan.

The Authors

Fernando Reinares is Professor of Political Science and Public Administration at the University of Burgos, Spain. He is also contributing editor of the journal, *Studies in Conflict and Terrorism*. Previously, he was the holder of a Jean Monnet Chair in European Studies at UNED, Madrid.

Oscar Jaime-Jiménez is Titular Professor of Political Science and Public Administration at the University of Burgos, Spain. Previously, he taught at the Public University of Navarre in Pamplona.

5 The Police Response to Terrorism in Italy from 1969 to 1983

LUCIANA STORTONI-WORTMANN

On 18 March 1978 the President of the Christian Democratic Party (DC) Aldo Moro was kidnapped and the five members of his escort were killed. During the following police inquiry many mistakes were committed, afterwards causing a parliamentary investigation of police operations. The depositions of the home minister and of the chiefs of police before the Parliamentary Commission on terrorism revealed a very limited knowledge of the terrorist world affecting the whole security system. Francesco Cossiga, home minister at the time of the Moro kidnapping, declared:

> through such a painful event we totally grasped the problem of terrorism and also the police forces perceived this phenomenon, its complexity and its originality, and the efficacy and weakness of existing structures, methods and techniques to fight it ... The police were prepared to fight sporadic events of terrorism ... but a security policy against terrorism had not been yet set up ... Such a policy which has only been developed later even in other countries requires a political, social and cultural analysis, and not just a technical one. (Senato, 1985, III: 191–2)

The statements of the two chiefs of the main Italian police agencies were even more explicit: 'We had at that time two huge organizations, police and carabineers, who had no eyes and no ears ... we had no intelligence ... we had no informants ... we had no possibility to address, identify a really serious track [on Moro's kidnapping]' (Parlato, in Senato, 1985, III: 343); 'We were managing terrorism in an ordinary way ... without knowing and understanding its deep roots in this country' (Corsini, in Senato, 1985, III: 397). By 1978 terrorism had almost a ten-year tradition in Italy and from 1969 until 1977 attacks seriously injuring people had been 106. The declared 'impreparedness' of police forces at the time of the Moro kidnapping therefore poses some questions to which many answers are possible.

In Italy the adoption of anti-terrorist measures was very slow and accompanied by many difficulties. Intelligence was sometimes scarce and sometimes of doubtful value. Furthermore, the whole intelligence system had been reformed in 1977 and, for two years, during the most critical terrorist emergency, its operational capability was weak. The adoption of a specific analytical methodology regarding terrorism was quite slow and, until the Moro kidnapping, terrorist attacks were mostly treated by the police as isolated incidents. Special anti-guerrilla techniques were introduced only at the end of the 1970s when other important instruments, such as data-banks and sophisticated equipment, were introduced or upgraded.

The strategy against terrorism tends to modify the traditional organizational assets of police forces. It requires different specializations and a consequent strong coordination. Better specialization can imply the establishment of new 'ad hoc' units, and information exchange is particularly relevant in view of the territorial mobility of terrorism. Even in this respect the Italian situation was very confusing: special structures were created at different times, inside different organizations, with different features and aims. The lack of a unique and durable strategy, and the sometimes difficult relations between the different structures, posed, at least until the end of the 1970s, serious problems affecting collection and transfer of information. Before going into detail we have to consider Italian terrorism: without providing a very detailed analysis, we shall just highlight the main features of Italian terrorism which seemed to affect both the perception and the reaction of the police.

The Italian Terrorism: some Relevant Peculiarities

From 1969 until nearly the middle of the 1980s, many terrorist groups, inspired by both right-wing and left-wing ideologies, were active in Italy. The Italian political system had been distinguished since the postwar period by the continuity in government of the DC and by the presence of the biggest western Communist Party (PCI), always confined to the opposition. From the 1960s, the stability of the centre–right government began to decrease because of the progressive electoral advance of the left-wing block and of a growing hostility towards the government, especially among the younger generation. Some innovations were adopted, such as the inclusion of the Socialist Party in the government, while the DC mantained a central position. The development of terrorism can be appreciated in such a political framework: on the one hand, terrorism can be considered as a reaction to the substantial immobility of the political system, as Luigi Bonanate (1979) argued, and this was especially the case of left-wing terrorism. On the other hand, terrorism was an instrument used to block any possible attempt to change the traditional power distribution, and this was especially the case of right-wing terrorism. The first feature of Italian terrorism we have to consider is, then, its heterogeneity: two main political areas, right-wing and left-wing, and quite different terrorist organizations inside them.

Right-wing terrorism aimed mainly, even if not entirely, to spread terror among people, to cause reactions of greater control and to shift the political system towards the right. This kind of terrorism was not really interested in propaganda, it was particularly bloody and enjoyed support from some members of crucial institutions: the police itself, the judiciary and, especially, the intelligence system. Some coups d'état, perhaps four up to 1974, were even planned and partially developed by such 'separate' institutional actors, assisted by right-wing extremists. Left-wing terrorist organizations aimed to propagate their political projects in order to obtain support from identified audiences. Their attacks were not indiscriminate, like the massacres committed by right-wing groups, and their choice of targets usually had a purpose often explained by written declarations. Left-wing terrorism groups were quite different in size, internal structure, activity and political projects. The Marxist-oriented Red Brigades (RB), the biggest, the most clandestine and militarily structured organization, tended to deal directly with state institutions. The smaller organizations were oriented towards post-industrial society perspectives, were less organized and were strictly connected with protest movements.

The second relevant feature we have to take into account is the development of Italian terrorism; that is, the presence of quite different phases. The first phase (1969–75) was dominated by a quite bloody right-wing terrorism; left-wing terrorist organizations were at that time poorly structured and they did not intentionally attack individuals. Between 1969 and 1975, the institutional protection accorded to right-wing terrorists before and after their attacks, which only emerged later, was particularly powerful. Left-wing organizations at this time were of relatively modest dimensions, had a quite simple organization and were still quite open to external movements. The first group of Brigadists was still close to worker groups active in north Italian factories: the Gruppi Armati Proletari were mainly gathered around Giangiacomo Feltrinelli and practically disappeared after his death; the Nuclei Armati Proletari were very active in prisons and even open to common criminals.

From 1977 until 1979, terrorist organizations and attacks increased enormously. Left-wing terrorism prevailed at this time. The Red Brigades were reorganized under a more military leadership and expanded their membership massively. Their targets were, beside industrial executives, even political representatives. Many less structured groups connected with the movement 'Autonomia operaia' attacked tradesmen and free professionals while Front Line, which appeared at the end of 1976, represented, because of its size, structure and activity, an intermediate organization between 'high and low' (well organized and spontaneous) terrorism. Front Line was quite active against industrial executives but also against judges and professional men. Right-wing terrorist attacks never exceeded, at that time, 25 per cent of the total. Two levels were present even here: one relatively organized, such as the Nuclei Armati Rivoluzionari, and a large number of more spontaneous groups. The contacts with separate institutional actors decreased in comparison with the past, and a revolutionary strategy against the state was developed whose main victims were policemen.

Such a short analysis reveals that Italian terrorism was, in a sense, particularly difficult to fight against, first of all because of the number of groups, the continuous exchange of members between them, the different actions adopted and the multitude of targets. We must then consider that some crucial difference between left- and right-wing terrorism affected the reaction of the police and partially explained different results of police inquiries. As former home minister Rognoni (1989) asserted, left-wing terrorism was in a sense more vulnerable because of its intention to win political consent of the far left-wing movement: terrorists' messages to the public exposed them to investigation. Right-wing terrorism, indifferent to consent and using relatively easy techniques such as attacks with bombs, was comparatively more difficult to analyse and to detect. Such observations bring us to consider carefully the development of terrorism previously described. The predominance between 1969 and 1974 of indiscriminate slaughter and the obstacles posed by institutional protection to inquiries on right-wing terrorism, on the one hand, and the presence of not very organized left-wing terrorist groups on the other, were certainly not likely to facilitate or even motivate the development of specialized anti-terrorist strategies. Lastly, we must consider the concurrent presence of extremist movements, both left and right wing-oriented, sometimes quite violent. Such extremist movements offered covert and logistic support to terrorists and, in addition, their activism occupied police forces in public order assignments, reducing the personnel available for investigation. We must even consider that the student and worker conflict persisted in Italy for a longer time than in other countries and around 1977 there was a new wave of violent conflict. The presence of collective and spontaneous violence made it difficult to discern the development of more structured violent projects. This was especially the case at the beginning of the terrorist experience, around 1969–72, and in 1976 after the electoral collapse of the extreme left-wing organizations. Such a deficiency was not confined to the police agencies but involved the whole political system, especially the political actors whose reaction to terrorism must be carefully considered.

The Political Reaction to Terrorism

Political comment on terrorism was quite scarce until the so-called 'emergency phase' around 1978–9. Political perceptions about the ideological origins and projects of terrorists were disparate. In a sense, every political actor tended to interpret terrorism in the context of its ideological values, its political position and political interest. Different interpretations can be ascribed to the rather wide ideological distance existing between Italian major parties and to the presence of two opposite terrorisms, ideologically contiguous to the opposite political poles. The DC, mainly interested in maintaining its hegemony on moderate public opinion,[1] tended then to present itself as the 'order party' (the party of public order) in the face of two opposite extremisms simply considered quite similar. The two institutional extreme poles, the PCI and the Movimento Sociale Italiano (MSI), mainly recognized the danger of the respective opposite terrorisms. Some MSI members had rather close contacts with right-wing terrorists, especially during the first half of the 1970s. The PCI tolerated a certain violence inside its more radical circles and until 1976 it did not recognize the reality of a terrorist movement emerging from the left-wing.[2] As Angelo Ventura (1984) pointed out, this fact had a significant relevance because of the PCI's hegemony on Italian cultural life.

By the middle of the 1970s, the attention of almost the whole Italian political system was concentrated on changes affecting relationships between institutional parties as a consequence of significant electoral variations. PCI electoral growth in 1975 and 1976 concentrated political attention on new alliances between the traditional classes, that is the workers and the middle class. This implied scant attention being paid to new social actors, new collective movements and new demands. It even implied a quite general neglect of terrorism and the lack of a common strategy during the maturation of the most dramatic terrorist phase.

Gianfranco Pasquino (1990) analyses the 'underevaluation' of terrorism emerging from the governments' programme during the 1970s which can also be seen in the parliamentary debates of the same period. Especially worth noting is the lack, at least until 1978–9, of analysis concerning the strategy of terrorism in connection both with collective movements and with state reactions. Only quite general references to social and economic dysfunction were made, together with a few allusions to political motivations, allusions often influenced by pre-constituted hypotheses.

From 1969 to 1974, the criminal legislation was directed to increasing individual rights and contained some limitations regarding police powers. From 1974, such a tendency was reversed as a reaction to a general 'social alarm'.[3] The measures introduced were not expressly aimed against terrorism; only crimes connected with the reconstruction of the Fascist Party were considered. Political debates did not reveal any conscious distinction between common and political criminality. The measures seemed to address just a few practices of the new criminality, such as the increasing number of attacks against the police. Police powers were the most critical issue. The centre–right pointed to the increase in police preventive powers as the key solution to public order problems considered as strongly challenging the ability to govern. The political left, strongly criticizing the lack of democratic accountability of police agencies, opposed any expansion of police powers, preferring to invoke structural modifications. The government being a left–centre coalition, the result was a limited increase in police powers of investigation. The intractability of opposite positions, the hostility of debates and the limited solutions seem to indicate a limited perception of the terrorist menace. The perception of the terrorist menace was anyway not deep enough to push all political parties towards a serious collaboration.

In 1977, criminal legislation showed a degree of political attention to terrorism,[4] but the social alarm was still ascribed to a 'general

increase of criminal violence' (*Report Bartolomei*, 1977). The attitude of political actors confronted by terrorism changed dramatically
only from 1978, especially after the Moro kidnapping. The 'emergency legislation' contained relevant modifications affecting both the
criminal code and the code of criminal procedure. It defined new
specific crimes connected with terrorism and contemplated for the
first time special treatment for those collaborating during inquiries.[5]
The widening of police powers was considerable and a general shift
of power from the judiciary to the police was introduced, even if for
a limited time and restricted to particular crimes.[6] A truly new preventive measure was introduced in March 1978: the home minister
had the power to ask for copies of legal proceedings and written
information about them[7] in order to prevent further crimes or in
order to include them in a new data bank. Through the same decree,
the police were allowed to collect summary information from suspects or detainees without the presence of a defending counsel.[8]
Previous limitations affecting phone interceptions were abolished[9]
and the police were permitted to take people to police stations in
order to check their identity.[10] In December 1979, a measure previously much discussed was introduced: the preventive arrest, detached
from any presumption of a committed crime, combined with the
allowance of searches and with the acquisition of summary information.[11] The measure was surrounded by two specific guarantees: there
would be parliamentary control of such arrests through six-monthly
reports presented by the home minister, and they would be limited to
one year (once renewable). The duration of normal arrest was length-
ened[12] and the conditions for house searches were extended.[13]

The whole legislation was directed to emphasizing preventive
intervention. It delineated a sphere of independent decision for the
police concerning 'open' situations susceptible of a criminal evolution over which the judiciary wielded only a formal control. The
role of the police was even strengthened in the sphere of criminal
investigation and such a trend was also related to organizational
difficulties of the whole juridical apparatus. Inquiries on terrorism
expanded enormously because of connections progressively emerging between many offences, to the point of completely jamming
proceedings (see Dalia, 1982). The progressive expansion of preventive imprisonment was a reaction to the same difficulties and the
loss of personal liberty was shaped as a measure of prevention and
deterrence (see Galli *et al.*, 1977).

Such measures were adopted with wide parliamentary support.[14]
The menace of terrorism was perceived widely if not unequivocally.

The DC was particularly threatened by the Red Brigades' assault directed against the party as the main representative and defender of the status quo. The PCI was mainly concerned by the anti-reformist aim of terrorists; that is, the assault directed against those political groups which could ameliorate and strengthen the current system. Different solutions were conceived: the DC focused on economic improvement and on a general recovery of moral values without bringing into the discussion the present political configuration. The PCI wanted a general reform of the state apparatus with the contribution of all representative political parties. The reform of police agencies and popular participation were considered the key solution to terrorism.[15] The 'emergency legislation' was adopted by a 'government of national unity', a consociative experiment lacking ideological homogeneity. The parliamentary majority coalesced mainly on general principles and produced a legislation which was mainly 'defensive', sometimes touching the limits of a liberal democracy,[16] responding to the most urgent problems, but it was not able to achieve substantial reforms (see Pasquino, 1985). That's why the reform of the police was significantly approved in 1981 after the end of the consociative experience. As consequences concerning criminal legislation, we may note the presence of frequent modifications of the same rules; the mixture of several aspects of the criminal codes, even producing uncertainties in application; the absence of political consent on basic questions, the delay in coping with the situation and the urgency hindered a more harmonious policy. Nevertheless, from 1979, political analysis of terrorism became much more precise and the reports on internal security presented from 1981 by the home minister to the Parliament, as requested by the Police Reform Act, contained detailed analysis of origins and objectives of left-wing terrorism, especially the Red Brigades. Reflections on right-wing terrorism remained scant in spite of two very bloody acts committed in 1980 and 1984.

The Italian Security System: some Relevant Features

The reaction of the Italian security system to anti-terrorism was certainly influenced by some 'internal' variables concerning organization and structures. The Italian security system is composed of a number of structures and presents two relevant peculiarities. Firstly, we must consider the presence of two police agencies differently organized but with very similar dimensions and functions: the Pubblica Sicurezza, denominated Polizia di Stato from 1981 (hereafter 'PS') and the Arma dei Carabinieri (hereafter 'CC'). Secondly, we must consider the involvement de facto of the military intelligence service in internal security issues. The intelligence service's denomination was SIFAR until 1965 and SID thereafter. It is worthy of emphasis that, in spite of the activity of numerous agencies, no stable form of central coordination was introduced until at least 1979.

The security system was characterized by a very low level of control over security agencies by representative political bodies, such as the Parliament. The security policy was mainly supervised by the home minister, exclusively guided since 1945 by the DC. The connection between the home minister and the PS was particularly stable, while the CC enjoyed comparatively more autonomy because it was part of the army.[17] The government's influence over the intelligence service appeared to be even feebler because of a very strong connection of the service with foreign intelligence agencies, especially the American one, often implying a greater loyalty to the latter than to the national rule. Attempts to change such procedures were introduced by the Intelligence System Reform Act (1977) and by the Police Reform Act (1981).

The Italian security system was, after the Second World War, mainly patterned on public order requirements in order to face quite frequent and sometimes violent political strife. Education, training, equipment and structures were mainly patterned on military criteria even inside the PS. Criminal investigation got relatively lower care. The personnel fighting criminality were invariably inadequate and the adoption of new instruments and techniques was quite slow. We have to consider that a distinct Criminal Investigation Department under the direction of the public prosecutor never existed in Italy. Moreover, geographical distribution of the Italian police was not related to the territorial incidence of criminality. The southern units were often overstaffed, while the northern units did not have enough personnel. The lack of personnel seriously affected metropolises like Milan and Rome.

All these features influenced during the 1970s the development of the fight against terrorism. First of all, the different institutional positions and internal situations of police agencies produced different adjustments. The PS experienced during the 1970s a deep internal crisis, leading to a structural reform in 1981. Demands for better working conditions and greater professionalism, which had already emerged in earlier years, were put in a concrete form by the internal union movement, which demanded a new civil status – the body was still militarized – and the creation of a union organization, which was still prohibited. The challenge of terrorism amplified already existing functional problems. The PS was burdened by a huge number of administrative duties and the personnel occupied in criminal investigation were very limited. Moreover, the rise of terrorism tied down a huge number of agents in surveillance of critical targets, especially in Rome, ultimately limiting the personnel assigned to analyse and investigate terrorism. A sort of spiral emerged because such a reduction necessarily implied a quite scattered prevention. Moreover, the already quite scarce operative training was further reduced, compromising agents' capability to react to terrorist assaults. During the 1970s, applications for jobs in the PS decreased significantly, while resignations increased. The internal rebellion, sometimes quite violent, was addressed by the police union movement with demands for greater autonomy from political pressure and a closer relationship with civil society. These were considered as the main requisites for a better professionalism. Terrorism on the one hand precipitated the reform of the police, putting already existing problems into dramatic evidence, but on the other it frustrated transformation, at least for a time. During the 1970s the reform was blocked by politicians' attempts to centralize and control the fight against terrorism. The Reform of the Police Act was introduced in 1981, when few terrorist groups were still active but already destined to fail.

In the same period, the CC presented a very different situation. The major internal compactness and structural autonomy, connected with its inclusion in the army, allowed a quicker adaptation in the face of new challenges.[18] Some difficulties were considered, deriving from recent structural changes affecting the CC's traditional scattered distribution over Italian territory, considered as one of the CC's more relevant resources. However, the care already accorded to anti-guerrilla training, concentrated into the 13 mobile troops, expedited the creation of the first special anti-terrorist unit. CC's greater autonomy was not confined to internal decisions. During the 1970s, carabineers were able to inhibit decisions pointing to a major centralization of the security system and potentially affecting CC's autonomy. Moreover, relevant positions in the security system were conferred on CC's representatives: from 1977, the external supervision of penitentiaries; from 1978 until 1981, the direction of SISDE, the new intelligence service for internal security; from 1981, advice on terrorism to the President of the Republic; from 1979, management of the more important anti-terrorism structure.

The political choice regarding distribution of responsibilities in the fight against terrorism seemed to take into consideration the different situation of the two police agencies. The contribution of PS, the most politically controlled agency, was given priority during situations having a serious political meaning and impact, like the inquiry into Moro's kidnapping and murder. The organization of the security system in the face of terrorism increasingly favoured CC's contribution in view of its specialization.

The whole intelligence system was modified in 1977 through a reform mainly aimed to ensuring stable political control over the intelligence services. The reform was a reaction to dangerous extra-institutional activities of SID's members, which were even connected with terrorism (see below). The SID was replaced by two distinct agencies: the SISMI, designated to protect military security, and the SISDE designated to protect internal political security. New rules defining responsibilities, control and coordination patterns were settled for the first time.[19]

The Fight against Terrorism: the Main Events

The First Phase: 1969–75

The reaction of the police faced with mass demonstrations at the end of the 1960s mainly followed typical public order control tactics. Extremist movements were infiltrated by undercover agents and, around 1971–2, the presence of some terrorist projects inside the left-wing extremist movement was detected by the police both in Rome[20] and in Milan.[21] At that time the most dangerous organizations belonged to the right-wing extremists, but the inquiry into the first bomb attack, in December 1969 in Milan, was quite confusing. The attack was initially ascribed to an anarchic group. The responsibility of right-wing extremists, emerged slowly, later. However such responsibility was widely covered following a strategy that will be analysed later.

The first massive police offensive against terrorist organizations took place around 1974–5 thanks to two new bodies created inside the PS and the CC. A new central body was created by the home minister at the top of the PS in 1974. This body was not, in spite of its denomination 'Ispettorato antiterrorismo', exclusively concerned with terrorism. The Ispettorato, from 1976 denominated Servizio di Sicurezza (SdS), was an investigating body collecting and then distributing information from and to regional bodies.[22] It is worth noting that the Ispettorato worked mainly in connection with peripheral bodies and had limited investigative autonomy. The Ispettorato and its peripheral bodies decimated left-wing organizations such as the Gruppi Armati Proletari (GAP) and the Nuclei Armati Proletari (NAP).[23] Its inquiries on right-wing terrorism achieved relevant successes,[24] but did not reach the key units. In the same year the first specialized structure on terrorism was created on the initiative of the CC in order to develop a deeper analysis, with operational aims directed at the Red Brigades. The first Nucleo Dalla Chiesa was territorial – it worked mainly in northern Italy – and temporally circumscribed: after gaining its main objective, the clearing up of the Judge Sossi kidnapping, it was dissolved. Investigation had been mainly concentrated on organizational features of terrorism and special attention was given to identification of contacts between militants.[25] The Nucleo's members, and their experience, were later distributed throughout the national territory.

The Second Phase: from 1975 until the Moro Kidnapping (March 1978)

After the success of 1974–5, police attention to terrorism decreased. The whole security system failed to appreciate the reconstruction of the Red Brigades around militants who had escaped previous arrests as well as the aggregation of new left-wing terrorist groups from the end of 1976. Such a failure can be ascribed to a sort of 'information gap' related to the structural changes introduced in 1977. The whole intelligence system had decreased its activity already before the reform because of a 'waiting situation'. The proliferation of new structures around 1977–8 caused the departure of many personnel and resources, sometimes meaning the loss of precious knowledge and experience, a particularly critical loss because of the then still limited development of the automatic information system. Both intelligence and investigative functions suffered: most personnel and resources of the old secret service, the SID, were transferred to the new service for military security, the SISMI, penalizing the new service for internal security, the SISDE.[26] Important members of the old Ispettorato antiterrorismo, even including its director Questore Santillo and some directors of regional units, were allocated to a number of different positions, and only a few of them were transferred to the new central organization of the police, the UCIGOS. The reform of the intelligence system and the contemporary reorganization of the PS headquarters in 1978 produced partially overlapping structures and activities,[27] while the deputed coordination structure, CESIS, was only slowly developed and organized.

During the inquiry into the Moro kidnapping, which was not anticipated although the Red Brigades had already in 1977 launched an explicit offensive against the Christian Democratic Party, the information the police had about the Red Brigades was not much greater than it had been three years before. The police seemed to know better the 'Autonomia Operaia', considered the most dangerous extremist wing in Rome, but the contacts between it and terrorist organizations were not really discerned. Really massive searches were then made inside the Autonomia Operaia, partly at random, exerting strong pressure as a way to get information. For the first time, a sort of central coordination of police forces was attempted in Italy, but with poor results. Immediately after the Moro kidnapping, a 'technical committee' was created following the example of 'crisis management committees' already existing in other countries. The technical committee was composed of the most relevant police representatives and was put under the direction of the home minister. This committee was in the end 'the seat where all frustrations deriving from failures converged' (Maggioranza, in Senato, 1985: 43) and after 20 days it was definitively abandoned. The inquiry into the Moro kidnapping led to a series of warrants for suspects belonging to the Red Brigades without evidence connected to the kidnapping. The inquiry had even been restrained by the priority accorded to the hostage's safety and the warrants were blocked by the attorney-general while Moro was still alive. The Moro kidnapping showed the inadequacy of police knowledge on terrorism, an inadequacy to which the whole security system reacted after the dramatic conclusion of this event.

The Third Phase: 1979–83

The recovery of efficiency first occurred through the second Nucleo Dalla Chiesa. Such a Nucleo was completely separated from the existing structures, it responded exclusively to the home minister and was mainly composed of CC members.[28] Its potency was the direct connection between analysis, information and operations, the so called 'antiguerrilla technique' (Dalla Chiesa in Senato, 1985, IV: 246–8), a connection supported by the exclusive concentration on terrorism and by a particularly flexible structure. The Nucleo Dalla Chiesa secured the first arrests and provided wide information about the structure and composition of the most important terrorist groups, the Red Brigades and Front Line. Territorial police organizations used such information as starting points for more complex investigations and, separately, all police agencies developed sophisticated analyses of terrorist groups. The CC headquarters composed a series of monographs on different organizations. These monographs concentrated on ideological leaflets written by terrorists and they were intended to help understand terrorists' modus operandi. The CC elaborated statistics on terrorist attacks in order to connect times, geographical distribution, targets and political events. The UCIGOS collected information from regional units in order to evaluate terrorists' ideological position. Particular efforts were directed to compare different terrorist groups, their structural organization, their ideology, their programme, and to identify relations with external extremist movements. Such analysis was even aimed at evaluating possibilities of further growth of terrorism. Terrorist attacks were correlated with economic and political events.[29] Information about critical geographical areas was used to improve the control of territory.[30] As a consequence gunfights between police and terrorists became quite frequent. The protection of human targets remained critical, in spite of the new development of specific training,[31] because of the huge number of potential targets, the scarcity of personnel, the high costs and the still existing coordination difficulties between the different units involved.[32] The increase in the number of murders of critical targets such as judges, in spite of a generally better organization against terrorism, can be ascribed to such difficulties. Some attacks on human targets were foiled thanks to documents found in terrorists' hideouts. Special operative secret commandos, created around 1978–9 inside both the CC and the PS, were frequently employed to deal with terrorist emergencies and they had quite relevant success, as with General Dozier's liberation. Such success can certainly be ascribed to the increase in information about the internal structure of terrorist organizations.

The flow of information increased at the end of the 1970s, partly thanks to the secret services' better functioning.[33] A new policy regarding prisoners aimed at stopping proselytizing[34] and at collecting information[35] and, especially, the collaboration of several terrorists rejecting their past militancy, were particularly relevant. The support coming from the development of the automatic information structure, greatly strengthened in 1979 and 1981, and the integration of the PS and CC electronic centres was also decisive. At the end of 1978, 21 warrants concerning the Moro kidnapping were issued and eight of the suspects were captured. By the end of 1979, nine suspects were still at large, while some members of the

Red Brigades' top echelon had been captured. Information given by Patrizio Peci in February 1980 led to the imprisonment of 85 members of the Red Brigades and indirectly to the imprisonment of about 100 members of Front Line. The political crisis of terrorism caused other defections and, for instance, Antonio Savasta's information caused the capture of 290 members of the Red Brigades in 1982. In June 1980, the police had identified 858 left-wing terrorists (Senato, 1985, III: 257); at the beginning of 1986 the number was 2173 (*Report Home Minister*, 13 February 1986).

Some Hypotheses on the Significant Variables

Some variables influencing police intervention against terrorism have already been mentioned in previous sections. We presumed the relevance of variables connected with terrorism, the political system and the security system. We can now try to detect some relationships emerging between them.

The first anti-terrorism phase (1969–75) was concluded by successful police operations, especially in relation to left-wing organizations, in spite of a still limited development of specialized police methodologies. The inadequacy of specialization against terrorism affected mainly the PS. This put into evidence the effects of the scarce attention of political actors to terrorism. The CC who gained a major autonomy were able to develop an ad hoc unit. Another example of such influence was the government's decision to publicize immediately the success gained against the Red Brigades by the first Nucleo Dalla Chiesa in 1975. Such a decision blocked further inquiries and was taken against the wishes of General Dalla Chiesa, who wanted to continue until the total defeat of the organization. The development of specialized methodologies and techniques was perhaps influenced by financial circumstances: we have to consider that the budget of the PS and CC during the 1970s was more or less unchanged and even suffered a considerable reduction within the overall state budget.[36] Comparing the different phases of anti-terrorism, we can maybe conclude that police successes in 1974–5 against left-wing terrorism can be mainly ascribed to variables internal to terrorism. The relative 'naivety' of the first terrorist organizations certainly played a part.

The information gap on terrorism around 1976–7 was also influenced by political variables. The procedure adopted to reform the intelligence system testifies to a certain political myopia. During a period of increased terrorist activity the system was completely dismantled, with a forecast of a period of six months' reconstruction while the experts had estimated at least two years. The implementation of this reform indicated the influence of the security system's internal variables that we can define as 'bureaucratic–military variables'. The difficulties affecting the appointment of new directors, the movement of personnel and resources, severely restraining the new services' efficiency, can be ascribed to fierce tussles between the civil administration and the military to maintain or win prerogatives. The most controversial structure was, significantly, the SISDE, an intelligence service for the first time detached from army headquarters and from NATO. The fight was mediated by the government distributing the leading positions among exponents of different organizations but causing relevant operational difficulties.[37]

The effects of political engagement against terrorism during the 'emergency phase' of police action was not unequivocal. Some of the measures introduced by the criminal legislation, especially the most politically controversial, were not really effective. The preventive arrest was quite narrowly utilized. The police felt uncertainty in applying such a controversial measure because of the possibility of misuse. The public prosecutor's veto on preventive arrests was then felt as a humiliation (Dalla Chiesa, in Senato, 1985, IV: 327). The measure enabling the home minister to ask for copies of legal proceedings was applied just three times.

Organizational measures, such as the criminal legislation, were dominated by the logic of special powers and special measures. The creation of new structures was, as even in the past, mainly not followed by more general adjustments concerning relations with the entire organization. Already existing coordination difficulties were sometimes even aggravated. The two Nuclei Dalla Chiesa, the first one exclusively and the second one mainly composed of Carabinieri, for instance, received quite limited support from the PS.[38] The coordination of different inquiries was, until at least the time of the Moro kidnapping, mainly performed by public prosecutors and it was consequently limited by secret proceeding regulations. Also the need to modernize was met by temporary 'special measures', that is, through a series of extraordinary funds assigned progressively from 1978 until 1984.[39] The most significant example of the logic of the special powers was the second Nucleo Dalla Chiesa which contradicted all emerging principles about major transparency and democratic accountability of the police system. The creation of this Nucleo in 1978 was approved by most of the political parties. It indicates the presence of two contemporary aims: the Nucleo's institutions were widely publicized, while its structure and its operations were kept strictly secret. The Nucleo was directed to fill the operational gap in the existing police structures and to cope with terrorist organizations by tactics used by terrorists, first of all surprise and secrecy. But such a structure was even intended, as its publicity indicates, to demonstrate the increasing commitment of the state to the fight against terrorism. It was intended to exemplify a strong state and, like the criminal legislation, it was a response to citizens' emotional need to be reassured by the active response of the state. Such a symbolic function was even intended, as the parliamentary debates show, to demonstrate the trust of the whole political class in the institutional actor most exposed to terrorism: the police (see Pulitanò, 1981). The decision to reject terrorists' demands during the Moro kidnapping was a response even to such a need. Five policemen had been killed during the attack and negotiation with terrorists aimed at saving the hostage could have had a strongly negative impact on the morale of the whole police force (see Cossiga, in Senato, 1985, III: 213). The political response to terrorism has been strongly criticized by Stefano Rodotà (1984) even concerning the post-Moro period; and the subsequent increased efficiency of state agencies has been considered as resulting from a 'natural adaptation' to the external environment much more than from a deliberate anti-terrorism strategy. Such a conclusion is in a sense correct, but it undervalues the impact of the political response's symbolic meaning in reacting to a kind of political violence with such symbolic content as terrorism. This impact is certainly difficult to measure, and we can simply report a comment from one chief of the CC: 'the new measures have helped the personnel who got some guarantees ... it is enough to give a bit of trust to the policeman and to the carabineer. In the past he was blamed because he exaggerated, because he went beyond the permitted limits and he felt frustrated' (Corsini, in Senato, 1985, III: 434).

Perhaps the most significant contribution of the emergency legislation to police operations was the 'pentiti' legislation, that is, the punishment discounts for terrorists collaborating with inquiries, progressively increased. Such a rule was particularly effective because of a kind of connection activated since 1979 between terrorism's political and military isolation causing many defections inside terrorist organizations. The decrease in collective movements' activism undermined the meaning and purpose of terrorist propaganda, causing defections and even internal conflict. Such a development facilitated police repression which pushed terrorist organizations to strengthen protective barriers and increase their isolation (Della Porta and Rossi, 1984). This sequence of events mainly explained the defeat of left-wing terrorism; it does not really apply to right-wing terrorism whose connections with police intervention are much more difficult to detect.

The history of right-wing terrorism is still not fully grasped and the perpetrators of some serious attacks remain even today unidentified. Decisive obstacles, aimed at 'deviating' the repression of terrorism, interfered with police investigations and with criminal trials. Responsibilities must be primarily ascribed to members of security institutions, especially of the secret service, but even of the police agencies, which in different ways manipulated right-wing terrorism in order to influence the political system. The origin of such a kind of 'invisible power' can be ascribed to a quite widespread custom inside the Italian political system: the massive development of fragmented linkages between political lobbies and military and bureaucratic circles (see Senato, 1986: 125). This system opened wide possibilities to achieve political and personal targets, acting outside institutional channels and without any institutional control. The intelligence system was the principal centre where, from the 1950s onwards, many intrigues evolved. Its natural secrecy was enhanced by very vague rules defining tasks and responsibilities, while the close linkage with the CC, from which SIFAR got almost 90 per cent of its members, represented a powerful vehicle for interfering with internal policy. Such resources were combined with precise ideological and political motivations: the strong opposition to communism, shared by the whole security system leadership, was here reinforced by international contacts. Plots coincided from the 1950s with the crisis affecting centre–right government stability, with the inclusion of the Socialist Party in the government during the 1960s, and increased at the end of the 1960s in the face of the expansion of the student protest and of PCI electoral growth. The close contacts already existing between some SID members and neo-fascist extremists, often working as confidants for the service, represented a further resource for the 'invisible power'. This entity coalesced during the 1970s around the masonic lodge P2, which enrolled 195 officials and even members of the home minister and of the judiciary. The 'strategy of tension' combined terrorism and attempt of coup d'etat probably aiming, considering its protagonists' heterogeneity, at different targets. It was maybe partly conceived as a means to install a military government and partly as a way to aggregate the conservative electorate in order to block new political experiments.

Terrorism was a quite suitable instrument. It provoked emotional reactions affecting political values on which public opinion could be aggregated. Terrorism offered in addition the possibility of criminalizing those constitutional parties and movements ideologically contiguous to terrorist organizations. These political functionalities of terrorism were widely exploited by some members of security institutions protecting right-wing terrorists in many ways. Information was the main instrument adopted: information about terrorists' plans were kept secret or sometimes they were only communicated later, false information was transmitted and some inquiries into right-wing terrorist attacks were intentionally manipulated in order to charge left-wing extremist groups. Relevant proofs were hidden, suspected right-wing extremists were widely assisted, while investigators and judges were sometimes censured even at a personal level.

The vast literature describing such events, such as the book of Franco Ferraresi (1995), is based on many preliminary proceedings. Many right-wing terrorists, members of the secret service and of police agencies and even some politicians involved in serious intrigues were acquitted, however, on grounds of insufficient proof, or else they were given only low penalties. Processes were often obstructed by the government's decisions to oppose military secrecy and certainly the invisible power received the support of many representatives of the judiciary.

From 1974 to 1975, the P2 adopted a new strategy directed at controlling the most relevant decision-making and productive centres of the country. Contacts with right-wing terrorists were reduced, while many eminent members of the institutional apparatus were enrolled; among them many members of the army staff headquarters, chiefs of the Guardia di Finanza and the first two directors of SISDE and SISMI. Seven of the nine members of CESIS were members of the P2 in 1978. Such data suggested some hypotheses about manipulations of left-wing terrorist repression during the second half of the 1970s. Police failures during the inquiry into the Moro kidnapping raised many doubts. Such an inefficiency was even suspected to be just a cover for the aim to block the investigation (Rodotà, in Senato, 1985, I: 175). Giorgio Galli (1986) wrote a detailed history of Italian terrorism, identifying tactical distributions of police capabilities between success and failures responding to a precise political aim: the presence of

left-wing terrorism should have facilitated the 'subordinate' integration of PCI into the government, granted the continuity of
DC's dominance. Evidence of interference with left-wing terrorist
repression is, however, quite scarce and, even if some episodes are
really questionable, a planned and continuous strategy is quite
difficult to detect. In a more realistic vision, security systems'
deficiencies and terrorist manipulation should be considered as
contextual rather than contradictory. We may consider that the
success of the frequent interference in police inquiries concerning
right-wing terrorism was probably assisted by the security system's weakness as regards specialization and coordination. On the
other hand, such interference certainly aggravated the security
system's difficulties: it led, for instance, to the reforming of the
intelligence service whose negative impact has been already considered. The possibility that the dissolution of the Ispettorato
antiterrorismo could have been caused by its investigation into the
P2 would then represent a further serious negative influence. A
deep analysis of relations between official and the 'invisible' power
should be developed in order to verify this, and many other,
incidents. Such an analysis would require detailed investigations
aimed at detecting coincidence of objectives and personal contacts
as a basis for proving real connivance.

Notes

1   In the face of electoral challenges coming, until 1974, mainly from
     the right and later from the left.

2   The PCI had adopted in 1973 the 'historical compromise' pro-
     gramme in order to challenge the then rising political influence of
     the right, the crisis of centre–left governments and the consequent
     possible re-emergence of centre–right governments. Great effort
     was then dedicated to fighting the new fascist extremists within
     which the PCI even included the 'so-called' left-wing terrorist groups,
     considered as part of a general authoritarian project.

3   In 1974–5, police powers regarding interrogations, searches and
     arrests were increased. Police interventions were protected, broad-
     ening police officers' right to use weapons and punishing several
     more crimes against them. Some preventive measures, already ex-
     isting for mafia crimes, were extended to preparing acts aimed at
     overthrowing the order of the state. Some trial constraints were
     introduced at the same time regarding specific crimes such as rob-

beries, kidnapping, use of weapons and crimes connected to the reconstitution of the neo-fascist party.

4 Some measures were adopted to protect the first trials of terrorists and a new law concerning sequestration of possible terrorist headquarters, later revealed as extremely effective, was introduced.

5 For the first time, terrorist purposes were considered as aggravating crimes such as kidnapping (D.L. 21 March 1978, no. 59). New crimes were defined, such as attacks for terrorist purposes and terrorist association, both included in 'crimes against state personality' (D.L. 15 December 1979, no. 625). Leniency for terrorists collaborating with inquiries was progressively amplified from 1978 to 1982 (D.L. 21 March 1978; D.L. 15 December 1979, no. 625; L. 29 May 1982, no. 304).

6 Such crimes, about 60 in number, were listed in the D.L. 21 March 1978, no. 59. Most of them presumed the presence of an organization.

7 The judge could refuse to give such information, but he had to explain his motivations.

8 Such information could be collected only in very urgent situations and could only be used as a way to carry on police inquiries. They could have no value in the legal proceeding.

9 The following new authorizations were introduced: indeterminate adjournment; verbal permission given by public prosecutors which was sufficient in particularly urgent situations; the operations could be conducted at the criminal police headquarters; the police were allowed to intercept telephone conversations on grounds of suspicion alone in order to continue inquiries but without resultant evidence being admissible in legal proceedings. Such authority was connected with permission given by the public prosecutor following requests coming from the home minister or, on his delegation, from other police officials.

10 This permission was limited to 24 hours and later it had to be controlled by the public prosecutor.

11 The hypothesis here considered was the urgent necessity to verify behaviour and actions possibly directed to committing one or more of the serious crimes listed in the D.L. 21 March 1978, no. 59.

12 The detainee could now be retained for 48 hours and the arrest could be communicated to the public prosecutor within the same period and not, as before, immediately.

13   Such searches were previously allowed only in the case of escapes
      or during the commission of a crime. Now, they were allowed even
      when the police supposed the presence of a person suspected or
      guilty of crimes connected with terrorism or the existence of evi-
      dence to be protected.

14   The D.L. 21 March 1978, no. 59 was approved by almost 90 per
      cent of Parliament and the D.L. 15 December 1979, no. 625 by 85
      per cent.

15   The PCI's great commitment in the fight against terrorism at the
      end of the 1970s was directed to cutting off social complicity with
      terrorists, and PCI leaders exhorted their popular base to collabo-
      rate actively with the police. The assent to the 'emergency
      legislation', to which their close relationship with the police inter-
      nal union movement certainly contributed, was not painless. Some
      goals were postponed and some dissension was given up for a
      superior common interest.

16   The emergency legislation certainly countered the trend enhancing
      civil rights which had inspired the reform of the code of criminal
      procedure whose proposal had been adopted in 1974 (L. 3 April
      1974, no. 108).

17   The CC is a military corps belonging to the army and shares the
      army's hierarchic and disciplinary system. The CC has a double
      ministerial dependency: organizational matters are managed by the
      defence minister, while security functions and public order assign-
      ments are supervised by the home minister.

18   During the 1970s, internal contrasts appeared only at the upper
      level, mainly between the CC headquarters and the chiefs ap-
      pointed externally. Chiefs of the CC came usually from the army.

19   The prime minister was appointed to direct the intelligence services
      with the advice of an executive committee (CESIS) designated to
      coordinate services and police agencies. Two patterns of parlia-
      mentary control, a stable one and a periodic one, were then
      introduced.

20   In September 1971, police headquarters in Rome produced a re-
      port on Potere Operaio describing its subversive programme, but
      the suspects were not prosecuted by the local judiciary.

21   In July 1972, the chief of police in Milan, Questore Bonanno,
      presented to the home minister a report describing, even if quite
      vaguely, the structure and methods of the Red Brigades.

22   The Ispettorato replaced a previous body restricted to dealing with information, the 'Divisione affari riservati'. The Ispettorato was conceived as a coordinating element for the provincial investigating departments, the 'Uffici politici', and later 13 regional bodies were created.

23   From 1974 until 1977, the Ispettorato processed files containing quite detailed information on about 200 left-wing terrorists.

24   At the end of 1977, the Ispettorato had processed 1800 files on right-wing terrorists.

25   The Nucleo Dalla Chiesa began its work by identifying 20 suspects belonging to the Red Brigades.

26   The SISDE was created on 30 January 1978, having just about 50 members coming from the central organization of the Ispettorato antiterrorismo and, on March 1978, about 20 people coming from the old SID. SISDE began to recruit its own personnel only from December 1979. SID's archives were transferred to SISMI and Ispettorato's archives were transferred to UCIGOS: SISDE could only ask for copies. General Grassini, the first Chief of SISDE, declared: 'SISDE should have begun to operate on June 22, 1978, but at that date it had not the structure and not the activity of an intelligence service' (Grassini, in Senato, 1985, IV: 194–241).

27   Because of SISDE's organizational problems, SISMI worked for a while on internal security. The UCIGOS, created at the same time by a government decree, got very broad competence, to retrieve information, without getting the usual resources of secret services. The result was the presence of overlapping structures, not one of them completely efficient.

28   It was composed of 180 members of the CC and 50 members of the PS.

29   The analysis considered terrorists' reaction to events such as worker conflict, changes in government and political scandals.

30   New training courses and methodologies directed at improving shooting and street barricade techniques were introduced at PS schools in Alessandria and Nettuno.

31   An ad hoc unit was created by the CC with a special 15 days' training in Sardinia, while the PS organized a special service trained by American and English instructors.

32   Difficulties emerged, for instance, because the armoured cars were controlled by the Justice Department.

33   In 1980, the SISDE, with 60 per cent of its staff, investigated right-
      wing terrorism and the Red Brigades. The SISMI worked on
      relationships between the Autonomia Operaia and the Red Bri-
      gades and on those between Italian and foreign terrorists, but
      without getting significant results. Major incentives came from the
      coordination unit of the secret services (CESIS) which at the end of
      the 1970s came fully into operation.

34   From 1978, all leaders of terrorist groups were gathered in a
      special security prison and kept separate from other prisoners.

35   In June 1978, a special unit of 8 CC, was created to control contacts
      of prisoners with the outside, especially by checking their mail.

36   In 1972, the two budgets represented 4 per cent of the entire state
      budget. In 1980, this had fallen to 1.4 per cent.

37   A soldier, General Grassini of the CC, was appointed as chief of
      SISDE even though the position had been intended at the time of
      the political debate for the civil administration. The combination
      of the organizational dependence on the home minister with the
      operational dependence on the military caused resistance from both
      sides affecting personnel transfer. CESIS' direction was assigned to
      a prefect, whose disagreements with the two military chiefs of
      SISMI and SISDE caused the breakdown of the coordinating struc-
      ture during the inquiry into the Moro kidnapping.

38   General Dalla Chiesa complained explicitly about the lack of sup-
      port for the second Nucleo: 'The CC headquarters alone distributed
      the official decree calling for the total collaboration of the periph-
      ery ... therefore [the PS peripheral units] always considered men
      belonging to the Nucleo as an irritating interference from the ex-
      ecutive' (Dalla Chiesa, in Senato 1985, IV: 248).

39   In all, 225 billion were assigned to computers and telecommunica-
      tions, 202 billion to transport, 201.5 billion to infrastructure, 100
      billion to individual equipment and 15 billion to both the scientific
      and traffic police.

References

Bonanate, Luigi, ed. 1979. *Dimensioni del terrorismo politico*. Milan:
    Angeli.
Dalia, Antonio. 1982. *Notizie segrete e banca dati*. Milan: Giuffrè.
Della Porta, Donatella and Maurizio Rossi. 1984. *Cifre crudeli. Bilancio
    dei terrorismi italiani*. Bologna: Istituto Cattaneo.

Ferraresi, Franco. 1995. *Minacce alla democrazia. La destra radicale e la strategia della tensione nell'Italia del dopoguerra.* Milan: Feltrinelli.

Galli, Giorgio. 1986. *Storia del partito armato.* Milan: Rizzoli.

Galli, Guido, Bruno Siclari and Francesco Siena. 1977. *Le recenti leggi contro la criminalità.* Milan: Giuffrè.

Pasquino, Gianfranco. 1985. 'Il partito comunista nel sistema politico italiano'. In *Il sistema politico italiano*, edited by G. Pasquino. Bari: Laterza.

Pasquino, Gianfranco. 1990. 'I soliti ignoti: gli opposti estremismi nelle analisi dei Presidenti del Consiglio (1969–1985)'. In *La politica della violenza*, edited by R. Catanzaro. Bologna: Il Mulino.

Pulitanò, Domenico. 1981. 'Misure antiterrorismo: un primo bilancio'. *Democrazia e diritto* 21: 1–2.

Report Bartolomei, L. 8 August 1977 no. 534. Modificazioni del codice di procedura penale.

Report of the Home Minister to the Parliament. 1986. IX Legislatura, Doc. LVII, no. 2.

Rodotà, Stefano. 1984. 'La risposta dello stato al terrorismo: gli apparati'. In *La prova delle armi*, edited by G. Pasquino. Bologna: Il Mulino.

Rognoni, Virginio, 1989. *Intervista sul terrorismo.* Bari: Laterza.

Senato della Repubblica, Camera dei Deputati, VIII Legislatura. 1985. *Commissione Parlamentare d'inchiesta sulla strage di via Fani, sul sequestro e l'assassinio di Aldo Moro e sul terrorismo in Italia.* DOC. XXIII no. 5, vol. I: Relazione di maggioranza; vol. II: Relazioni di minoranza; vols III–XIII: Allegati alla relazione.

Senato della Repubblica, Camera dei Deputati, IX Legislatura. 1986. *Prerelazione Anselmi alla Commissione Parlamentare d'inchiesta sulla loggia massonica P2.* DOC. XXII, vol. XV.

Ventura, Angelo. 1984. 'La responsabilità degli intellettuali e le radici culturali del terrorismo di sinistra'. In *Università cultura e terrorismo*, edited by C. Ceolin. Milan: Angeli.

The Author

Luciana Stortoni-Wortmann, formerly Research Fellow in Political and Social Sciences at the European University Institute in Florence, Italy, is now an independent consultant based in Germany.

Part II
Intergovernmental Cooperation

6 The Third Pillar on Judicial and Home Affairs Cooperation, Anti-terrorist Collaboration and Liberal Democratic Acceptability

PETER CHALK

Introduction

The European Union's (EU) third pillar of judicial and home affairs cooperation for the first time specifically makes internal security affairs a matter for intergovernmental cooperation between the EU member states. Its aim is to allow the 15 members to deal with major threats to their internal security (such as drug trafficking, major organized crime and terrorism) with the same means and instruments on a single, Union-wide basis. These have been legitimately included within the ambit of the EU by virtue of its role as a liberal democratic institution and its concomitant 'duty of ensuring that [liberal] democratic values are fully respected ... and [obligation] to combat all subversive movements and tendencies liable to present a threat to democracy, democratic values and the fundamental rights of the individual' (De Piccoli, 1993).

Article C of the 1992 Maastricht Treaty on European Union (TEU), the original founding document upon which the third pillar rests, affirms the intention to achieve its objectives while respecting and building upon the *acquis communautaire*. This describes the instruments and agreements which all members are required and expected to accept, covering both legally binding conventions and intergovernmental agreements (*Statewatch*, 1993, 3/4). It has developed on the basis of constitutional customs and traditions common to all member states, philosophically defined as liberal democratic polities which is, itself, a fundamental requirement of Union membership. This commitment is backed up by Art. F, paras 1 and 2, which state:

> 1. The Union is founded on the principles of liberty, democracy, respect for human rights and fundamental freedoms, and the rule of law, principles which are common to the Member States.
> 2. The Union shall respect fundamental rights, as guaranteed by the European Convention for the Protection of Human Rights and Fundamental Freedoms signed in Rome on 4 November 1950 and as they result from the constitutional traditions common to the Member States, as general principles of Community law. (*The European*, 1992; European Union, 1997; *Statewatch*; see also De Piccoli, 1993: 12)

One of the most basic features of any liberal political entity is the need to constrain power within acceptable bounds. Given the fact that anti-terrorist cooperation has now been made a legitimate matter for intergovernmental cooperation, and given the fact that the member states of the EU are required both singly and collectively to uphold liberal assumptions of constitutional authority, it is vital that any response initiated conforms to, and is constrained by, the overall guiding principles of action as developed here: namely, limitation, credibility and accountability (Chalk, 1995: 10–45; 1996). It is these features which both (should) characterize the liberal democratic response to terrorism and, more importantly, ensure the type of public support and consent that is required for democratic legitimacy.

The theme of this chapter is to assess how effective the third pillar's provisions are with respect to the fight against terrorism when they are measured against the criteria of limitation, credibility and accountability. It is argued that, unless critical considerations of democratic control are incorporated within the third pillar, its various stipulations will almost certainly fail to gain the type of public support and consent that is so necessary for effective anti-terrorist policing in open, liberal democratic societies.

The EU Third Pillar of Judicial and Home Affairs Cooperation

Like Schengen before it, impetus for the third pillar of judicial and home affairs cooperation initially derived from the realization that any moves made to relax internal frontiers needed to be balanced by providing for an enhanced level of Community-wide cross-border law enforcement and judicial cooperation. The collapse of the USSR and the ensuing instability that has been caused as a result of the dramatic transformation of the East European geopolitical landscape, however, radically increased the importance of achieving such a state of affairs.

Maastricht provided the opportunity that the (then) 12 members needed to renegotiate an internal security deal that would, unlike Schengen, be able to incorporate all member states within its overall framework. The agreements signed at Maastricht – many of which have been further developed since 1992 – form the basis of what has now become an integral part of EU integration: judicial and home affairs cooperation.[1] Specifically, the internal security provisions of the third pillar[2] cover, on an intergovernmental basis (although the 'passarelle' provision of the Treaty does allow for the transfer of any subject to 'Community Title' should the 15 members deem it desirable at a later date), the following areas of common interest:

- Asylum policy.
- Rules governing the crossing of EU external borders.
- Immigration policy and policy with regard to nationals of third countries, including:

  (a) conditions of entry and movement by nationals of third countries on EU territory;
  (b) conditions of residence by nationals of third countries on EU territory, including family reunion and access to employment;
  (c) combating unauthorized immigration, residence and work by nationals of third countries on EU territory.

- Combating fraud.
- Combating drug addiction.
- Judicial cooperation in civil and criminal matters.
- Customs cooperation.
- Police cooperation to combat terrorism (which for the purposes of the TEU is defined as 'the use and attempt to use violence by a structured group to obtain political objectives': *Statewatch*, 1993, 3/1),[3] drug trafficking and other international organized crime (defined as 'an uninterrupted series of criminal activities committed by a group of individuals with the intention of obtaining benefits, influence or power': *Statewatch*, 1993, 3/1).[4]
- The organization of a union-wide system for exchanging information within a European Police Office (Europol). (European Communities, 1992a; 1992b; *The European*, 1992: 18–19.)

The first step in establishing Europol was taken in June 1993 when the Europol Drugs Unit (EDU) was created, the headquarters of which were opened in the Hague in February 1994. Europol formally came into existence in June 1996, following the UK's ratification of a governing Convention (Britain being the last state to do so).

Following the 1997 Treaty of Amsterdam, it was resolved that Europol should aim to commence operations within the next five years. Until then, the EDU will operate as the main coordinating body for criminal intelligence between EU police forces. In December 1994, the ambit of the unit was extended from an exclusive focus on drug trafficking to a number of other areas, including crime involving nuclear substances, illegal immigration networks, vehicle trafficking and associated money-laundering operations. A further responsibility was added in July 1996: the sex trade, especially with regard to the sexual exploitation of children (*New York Times*, 1994; *Statewatch*, 1994, 4/6; 1995, 4/3; 1996, 5/6; 6/2; *Keesing's Record of World Events*, 1996: 41285–6; 41157; 41207: European Union, 1997).

Overseeing the above areas of common interest is an executive coordinating committee of senior officials (known informally as the 'K4 Committee', after Art. K4 of the Maastricht Treaty which first established the Committee). This structure represents the real power within the third pillar.[5] The Committee has three steering groups, each with a number of working parties:

- Immigration and Asylum: working parties on asylum, immigration, visas, control of external frontiers and clearing houses on asylum and immigration (CIREA – the Centre for Information, Discussion and Exchange on Asylum – and CIREFI – the Centre for Information, Discussion and Exchange on the Crossing of Borders and Immigration).
- Security, Law Enforcement, Police and Customs: working parties on counterterrorism, public order, combating serious crime, Europol, customs and drugs.
- Judicial Cooperation: also working parties on civil and criminal matters. The Committee will also have responsibility for the setting up of two planned EU-wide computer systems, the European Information System (EIS) and the Customs Information System (CIS) (*Statewatch*, 1993, 3/4).

In addition to a strict coordinating role, the K4 Committee also has a fair degree of latitude with respect to initiating and implementing executive decisions. Under the terms of the 1997 Amsterdam Treaty, for example, the Committee is empowered to:

- give opinions for the attention of the Council of Justice and Interior Ministers, either at the Council's request or on its own initiative;
- contribute to the preparation of the Council of Justice and Interior Ministers' discussions and decisions in any area dealing with police and judicial cooperation in the third pillar (European Union, 1997).

Membership of the K4 Committee is made up with one official from each EU state plus one from the Commission. In practice, however, it essentially mirrors the representative make-up of the Group of Coordinators which wrote the initial report recommending its creation. The Committee was formally established when Germany completed the ratification process of the TEU in October 1993 (*Statewatch*, 1993, 3/4; European Union, 1997).

Central to the process of harmonizing the rules governing the crossing of the EU external borders is the implementation of the External Borders Convention, signed by the (then) 12 members in June 1991. Its main provisions include the following:

- sanctions for the crossing of external borders other than at authorized times and places;
- 'Effective surveillance' of all external frontiers by member states;
- rigorous controls (by visa and other 'requirements') on the entry of third country nationals;
- carrier sanctions for airlines and other passenger carriers who fail to ensure that third country nationals have the required travel documents/visas;
- a common list of countries whose nationals require a visa to enter the EU;
- the establishment of a joint computerized list, contained within a European Information System (EIS – a EU-wide computer system covering immigration, asylum, security and policing),[6] of 'inadmissible' third country nationals who are to be refused entry to the Union;
- limited 'visiting rights' of reunification with respect to family members of third country nationals already living within the Community.

Implementation of the External Borders Convention is currently being held up by a dispute between the UK and Spain over the status of Gibraltar,[7] although the 1997 Treaty of Amsterdam does impose a deadline of 2002 for the introduction of a fully harmonized immigration policy (European Union, 1997; *The Australian*, 1996; *Statewatch*, 1992, 2/4; 1996, 6/3).

Given the urgency of the matter, visa policy was made an immediate area of Community (not intergovernmental) responsibility in 1992 (Art. 100c of the TEU). Decisions as to which third countries will require a visa to enter the EU are taken by the Council of Ministers (acting on proposals made by the Commission and after consulting the Parliament) on the basis of unanimity. In an emergency, however, it may act by qualified majority vote (QMV) which, since the end of 1996, has become the rule (*The Independent on Sunday*, 1992).[8]

To facilitate customs cooperation, the third pillar provides for the establishment of a CIS. Based on the existing encrypted message system, SCENT (Systems Customs Enforcement Network), it will link Community customs officials through 300 terminals allowing them to exchange information and intelligence on drugs, fraud and current smuggling techniques.[9]

The third pillar also includes provisions on asylum policy, police cooperation and extradition. Although it proved impossible to agree on a common asylum policy at Maastricht, the (then) 12 members did, nevertheless, stipulate it as a priority issue, committing themselves to the harmonization of certain aspects of their asylum policies by the end of 1993. Following the 1997 Treaty of Amsterdam, the EU member states resolved to have a fully harmonized asylum policy in place by 2002 (European Union, 1997; *Statewatch*, 1996, 6/3; *The Australian*, 1997; Lodge, 1992: 14). Central to this objective is the implementation of the Dublin Convention, signed by the EU member states in June 1990. It applies the 'first safe country' principle whereby asylum seekers have to make their application for political asylum in their first 'safe' country of origin. This ensures that applications are, in theory, processed by only one of the 15 members so as to prevent the phenomenon commonly referred to as 'asylum shopping'.

In effect, the Dublin Convention means that asylum seekers do not have a second chance to apply for political asylum in another EU state once they have been refused entry by their first country of application, whose decision is thus binding on all other member states.[10] The Convention cannot, however, come into force until it has been ratified by all 15 members of the EU states. At the time of writing, this had yet to be achieved.

With respect to police cooperation, the member states have also confirmed their endorsement of the general principles governing such collaboration by agreeing to consider the adoption of practical measures on information exchange and experience (European Union, 1997: 373). Under the terms of the 1997 Treaty of Amsterdam these are taken to include the following.

• Operational cooperation between the competent authorities of the member states in relation to the prevention, detection and investigation of criminal offences.
• The collection, storage, processing, analysis and exchange of relevant information, including data held by law enforcement agencies of reports on suspicious financial transactions.
• Cooperation and joint initiatives in forensic research, the use of equipment, the exchange of liaison officers and secondments.
• The common evaluation of particular investigative techniques with regard to the detection of serious forms of organized crime (European Union, 1997).

Finally, to further strengthen judicial cooperation in criminal matters within the third pillar, an EU Extradition Convention was adopted in September 1996. The main objective of this accord is to supplement and improve the functioning of both the 1957 European Convention on Extradition and the 1977 European Convention on the Suppression of Terrorism (ECST). The major aspects of the 1996 Convention include the following.

• A lower threshold for extraditable offences. Once the Convention has been fully ratified, any person committing an offence punishable by a prison sentence of 12 months in the requesting state and six months in the requested state can be extradited.
• A specification of those offences for which extradition may not be refused, including those:

(a) classified as a conspiracy or an association to commit offences under the law of the requesting state (even if the law of the requested state does not provide for the same classification);
(b) classified as a conspiracy or an association to commit terrorist acts;
(c) classified as conspiracy or an association to commit offences

in certain other sensitive fields such as drug trafficking and other forms of organized crime and/or acts of violence.

- Provision that, if extradition is refused by a requested state for any of the above offences, the state in question must provide in its own national legislation means by which to punish and prosecute such offences (the principle of 'extradite or try').
- An easier means by which to extradite those charged with offences regarded as political. As a general principle, the Convention affirms that no offence may be regarded by the requested state as a political offence. Although member states may make reservations to this general principle, they may not do so in the case of any terrorist offence or conspiracy to commit such an offence.
- Provision that extradition may not be refused on the grounds that the person claimed is a national of the requested state. Those member states whose Constitutions prohibit the extradition of one of their nationals have the right to reserve extradition in this area for five years following the enactment of the Convention. On the expiry of this period, such reservations may be renewed (again for a period of five years), amended so as to ease the conditions of extradition or terminated.
- An easier means by which to extradite those charged with fiscal and amnesty offences.
- Inclusion of facilitative provisions to cover lapse of time (that is, when a person would be statute-barred according to the law of the requested state), re-extradition to another state, transit and exchange of information (see *Official Journal of the European Communities*, 23 November 1996, no. C313/11).

The Convention will come into force 90 days after it has been fully ratified by all 15 EU states. The Treaty of Amsterdam affirms that common action on extradition is now to be an integral part of the third pillar's activities (European Union, 1997).

The Maastricht Third Pillar and its Positive Contribution to the Fight against Terrorism

Whilst a valid assessment of the operational effectiveness of the third pillar with respect to the fight against terrorism can only be made once its performance becomes more apparent over time, it is possible to identify a number of ways in which it could have a positive impact on the fight against terrorism.

First, the third pillar incorporates all the member states into one, Union-wide system, vital for a fully integrated approach to terrorism. Unlike Schengen, which significantly does not include either Ireland or the UK in its membership,[11] the third pillar does not start out with the a priori abolishing of all internal frontier controls as the necessary prerequisite for enhancing internal security cooperation. It merely reaffirms the objective of facilitating the free movement of people by providing for enhanced cooperation in the areas of justice and home affairs (*The Independent on Sunday*, 1992). This, in effect, means that one can still be party to the EU's internal security provisions even if one is not prepared to fully abolish one's own border controls – something that Schengen did not allow.

As an option, neither the UK nor Ireland ever seriously considered involvement with the Schengen arrangements. Both are island states whose internal frontiers, it is argued, give them a unique advantage in controlling the inflow of terrorists, criminals, illegal immigrants and drug traffickers. As the then Home Secretary David Waddington stated in 1990: 'it would be absurd to throw away the natural advantages we have from being an island ... common sense dictates we should use our geographical advantage and keep our [internal] controls' (David Waddington, cited in House of Commons, 1990: 157).

Moreover, in the absence of any land contact with other EU states (except that which exists between the Republic of Ireland and Northern Ireland, which is anyway designated as a 'passport-free' common travel area),[12] neither the UK nor Ireland has been required to develop a concerted system of 'in-depth' defence, such as the mandatory carrying of identity cards. Furthermore they have not been involved in the type of concerted cross-land police cooperation that routinely takes place on the continent. In short, they have not 'enjoyed' the type of law enforcement background that would make the abolition of internal frontiers considerably easier to contemplate.

Finally, both countries interpret the EU's commitment to the 'free movement of people' as something that applies only to EU nationals. Consequently, each state wants to retain the right to check all third country nationals, irrespective of where they arrive from (Schengen allows free movement of people to all who are in Schengen territory, whether they are EU nationals or not: see, for instance, *The Economist*, 1990; *Statewatch*, 1992, 2/1).[13]

The failure of Schengen to consolidate all EU member states into its framework effectively created two categories of EU state: those who were incorporated within the Convention and those who were not. This flies in the face of EU integration and is completely incompatible with the notion of an integrated and unified system of Union-wide law enforcement cooperation.[14]

Second, the Maastricht third pillar provisions establish the beginnings of a truly effective EU crisis management structure that brings together disparate police, customs and judicial authorities under one clearly defined, legally based, authority framework. Such an arrangement will have a greater capacity to set priorities and determine the command, control and jurisdictional parameters of effective organization. This should lead to the emergence of a more coordinated, integrated and rationalized Union-wide strategy between police, immigration, customs, narcotics and anti-terrorist officials.

The current terrorist phenomenon is closely linked to issues of illegal immigration, narcotics and smuggling. By bringing these separate areas together under one overarching forum, the K4 Committee, it will be far easier to achieve the level of inter-service coordination that is necessary for any effective counterterrorist strategy. Schengen was the first attempt that the EU states had made to achieve this state of affairs. However, as noted above, it failed to embrace all member states within its framework.

Third, the Maastricht third pillar provides European internal security policing with a solid legal basis. By officially recognizing terrorism (together with organized crime and drug trafficking) as a matter of common interest and providing the Council of Interior and Justice Ministers and the K4 Committee with clear areas of responsibility in this field, the 15 members are paving the way for more systematic regulation over an area in which only sporadic progress has so far been achieved.

Fourth, a common visa policy and the commitment to work towards integrated immigration and asylum policies through the External Borders and Dublin Conventions, respectively, will contribute greatly to the strengthening of the EU's outer frontier. This, in turn, will minimize the associated risk of terrorists exploiting lenient border formalities and so gaining unhindered access to some 320 million people and a variety of highly visible and vulnerable targets in a geographical zone that stretches from Dublin to Athens.

Fifth, Europol has the potential to develop into a truly coherent intelligence initiative for serious international crime, its foundational provision envisaging a system of information exchange for the purposes of preventing and combating terrorism, drug trafficking and other forms of serious international organized crime. Such a centralized body is crucial for dealing with transnational criminal activities such as terrorism, where single pieces of information are often meaningless until they are pieced together in a larger picture with the intelligence data from other states.

It needs to be noted that there has been some initial reluctance to include sensitive terrorist intelligence in the overall ambit of Europol, particularly from the UK.[15] Thus far, the mandate of the office has been restricted to the coordinated exchange of information pertaining to drug trafficking, major organized crime and illegal immigration (reaffirmed in 1997), although, presumably, the office will take on the full range of responsibilities at present falling to the EDU. Nevertheless, there are a number of indicators which suggest that terrorism will eventually be included within the overall remit of Europol.

- Counterterrorism, Europol, organized crime and drug trafficking have already been placed within the same K4 Committee steering group, suggesting that a recognition at least exists that they are all, in some way, linked (*Statewatch*, 1994, 4/5).
- The objectives set out in the Europol Convention specifically include provision to incorporate terrorism within the ambit of Europol should the EU member states deem this desirable (*Statewatch*, 1994, 4/5).
- There is speculation that the general remit of terrorism could be included within the ambit of EDU in the not-too-distant future, so long as states are given the right to withhold information on specific forms of political violence (such as Northern Irish terrorism) (*Statewatch*, 1993, 3/3).[16]
- Finally, the 1997 Treaty of Amsterdam reaffirms the objective of preventing major crime – particularly 'terrorism, trafficking in persons and offences against children, illicit drug trafficking and illicit arms trafficking, corruption and fraud' – through closer cooperation between police forces, both directly and within the context of Europol (European Union, 1997).

The EU Third Pillar and Liberal Democratic Acceptability

As is argued above, in a number of significant ways the third pillar provides the EU member states with the means to develop a truly integrated and coherent anti-terrorist policy. However, successful anti-terrorist cooperation cannot be measured purely in terms of operational effectiveness. For a liberal anti-terrorist policy to be truly effective, it has to be regarded as socially legitimate. If this is in fact to occur, it is vital that any strategy initiated is tempered by those overall guiding principles which help to prevent an erosion of the standards and traditions which make a democratically liberal way of life possible in the first place. The following observations, made in respect of the general character of the third pillar, suggest that achieving such a state of affairs could be highly problematic.

Limitation

The first requirement of any liberal response to terrorism is a limited, well defined strategy that does not go beyond what is demanded by the exigencies of the situation and which is directed only against the terrorists themselves. By contrast, it appears that much of the substance of the third pillar is being guided by an underlying ideological rationale that implicitly, and increasingly explicitly, identifies immigrants and foreigners as a major, or at least significant, threat to internal security. No longer preoccupied by the external menace of communism, EU member states have begun to address a 'new enemy within', defined as terrorism, drug trafficking and organized crime – dangers which are seen to emanate from immigrant organizations, refugees and asylum seekers.

This process can be conceptualized as the result of a 'paradigmatic shift', a transformation which has led to a major negative change in the way security services perceive political movements or particular socioethnic groupings. According to one of its most vehement critics, Didier Bigo (1994a; 1994b), it is the consequence of an ideological merging that has occurred within European law enforcement agencies where internal security has progressively been redefined from something that is seen to be totally separate from external security to something that is regarded as closely related to it. The old external threat of communism is replaced by the new external threat of mass immigration – a phenomenon which is, itself, associated with imported organized crime, terrorism and general internal destabilization – often on highly questionable evidence. This shift, Bigo maintains, is reflected by the increasing concern shown by police and intelligence services with organized crime as opposed to the old preoccupation with foreign subversive activities. (For a good account of this process at work in the USA and Central America, see Bertlet, 1992.)

The equating of ethnic groups with crime by West European police and security forces is nothing new. It arises as a result of two interrelated suspicions. The first stems from the notion that those deprived of adequate living standards in their own societies will be attracted to the relative prosperity of Western Europe and, hence, will try to infiltrate these societies illegally by exploiting liberal legal frameworks (Bigo and Leveau, cited in den Boer, 1993: 51). The second flows from the first, in that it obscures the status of those already established within an immigrant community by reinforcing the view that these populations have a 'natural' propensity for crime and are therefore more susceptible to illicit, underground activities than are non-immigrants (den Boer, 1994: 9). Moreover, it is argued that, since illegal immigrants are largely prevented from obtaining welfare services or gaining legal employment, they will be forced into crime in order to establish a living for themselves.[17] Each of these strands reinforces a negative image of immigrants, promoting a perception that they represent a threat to public order while simultaneously justifying an a priori extension of external and internal controls by law enforcement agencies.

The rise of Islamic fundamentalism and ethnic conflict in the post-cold war era, however, has encouraged a gradual extension of this stereotypical association from one which associates immigrants with simple crime to one which now identifies them as a fundamental source of political instability. On the one hand, the increased presence of immigrants and asylum seekers in Western societies is seen to be a cause, if not the major reason, for the rise of neo-Nazi violence currently being experienced within the EU. More importantly, the perception that foreigners themselves constitute a 'potential high risk category' (by being equated with such threats as major organized crime, drugs and terrorism) is increasingly spreading across Europe, to the extent that it is now beginning to form the basis of a new European state (Bunyan, 1991: 19). As Gil Loescher (1992) observes:

> The rise of Islamic fundamentalism, Sikh militancy and other ethnoreligious political movements has not only introduced a new element into Europe's emerging multicultural societies, [it is] also seen to present a major security risk to governments. In recent years, most European states have experienced a rise in terrorist activities and drug trafficking. Governments ... associate these problems with greater numbers of illegal immigrants, and this further complicates the already tense relations between immigrant communities and local police.

The inclusion of the fight against terrorism (and other forms of serious crime) and illegal immigration in one single framework of internal security cooperation has been interpreted by numerous commentators as an internationalization of the national police agenda which routinely identifies 'aliens' as a potential 'high-risk' category (den Boer, 1993; 1994; Bigo, 1994a; Hudson, 1993: 1–27).

When one considers the number of initiatives that have been developed which concentrate purely on immigrants, it is difficult not to reach the same conclusion. Indeed, in addition to the EIS, the EU member states are now pushing to establish yet another data bank on third country nationals, EURASYL, a computerized system to hold information on the fingerprints of asylum seekers. Furthermore, the sole purpose of CIREA and CIREFI – the two working groups in the K4 Immigration and Asylum steering group – has thus far essentially been restricted to the development of means to better identify and apprehend aliens already resident within the EU who are deemed to be in an 'irregular' situation (*Statewatch*, 1993, 3/1; 3/3).

Moreover, an increasingly militaristic attitude now appears to have pervaded EU discourse on the best way to control migratory flows. This is reflected in the strong endorsement that the (then) 12 members' immigration ministers gave to a proposal, made at the second European Conference to Prevent Uncontrolled Migration, held on 15/16 February 1993, which called for the use of mobile surveillance forces to secure external borders. According to the recommendation, these units would perform their tasks at sea borders:

> by using patrol boats or appropriate helicopters without, however, dispensing with the use of operational forces on land, whose mission primarily consists of apprehending illegal migrants reported by the airborne surveillance forces. [The units are to be] integrated into a close network of telephone, radio, telex and other connections [and will] use highly efficient equipment ... which should be harmonised step by step on the basis of an all-European standard. (*Statewatch*, 1993, 3/2)

Given that the EU External Borders Convention calls for the effective surveillance of all external frontiers and a duty of cooperation with respect to surveillance services, it is not difficult to see how this restrictive concept could find its way into the Maastricht third pillar. Using methods such as these is normally something that is reserved for the control and monitoring of foreign hostile states. However, as Bigo points out:

The police [now] assume a major role and replace the army as the central instrument of coercion. The enemy is no longer a foreign state, but the world of crime, drugs [terrorism], the immigrant and ... the asylum seeker. The post-Hobbesian state is therefore quite possibly a new reality, but it is as security conscious as its predecessor. It has a new concept, introduces new provisions and creates new control systems. (Bigo, 1994a: 8)

All of this raises the crucial question of the extent to which the protection of basic human rights within the EU has now become a function of Union nationality. A major concern exists that prejudice and stereotyping will play a significant role in identifying immigrants as the main source of these and other dangers. As a result, many members of certain ethnic groupings could well fall victim to an unwarranted intrusion in, and examination of, their private lives on the arbitrary grounds of being foreign or carrying an uncommon name (den Boer, 1993: 70). Indeed an extremely restrictive proposal for joint action against illegal immigration, initially made by France in early 1995, has already been adopted by the EU member states. This specifically gives security officials the right to carry out systematic checks on 'foreigners': 'either when an offence has been committed; or to ward off threats to the public on specific occasions (especially with respect to frontier zones); or whenever the competent authorities have "questioned a foreign national *for any reason whatsoever*"' (emphasis added) (*Statewatch*, 1995, 5/2).

The issue of non-EU nationals' human rights is particularly problematic given the fact that there is a legal vacuum with respect to the protection of non-EU nationals' human rights in the third pillar. Although the TEU affirms that its provisions shall respect basic rights as protected by the European Convention for the Protection of Human Rights and Fundamental Freedoms, the EU as an organization has as yet not acceded to the Convention (nor has it yet developed a charter of its own). This means that actions taken by any one of its institutions or pillars which violate human rights will not be subject to direct control. Although accession of the EU to the ECHR was raised by the Belgian presidency in 1993, the initiative has yet to receive substantial support from member state governments (*Statewatch*, 1993, 3/6; den Boer, 1993: 70).

This legal vacuum is further compounded by the fact that the third pillar remains in an intergovernmental framework of cooperation. This means that its actions will remain beyond the jurisdictional purview of both national courts and parliaments and official EU institutions such as the European Court of Justice (see the section on accountability below). If domestic remedies for accountability are rendered ineffective without providing for alternatives at the European level, there is a very real danger that human rights will be violated in the process of internationalization. Whilst EU nationals would at least have the protection that is afforded by their own constitutional guarantees and the ECHR, it is not at all clear whether non-EU nationals would have access to any effective forum to which they could appeal against unjust police and judicial actions and decisions (den Boer, 1993: 70).

Credibility

The second requirement of any liberal democratic response to terrorism is credibility. The general populace has to be convinced that the action initiated is both necessary and effective in producing results. Again this is problematic with respect to the third pillar. A widespread fear already exists that many of its provisions will have no discernible effect on serious crime and will have been initiated merely to enhance police and law enforcement powers of surveillance.

A significant reason for this is the secrecy that has surrounded its development. Although interior ministers and police chiefs insist that structures such as the K4 Committee, the CIS, EIS and Europol are absolutely necessary for the overall security of a borderless EU in the 1990s, it is perfectly understandable that the less people know about these bodies, the more suspicious they will become of them. The lines of communication between the general populace and those involved with the third pillar are extremely limited. This is essentially because internal security remains a matter for inter-governmental cooperation only. As a result, neither the European Parliament nor the European Commission is able to provide any meaningful information which can be transmitted, via Members of the European Parliament (MEPs), to individual citizens in a manner that will stimulate critical public debate. The problem is well captured in the following observation made by Lode Van Outrive (1992b: 11), the European Parliament's Committee for Civil Liberties and Internal Affairs *rapporteur* on Europol:

> Disadvantages of intergovernmental decision-making: let us first proceed on the assumption that the Maastricht Treaty is not yet in place. Experience shows that it is very difficult, both for the European Parliament and for the national parliaments – and certainly for interest

groups as well – to find out when decisions are taking place, what is being discussed, what progress has been made etc. It is virtually impossible for matters to be publicly debated in advance. Members of parliament are dependent on the goodwill of national ministers and of the Council for information. Moreover, the legal and political status of documents is never clear: are they public, secret or confidential, and who decides this? Their confidential nature is certainly exaggerated – but it is enough to create ample opportunities for governments to manipulate the national and European political debate ... Public debate is thus rendered impossible.

A lack of public debate not only promotes the idea that member state governments are trying to hide something that will not be particularly popular with their electorate, it also makes it extremely difficult for political leaders to show that their actions are necessary and being initiated for the general good. This is a serious problem when one remembers that, in the final analysis, policing is nothing other than a community service. What law enforcement authorities do must be in response to what people want them to do. Consequently, the more decisions are made behind closed doors, the more one can expect to see a gradual decline in the public's confidence that these are in fact being made for the general good.

This particular problem has already been reflected by the somewhat sinister public image Europol has developed as an all-encompassing trans-European operational police force which is capable of 'seizing people and searching houses at the behest of another country's police, and spiriting them into a foreign cell' (Woodward, 1993: 23). The fact that Europol has no power of arrest at its disposal – its role limited to the collection and dissemination of criminal intelligence – suggests that the EU's interior ministers and police chiefs have not done a particularly effective job in explaining either the purpose, value, necessity or nature of their actions.

The public's confidence in the utility of the third pillar has been further undermined by the fact that the various intelligence initiatives incorporated within the TEU have been planned in the absence of any common data protection law. This means that there is no international legal requirement, at present, to ensure that information stored on systems such as Europol, the CIS and the EIS (all of whose data protection provisions revert to the national level) is correct or even useful in the fight against serious international crime. This is an important shortcoming, for an essential aspect of

any liberal democratic system of law enforcement is the requirement that the individual be protected against the arbitrary actions
committed by the state. It is therefore vital that a liberal citizenry is
convinced that official agents/institutions of coercion/control do
not have the power to intimidate any one of their members except
through the use of well understood and accepted legal procedures.

For this to occur, the use of restrictive measures such as intelligence gathering has to be controlled in its scope and modified by
legally enforced rules of fairness. Consequently, if *international*
exchanges of data are to take place, it is vital that they be accompanied by *international* safeguards. This ensures that they will always
be maintained in a defensive (as opposed to an offensive) role and
limited to proportionate and necessary actions that are excused
only as a legitimate response to the threat posed by serious criminality
(Shaklar, 1989: 21–80).

Both the European Court of Human Rights and the European
Parliament have made it quite clear that the collection of personal
data constitutes a serious interference with the private life of the
individual concerned. Such action can only be justified if it is pre-
scribed by law, and if it is regarded as both necessary and
proportionate for an aim that is regarded as socially legitimate. As
Karel de Gucht (1993: 49), *rapporteur* for the European Parliament's Committee on Civil Liberties and Internal Affairs on Respect
for Human Rights in the European Community, observes:

> The main issue is to what extent the threat to public order justifies
> restricting individual freedoms. There is only a very thin dividing line
> between the maintenance of law and order and its misuse as a basis for
> arbitrary control ... There is an important and tangible link between
> institutions and the population as a whole; the State will be weakened if
> it opts for policy to combat crime and terrorism that does not guaran-
> tee a free society and human rights.

The EIS, CIS and Europol all leave very serious questions concerning data protection unanswered. The information collection,
storage and dissemination provisions for these various intelligence
initiatives are to be contained within their respective conventions
which mirror the relevant stipulations as set out for the Schengen
Information System (SIS) Convention (*Statewatch*, 1995, 5/4). This
essentially bases data protection on two main mechanisms: (a) the
Council of Europe's 1981 Convention on Data Protection, and (b)
the 1987 Committee of Ministers of the Council of Europe Recom-

mendation (87)15, Regulating the Use of Personal Data in the Police Sector (Grange, 1994: 8).

The 1981 Convention attempts to achieve a limited degree of harmonization with respect to data protection procedures by establishing certain principles, which contracting parties are required to implement in their domestic legislation. These include norms relating to the quality of data, the use of 'sensitive' data, data security and personal access to and correction of data. Recommendation (87)15 supplements the 1981 Convention, having particular regard for Article 8 of the ECHR which lays down rules for the protection of individual rights. Accordingly, regulations are set out governing the collection, storage and communication of data, together with data subjects' rights of notification, rectification and erasure (Baldwin-Edwards and Hebeton, 1994: 12–4).

Despite these provisions, however, neither the 1981 Convention nor Recommendation (87)15 provides the sort of adequate international protection that is required for transnational data exchanges. The extent to which the 1981 Convention achieves harmonization of data protection procedures is highly questionable largely because the general character of its norms fails to overcome divergent domestic rules and/or provide legal certainty with respect to the application of the Convention in different national systems. As Vassilaki notes, even where largely corresponding legislation does exist between sending and receiving states, 'small differences between national provisions which determine the transport of data are enough to cause questions and uncertainties' (Vassilaki, 1993: 36).

As far as R(87)15 is concerned, the recommendation has no binding force, nor is there even a requirement, as far as data in the police sector are concerned, to ensure that its provisions are incorporated within national legislation. In addition to these weaknesses, the SIS Convention excludes many of the types of data exchange from the provisions of the 1981 Convention and R(87)15 that are typically used to track terrorists. These include the following:

- information on asylum applications (full exemption);
- extradition, mutual assistance in criminal matters and application of the non bis in idem[18] principle (partial exemption with respect to automated data files);
- extradition, mutual assistance in criminal matters and application of the non bis in idem principle (full exemption with respect to non-automated data files/personal data files recorded in another manner) (Baldwin-Edwards and Hebeton, 1994: 12–13).

Given that the EIS, CIS and Europol Conventions are all modelled on the SIS Convention, these exemptions and weaknesses have equally as forceful relevance to the former three intelligence initiatives.

With regard to Europol's predecessor, the EDU (the existence of which has never had to be ratified by national parliaments), provisional rules on technical security and protection have been drawn up which prohibit the holding of all personal data other than at the national level (a restriction which will hold until Europol becomes fully operational). Such information will be covered by the respective data protection laws of the country concerned. The EDU, itself, will act as a centralized body to facilitate the international exchange of information between EU states. The decision to pass data from one country to another will be at the discretion of each respective liaison officer working within his/her own data protection laws (Grange, 1994: 12–13; *Statewatch*, 1993, 3/3; *EU Official Journal*, 1995).

These provisions are even weaker than those for the SIS, EIS, CIS and Europol. One can identify at least two major problems. First, the data protection standards of the EU states vary greatly. Indeed, the 1981 Convention has yet to be ratified by some member states, including, Belgium, Greece, Italy, the Netherlands and Portugal. Of these, only the Netherlands has any longstanding tradition of domestic data protection legislation (Baldwin-Edwards and Hebeton, 1994; *Statewatch*, 1993, 3/2). Second, the rules make no attempt to harmonize the data protection standards of those states participating within the EDU. The EIS, CIS and Europol at least require the adoption of standards equivalent to those set out in the 1981 Convention.

Given that the EDU is currently the EU's main, operational, criminal intelligence body, the lack of adequate data protection laws to cover transnational exchanges of information is somewhat worrying. This is particularly so when one considers that the mandate of the unit has already been expanded twice since it was first set up in 1994. As one civil liberties lawyer has commented:

> This is a quite extraordinary move. The EDU was only set up as a temporary measure under a 'ministerial agreement' … It does not have to be ratified by national parliaments, has no mechanism for accounting to the European Parliament, for subject access or appeal to the European Court of Justice … Giving new powers to the [unit] 'at a stroke' and in this manner is bad law-making and undermines democracy. (Quoted in *Statewatch*, 1994, 4/6)

In addition to the EIS, CIS, Europol and the EDU, a certain level of informal information exchange will also undoubtedly take place within the third pillar. Indeed, a feasibility study for the establishment of a European automated fingerprint recognition system, EURODAC, to be incorporated under the aegis of the Dublin Convention in order to prevent asylum fraud and multiple applications, is already well under way. Owing to the excessive secrecy that currently surrounds the third pillar's intelligence initiatives, it is not at all clear what, if any, procedures are being planned for dealing with mistakes and complaints with respect to data collection on this system.

It could be that, in the final analysis, one has to rely on the integrity of those involved with intelligence not to misuse information that they come into contact with. However, comments such as the following, made by Sir Peter Imbert at the Crime in Europe Conference in September 1993, do little to inspire public confidence in this form of 'data protection': 'The last thing that you think about when exchanging information is whether or not such procedures conform to data protection standards.'[19] Civil rights groups throughout the Union have consistently raised objections to the above shortcomings. They especially air concern over how accurate information stored on these data banks will be, stressing the examples of people who have been arrested within their own countries as a result of mistaken identity or false information. If one adds on an international dimension that is essentially unregulated with respect to data protection, the potential for such mistakes obviously becomes manifestly higher.

This was vividly demonstrated by the case of the wrongful arrest of one Welsh football fan, Mr Williams (not his real name), in 1993. Incorrect information passed by Belgian authorities to the UK National Criminal Intelligence Service (NCIS) in 1990 led to the inclusion of Williams on a British list of 'football hooligans'. This list was sent back, in 1992, to the Belgian police, who, acting on the information, detained and expelled Williams when he subsequently tried to enter the country later that year. This information was sent back to the NCIS who duly recorded it, so compounding and exacerbating the original error (*Statewatch*, 1993, 3/2).

Although it is true that an EU draft directive on data protection does exist[20] which seeks to go some way beyond the harmonizing provisions of data protection as contained within the 1981 Convention, it will require substantial modification of existing national legislation before it can enter into effect. There is nothing to suggest that the EU states will delay the initiation of the third pillar's data banks until this is in fact achieved. The EDU is already operational and although the EIS and CIS include the principles of the 1981 Convention and R(87)15 in their respective conventions, both conspicuously exclude any reference to the more restrictive draft directive.

Indeed, as things stand, the standards of data protection envisioned for the third pillar amount to little more than the legitimation of the invasion of personal privacy by inter-state actors (such as Europol, EIS) which effectively exist in the absence of any appropriate form of legal control. Such a state of affairs can hardly be expected to inspire the level of public support and confidence that is required for effective policing in an open liberal democratic political system.

Accountability

The third requirement of any liberal democratic response to terrorism is constant parliamentary supervision and judicial oversight. Visible and workable structures of accountability are absolutely essential to ensure that official agents of coercion are held publicly accountable for their actions and, hence, prevented from carrying out arbitrary, unexpected and unlicensed acts of force.

It is the lack of such structures of control that gives cause for most concern with respect to the third pillar. The EU's internal security provisions remain lodged in an intergovernmental framework of cooperation. This essentially means that they exist beyond the purview of both national and EU mechanisms of oversight. As a result, a 'democratic deficit' has grown up whereby decisions that have the potential to affect a great number of people can now be made without reference to either national parliaments or official EU institutions such as the European Parliament and Court of Justice. This is a serious problem, as John Benyon points out:

> Police cooperation in Europe is developing at various levels ... Whether the initiatives are inspired by ministers or generated by police officers, there appears to be a widespread neglect of mechanisms to ensure political and social accountability. These are [absolutely] necessary to ensure legitimacy and public consent, both of which are vital for effective policing in open, democratic societies. (Benyon, 1992: 34)

Member state governments tend to disagree with both aspects of the above view. With respect to national oversight, it is argued that, because judicial and home affairs cooperation remains intergovern-mental in nature, any decisions that are enacted still have to be approved by national legislatures. Whilst this may be true in theory, it is far from accurate in practice. Intergovernmental agreements are never concluded in a particularly democratic manner. National parliaments are excluded from the overall process of negotiation, typically only being brought in at the last minute as a 'rubber stamp' to ratify or reject the end result. This, as Lode van Outrive observes, reduces the legislative process to a mere formality as it essentially eliminates the possibility of introducing any statutory amendments (Van Outrive, 1992a: 18; 1992b: 11).

Furthermore, certain actions that are taken within the third pil-lar may never be required to reach the legislative and judicial branches of national government. Article K6 of the TEU gives member states the power to adopt any joint positions and actions that are deemed necessary to the pursuit of the objectives of the Union (European Communities, 1992a: 328). However, if these 'actions' are framed as purely administrative agreements (such as the setting up of information networks or the exchange of police officers) they do not need to be formally ratified by parliaments (Van Outrive, 1992a: 18; 1992b: 11).

Finally, it should be remembered that national parliaments can only call their own government representatives to account. They have no direct influence over the collective element of the decision making process that is to take place within the third pillar (Piquer, 1993: 17).

With respect to international oversight, member states also argue that, in many ways, the third pillar introduces far more openness into the traditionally secretive world of internal security policy. It is pointed out that both the TEU and Treaty of Amsterdam give the European Parliament (EP) the right to be informed of the discus-sions taking place with regard to EU police and judicial cooperation. Equally, it is affirmed that both treaties give the European Court of Justice (ECJ) the right to interpret and make preliminary rulings on disputes regarding the application of conventions made within the third pillar (European Communities, 1992a: 328–9; European Un-ion, 1997).

As with national oversight, theory does not reflect practice. Un-der the terms of the third pillar, internal security cooperation is to proceed outside the formal structures of the Community legal frame-work and, hence, outside its system of checks and balances. All decisions are to be taken on an intergovernmental basis by the member states themselves (as opposed to the European Commission) acting through the Council of Interior and Justice Ministers. This essentially sidelines both the EP and ECJ who have legitimate powers of oversight only over Union (that is not intergovernmental) legislation.

Moreover, although member state governments are required to report to the EP on their activities within the third pillar, it is only required that they do so *annually* (within the context of a once-yearly debate) (European Communities, 1992a: 328–9; European Union, 1997). This obviously eliminates the possibility of regular scrutiny. Equally, there is no provision in either the TEU or Treaty of Amsterdam that obliges the Council of Interior and Justice Ministers to grant full legal competence to the ECJ with regard to actions and decisions taken within the third pillar; it is merely affirmed that the Council *may* grant jurisdiction to the Court if it so wishes, and then, essentially, only over issues of interpretation (European Communities, 1992a: 328–9; European Union, 1997). To ensure that there is no confusion over this point, the text of the Treaty of Amsterdam specifically states:

> the Court of Justice shall not have jurisdiction to rule on any measure or decision taken pursuant to ... the maintenance of law and order and internal security. The Council, the Commission or a Member State may request the Court of Justice to give a ruling on a question of interpretation of this Title or acts of the institutions of the Community based on this Title. (European Union, 1997)

A further way in which the intergovernmental nature of the third pillar undermines the concept of political accountability is through the power that it will inevitably place in the hands of unelected officials. Already bureaucrats have been dubbed the 'fifth power' within the context of national politics as a result of the decision-making responsibilities that have been delegated to them by increasingly overworked ministers. This process is bound to be exacerbated if national ministers are forced to take on new and added obligations with respect to EU-related affairs which must come second in line of priority to national affairs. As Carlos Piquer observes:

> The real nature of the political responsibility of Ministers of Justice and Interior [must] degenerate: they are preoccupied with their respective national problems, of which they have only a superficial knowledge and

which they only too often delegate to their staff, who have none of the political responsibility. Frequently, when a minister does attend [justice and home affairs] meetings, he is briefed in the plane on the way to the conference. It goes without saying that, as a consequence, his responsibility for the decisions taken is much more theoretical than practical. (Piquer, 1993: 12)

The intergovernmental nature of the Maastricht third pillar has been severely criticized by Charta '91, the 'watchdog' committee set up to oversee the fields of justice, law, racism and policing during the Belgian presidency of the EU. One of the most consistent points to emerge during their conference, 'Europe without Frontiers? Democracy without Citizens' (held in Brussels during June 1993) for instance was the view that the idea of European 'citizenship' (as advocated in Art. 8 of the TEU) was meaningless unless it had a practical content for all those living within the Union. This, the participants argued, can never happen so long as the individual citizen within the Union feels isolated from the dynamic of the political process – a phenomenon bound to be exacerbated when elected representatives and their institutions are consistently bypassed in favour of intergovernmental decision making that exists in the absence of democratic control (*Statewatch*, 1993, 3/4).

The EP's Committee on Civil Liberties and Internal Affairs has equally consistently stressed its objection to intergovernmentalism in the fields of justice and home affairs. It especially highlighted this aspect of the third pillar when considering the report made by Jeannou Lacaze for the Committee on Foreign Affairs and Security on *Terrorism and its Effects on Security in Europe*. Indeed, at its meeting of 22 April 1992, the Committee on Civil Liberties and Internal Affairs specifically called on the Committee for Foreign Affairs and Security to include (among others) the following statement in its report:

[The European parliament], deploring the fact that under the new draft on Political Union, the fight against terrorism is still basically the subject of intergovernmental cooperation ... reiterates that terrorism cannot continue to be dealt with by intergovernmental working parties without any democratic control. (Lacaze, 1994, 16–17)

More recently, the EP urged national parliaments not to ratify the Europol Convention until provisions relating to judicial oversight by the ECJ had been verified (*Statewatch*, 1996, 6/2). Although a protocol subsequently attached to the Convention in July 1996 does allow states to choose to accept the jurisdiction of the ECJ in relation to the operation and management of Europol, it does not oblige them to do so. The UK has already retained such a right of 'opt out' (this being London's condition for ratifying the Convention) – an action which the EP has already vigorously deplored (Van Outrive, 1992b: 12).

A final area of concern that needs to be stressed with respect to the accountability of the third pillar is that which rests with its executive coordinating committee, the K4 Committee. Many commentators have pointed out that it constitutes an extremely powerful entity that exists in the absence of any form of democratic control. Van Outrive identifies the K4 Committee with legislative, executive and judicial power:

- legislative in that it has the capacity to adopt rules, measures and provisions together with the power to amend and/or supplement such measures;
- executive in that it has the capacity to decide on the suspension or otherwise of initiatives made before it;
- judicial in that it has the capacity to monitor, interpret and settle disputes.

This, he argues, is contrary to the constitutional separation of powers that forms an essential feature of the political structures of all member states (as well as that of the EU) (Van Outrive, 1992b: 12).

Moreover, there is no effective provision for publishing the decisions of the K4 Committee, nor is it accountable to an electorate, as its members essentially consist of senior civil servants. Policies will be drawn up in secret by unelected bureaucrats, police, immigration, customs and internal security service officers. These will then be presented to the Council of Ministers for 'rubber-stamping' and only after this will they be made public. The press, public, parliaments and courts of the EU will thus be presented with a fait accompli over which they will have extremely limited influence (*Statewatch*, 1993, 3/4). This is far from satisfactory. If a liberal citizenry is ultimately to accept law enforcement decisions as ones that are being enacted for their own good, they must be confident that their coercive power will never be used against them in an arbitrary and unlicensed manner. This can only occur if there is effective and continual parliamentary and judicial oversight to ensure that the threat of punishment is both controlled in its scope and modified by legally enforced rules of fairness.

The lack of democratic accountability is especially worrying given the underlying ideological rationale that seems to be guiding EU internal security cooperation. It has already been shown how the Maastricht third pillar seems implicitly to identify immigrants as the major source of terrorism, drug trafficking and organized crime within Western Europe. If there are no means to ensure that police and law enforcement agencies are made to answer for their actions, there is a very great possibility that foreigners will be made subject to unwarranted harassment and surveillance. This could have potentially serious repercussions from an anti-terrorist perspective. Initiating measures that discriminate (or at least are seen to discriminate) against the basic rights of immigrants will almost certainly lead to a dramatic increase in xenophobia throughout the Union. Identifying non-EU nationals as a major threat to internal security will merely serve to promote and reinforce a negative perception of these communities, so facilitating an increase in racist tendencies and sentiments. This can only work to the advantage of the numerous and dangerous militant, neo-fascist organizations that have already sprung up in Western Europe in recent years.

Moreover, it has the potential to radicalize and alienate immigrant groups within the EU. It is important to remember that feeling confused, disoriented and resentful, discriminated ethnic groupings become extremely vulnerable to extremist propaganda and rhetoric. Such a development is not only likely to furnish subversives with a ready-made recruiting ground for activists (so, ironically, causing the fear of immigrants acting as a source of political instability to become a self-fulfilling prophecy), it is also liable to provide a useful pool of passive support that is capable of supplying sanctuary, information and logistical assistance.

The Consequences of Failing to Adhere to a Limited, Credible and Accountable Anti-terrorist Policy

What then would be the consequences of failing to uphold the rule of law by initiating unlimited, non-credible and unaccountable anti-terrorist policies? Philosophically, it would undercut the essential liberal democratic belief that is common to every EU member state, the notion that all human beings have the right to be protected against the arbitrary and coercive actions of institutions imbued with power. Ignoring this fundamental dictum brings the liberal polity one step closer to the type of illegitimate and indiscriminate strategies that are characteristically employed by totalitarian and authoritarian states. Systematic fear, aroused by the expectation of institutionalized cruelty, is the very antithesis of the liberal democratic way of life. It is for this reason that liberalism adopts a strong defence of equal rights and their legal protection. If individuals do not have the means to assert and protect themselves against bureaucratized abuse, freedom, the most highly prized ideal of any liberal polity, is nothing but a forlorn hope.

Strategically, failure to uphold the rule of law would run the risk of undermining the perceived legitimacy of the fight against terrorism. It should be remembered that terrorists thrive on the injustices, both imagined and real, that are inflicted by special anti-terrorist measures. One of the classic uses of this mode of warfare is the attempt to try and trap authorities into overreaction by provoking the use of illegal or unconstitutional countermeasures. When authorities do in fact violate accepted constitutional norms, they destroy their legitimacy and allow terrorists to set themselves up as the true protectors of freedom, so drawing support away from official authorities while aiding their own cause. Moreover, any victory that is ultimately achieved over the terrorists is likely to be hollow, as the fundamental nature of the state would be altered from liberal to authoritarian, changing it in the process to a regime that threatens the basic civil liberties of all.

Conclusion

This chapter has approached the issue of EU anti-terrorist collaboration within the third pillar from a largely philosophical angle. Such an approach has been adopted because, in the final analysis, EU counterterrorism is all about protecting a particular, philosophically defined, common way of life – liberal democracy. It is therefore vital that, in the headlong rush to provide for an enhanced international capacity to deal with terrorism, democratic legitimacy is not lost. However, judging from the above analysis, it appears that much of the substance of the third pillar has been driven almost exclusively by operational requirements.

This is a serious problem with respect to counterterrorism, as success in this field ultimately depends on the extent to which it is publicly supported. It has to be seen to be upholding the rule of law and working for the general good. This obviously cannot happen if the manner of that defence serves, itself, to undermine the very principles and traditions which make a liberal democratic way of life possible in the first place.

Many of the problems concerning the democratic acceptability of the third pillar stem from its intergovernmental nature. Creating an internal security system in this manner has led to the development of an arrangement that now exists in the absence of any real political structures of control. Problems of limitation, credibility and accountability would all be greatly reduced if internal security measures were, accordingly, made subject to more effective scrutiny and oversight at the Union level. Elevating the supervisory role of bodies such as the EP and ECJ would, for instance, allow for a clearer definition and protection of suspects' legal rights, tighter political and judicial control of criminal investigations and increased openness in the administration of EU justice. The 'passarelle' provision contained in Art. K14 of the TEU is the 'bridge' by which this could take place. It offers the long-term opportunity of transferring any matter pertaining to the third pillar from an intergovernmental framework of cooperation to one in which decision making and oversight would be exercised directly by the federal structures of the EU.

The lack of adequate legislative and judicial oversight would be of lesser consequence if technical matters alone were concerned. However, by enacting the third pillar through the TEU, and reaffirming its role in the Treaty of Amsterdam, the EU member states have created a whole new internal security structure that now has the ability to make decisions directly affecting the EU as a whole as well as people individually. In such instances, a lack of democratic control and supervision, essential if co-decision making is to be accorded democratic legitimacy, becomes unacceptable.

If closer anti-terrorist police cooperation is genuinely to offer greater liberty for those within the EU, the requirements of limitation, credibility and accountability must be incorporated and adhered to at a European level. Mechanisms have to be in place to ensure civil rights and maintain the even-handed administration of justice that is necessary to any healthy liberal democratic system of law. Only then will it be possible to talk about real progress in this field as only then will departures from the normal operation of the rule of law be accepted as a necessary evil that has been forced on the citizens of the EU by the threat of terrorism, rather than conveniently excused by it.

Notes

1   In the 1997 Treaty of Amsterdam, judicial and home affairs coop-
     eration is referred to as an EU area of 'freedom, security and
     justice'. However, throughout this chapter, the Maastricht TEU
     designation will be adopted.

2   Much of the substance of the third pillar reflects the recommenda-
     tions that were first made by the Group of Coordinators (set up in
     Rhodes in 1988 to oversee the work of the TREVI WG'92) in their
     Palma Document of 1989. These designated those law enforcement
     and judicial measures that needed to be taken if the member states
     were to give effect to the objective of establishing the free move-
     ment of goods and persons within their territory.

3   The definition is based on the terminology that was worked out by
     the TREVI WG3. It reflects the political component stressed in
     most definitions and, by emphasizing the idea of 'structure', ap-
     pears to accept the idea of terrorism as a deliberately planned
     campaign of violence, so differentiating it as an explicitly intended,
     systematic mode of psychological 'warfare'. It is noteworthy, how-
     ever, that the definition excludes two major characteristics that are
     often included in conceptions of terrorism: non-combatant activity
     and indiscrimination.

4   Again this definition is based on terminology worked out by TREVI
     WG3.

5   Technically, however, the work of the K4 Committee comes under
     the Council of Interior and Justice Ministers and the Committee of
     Permanent Representatives (COREPER), the latter having the re-
     sponsibility for agreeing an agenda and negotiating a consensus.

6   A person can be included on the EIS if he/she has served a custodial
     sentence of one year or more; if there is information to the effect
     that he/she has committed a serious crime; if there are serious
     grounds for believing that he/she is planning to commit a serious
     crime and/or represents a threat to the public order and national
     security of a member state; and if he/she has committed a serious
     offence in relation to the entry or residence of alien persons.

7   The dispute between the UK and Spain essentially revolves around
     the issue of whether the border of a future decolonized Gibraltar
     should be an internal or external border. The UK argues that,
     should the colony be granted independence, it would become a
     separate sovereign state and thus its frontier should be treated as
     an external border. Spain, however, maintains that, if the British

renounce sovereignty, under the terms of the 1713 Treaty of Utrecht, control of the colony would pass to it, thus designating Gibraltar's frontier as an internal border (see *Statewatch*, 1992, 2/4).

8   Under the terms of the Amsterdam Treaty, however, decisions taken in the third pillar on asylum and immigration will require unanimity for until at least 2002 (European Union, 1997; *The Australian*, 1997).

9   The preparatory work for the CIS was carried out by the Mutual Assistance Group 1992 (MAG '92). The system will incorporate standard messages such as 'stop and search', and will hold information on five main categories: persons, businesses, methods of transport, commodities and trends. In each category there is a space for intelligence to be added. The effect of the CIS will be that, instead of trying to watch every person or vehicle crossing an EU external border, customs officials will concentrate on suspects if they fit the 'profile' of a likely smuggler according to intelligence reports. A CIS Convention was adopted by the EU member states in July 1995; under a 'rolling ratification' procedure (which does not apply either to the EIS or to Europol), the CIS can become 'provisionally' operational once two or more member states have ratified it. (Information obtained from Sandy Russell during the Conference on Crime in Europe, University of Leicester, 23 September 1993. See also *Statewatch*, 1993, 3/1; 1995, 5/4.)

10   Information obtained from Dr Michael Spencer during the Conference on Justice in the European Community, University of Leicester, 30 September 1993. (See also *The Australian*, 1996.)

11   The Schengen Agreement, which came into force in March 1995, includes Belgium, France, Germany, Luxembourg, the Netherlands, Spain and Portugal. In May 1996, five observer members were also admitted: Denmark, Finland, Sweden, Iceland and Norway. Schengen has been described as a 'fast-track' EU which aims to achieve quicker, and more comprehensive, integration among its members.

12   The land border between Southern and Northern Ireland is not subject to any frontier controls, except for security purposes with respect to the activities of terrorist organizations in the north.

13   The Schengen Convention on the elimination of passport controls among continental EU members was signed in March 1995. However, the full implementation of the Convention has been held up by disagreements among participants, notably over France's con-

cern about opening its land border with the Netherlands in view of the latter country's more liberal government and, allegedly, lax control of drugs. Under the terms of the 1997 Treaty of Amsterdam, continental EU members have until 2004 to lift their border formalities (see *Keesing's Record of World Events*, 1996: 41067; European Union, 1997; *The Australian*, 1997).

14   For the purposes of the internal market as set out by the Treaty on European Union, the UK and Ireland were given a special dispensation allowing their ports and airports to be treated as an external frontier with respect to nationals from third countries. Although Schengen's provisions on frontier checks were integrated into the EU structure under the terms of the 1997 Treaty of Amsterdam, the right of both the UK and Ireland to retain their own border controls was reaffirmed (see *Statewatch*, 1992, 2/1; 2/6; 1993, 3/1; *European Union News*, 1997; European Union, 1997).

15   The UK has expressed reservations about entrusting anti-terrorism intelligence to Europol. London's main fear is that the information will be compromised (or even destroyed) in the process of international exchange by 'untrustworthy' police officers from certain EU states. In general, the UK prefers the system of informal exchange of intelligence that currently takes place between TREVI CTLOs. (See, for instance, *Statewatch*, 1995, 5/2.)

16   It is noteworthy, in this regard, that the EDU's operational budget for 1996 was adopted only after the EU member state governments had the opportunity to analyse the Council of Justice and Interior Ministers' traditional six-monthly report on 'The Assessment of the Terrorist Threat in the EU'.

17   Numerous academic studies have been conducted which focus on the relative overrepresentation of ethnic minorities in West European prisons. (See, for instance, Bernheim and Borgese, 1991; Fielding, 1991; Henry-Layton, 1992. For a detailed overview of statistics, see Brian *et al.*, 1994.)

18   The 'no double jeopardy' principle. This is the legal stipulation which states that a person cannot be tried for the same crime twice.

19   Sir Peter Imbert, comment made during the panel discussion at the Conference on Crime in Europe, University of Leicester, 23 September 1993.

20   Proposal for a Council Directive Concerning the Protection of Individuals in Relation to the Processing of Personal Data, Commission proposal COM(90)314 Final. For further details of the

original proposal, see Commission of the European Communities (1992: 54–6).

References

Baldwin-Edwards, Martin and Bill Hebeton. 1994. 'Will SIS be Europe's Big Brother?' In *Policing Across National Boundaries*, edited by Malcolm Anderson and Monica den Boer. London: Pinter.

Benyon, John. 1992. *Issues in European Police Cooperation*. Leicester University Discussion Papers in Politics. Leicester: Leicester University Press.

Bernheim, Jean-Claude and Giovana Borgese. 1991. *Racisme et Police en France*. Féderation Internationale des Droits de l'Homme. Rapport 153.

Bertlet, Chip. 1992. 'The Subversion Myth'. *Covert Action*. Summer.

Bigo, Didier. 1994a. 'Borders, Security, State, Transnational'. Paper presented before the 'Police and Immigration: Towards a Europe of Internal Security' Workshop, European Consortium for Political Research Joint Session of Workshops, Madrid.

Bigo, Didier. 1994b. 'The European Security Field: Stakes and Rivalries in a Newly Developing Area of Police Intervention'. In *Policing Across National Boundaries*, edited by Malcolm Anderson and Monica den Boer. London: Pinter.

Boer, Monica den. 1993. *Immigration, Internal Security and Policing in Europe*. Working Paper VIII in Series 'A System of European Police Cooperation in 1992'. University of Edinburgh.

Boer, Monica den. 1994. 'Rhetorics of Crime and Ethnicity in the Construction of Europe'. Paper presented before the 'Police and Immigration: Towards a Europe of Internal Security' Workshop, European Consortium for Political Research Joint Sessions of Workshops. Madrid.

Brian, Fabienne, Luc Verheyen, Greet Spiessens, Françoise Tulkens, Frank Hutsebaut and Lode van Outrive. 1994. *Etudes de l'Immigration. L'Inégalité Pénale; Immigration, criminalité et système d'administration de la justice pénale*. Paris: Programme de Recherche en Sciences Sociales, Service de la Programmation Politique Scientifique.

Bunyan, Tony. 1991. 'Towards an Authoritarian European State'. *Race and Class 32*.

Chalk, Peter. 1995. 'The Liberal Response to Terrorism'. *Terrorism and Political Violence 7*: 10–45.

Chalk, Peter. 1996. *West European Terrorism and Counter-Terrorism: The Evolving Dynamic*. London: Macmillan.

Commission of the European Communities. 1992. *Completing the Internal Market '92: The Elimination of Frontier Controls*. Luxembourg: Office of the Official Publications of the European Communities.

De Gucht, Karel. 1993. *Annual Report of the Committee on Civil Liberties and Internal Affairs on Respect for Human Rights in the European Community*. Strasbourg: European Parliament Session Documents, A3-0025/93.

De Piccoli, Cesare. 1993. *Report of the Committee on Civil Liberties and Internal Affairs on the Resurgence of Racism and Xenophobia in Europe and the Danger of Right Wing Extremist Violence*. Strasbourg: European Parliament Session Documents, A3-0127/93.

EU Official Journal. 1995. 'Joint Action on Europol Drugs Unit'. 20 March.

European Communities. 1992a. 'Treaty on European Union'. *International Legal Matters* 31: 327–9.

European Communities. 1992b. 'The Treaty on European Union'. *Commission of the European Communities Background Report*, ISEC/B25/92, 5.

European Union. 1997. *The Treaty of Amsterdam: Full Text*. Luxembourg: Office of the Official Publications of the European Communities.

European Union News. 1997. 'The Amsterdam Summit: a New Treaty for the European Union'. 15 July: 1–2.

Fielding, Nigel. 1991. *The Police and Social Conflict. Rhetoric and Reality*. London: Athlone Press.

Franks, John. 1996. 'Euro Enthusiast'. *Policing Today* 2.

Grange, Ken. 1994. 'The Impact of Data Protection upon European Police Information Flows and the Specific Implications for Immigration and Asylum'. Paper presented before the 'Police and Immigration: Towards a Europe of Internal Security' Workshop, European Consortium for Political Research Joint Session of Workshops, Madrid.

Gregory, Frank. 1991. 'Police Cooperation and Integration in the European Community: Problems, Proposals and Prospects'. *Terrorism: An International Journal* 14: 148–50.

Henry-Layton, Zig. 1992. *The Politics of Immigration. Immigration, 'Race' and 'Race' Relations in Post-War Britain*. Oxford: Blackwell.

House of Commons, Select Committee on Home Affairs, Session 1989–1990. 1990. *Practical Police Cooperation in the European Community*. London: HMSO.

Hudson, Barbara. 1993. 'Racism and Criminology: Concepts and Controversies'. In *Racism and Criminology*, edited by Dee Cook and Barbara Hudson. London: Sage.

Keesing's Record of World Events. 1996. April.

Keesing's Record of World Events. 1996. June.

Keesing's Record of World Events. 1996. July.

Lacaze, Jeannou. 1994. *Report of the Committee on Foreign Affairs and*

Security and Terrorism and its Effects on Security in Europe. Strasbourg: European Parliament Session Documents, A3-0058/94.

Lodge, Juliet. 1992. 'Internal Security and Judicial Cooperation Beyond Maastricht'. *Terrorism and Political Violence* 4.

Loescher, Gil. 1992. 'Refugee Movements and International Security'. *Adelphi Paper* 268.

New York Times. 1994. 'New European Police to Fight Regional Crime'. New York, 17 February.

Piquer, Carlos. 1993. *Report of the Committee on Civil Liberties and Internal Affairs on Cooperation in the Field of Justice and Internal Affairs under the Treaty on European Union (Title VI and other Provisions)*. Strasbourg: European Parliament Session Documents, A3-0215/93.

Shaklar, Judith. 1989. 'The Liberalism of Fear'. In *Liberalism and the Moral Life*, edited by Nancy Rosenblum. Cambridge, MA.: Harvard University Press.

Statewatch, 1992. Vol. 2, no. 1 (January–February).

Statewatch, 1992. Vol. 2, no. 4 (July–August).

Statewatch, 1992. Vol. 2, no. 6 (November–December).

Statewatch, 1993. Vol. 3, no. 1 (January–February).

Statewatch, 1993. Vol. 3, no. 2 (March–April).

Statewatch, 1993. Vol. 3, no. 3 (May–June).

Statewatch, 1993. Vol. 3, no. 4 (July–August).

Statewatch, 1993. Vol. 3, no. 6 (November–December).

Statewatch, 1994. Vol. 4, no. 3 (May–June).

Statewatch, 1994. Vol. 4, no. 5 (September–October).

Statewatch, 1994. Vol. 4, no. 6 (November–December).

Statewatch, 1995. Vol. 5, no. 2 (March–April).

Statewatch, 1995. Vol. 5, no. 4 (July–August).

Statewatch, 1995. Vol. 5, no. 6 (November–December).

Statewatch, 1996. Vol. 6, no. 2 (March–April).

Statewatch, 1996. Vol. 6, no. 3 (May–June).

Statewatch, 1997. 'The Treaty of Amsterdam: Full Text'. bacdoc (June). [http://www/poptel.org.uk].

The Australian. 1996. 'Europe in Harmony Against Asylum-Seekers'. 16 January.

The Australian. 1997. 'Europe's Leaders Agree on a Lesser Design'. 19 June.

The Economist. 1990. 'Schengen Agreement: Jeux Sans Frontières'. 16 June.

The European. 1992. 'Maastricht Made Simple'. Milton Keynes: *The European*.

The Independent on Sunday. 1992. 'The Treaty of Maastricht: What it Says and What it Means'. 11 October.

Van Outrive, Lode. 1992a. *Report of the Committee on Civil Liberties and Internal Affairs on the Entry into Force of the Schengen Agreements.* Strasbourg: European Parliament Session Documents, A3-0288/92.

Van Outrive, Lode. 1992b. *Report of the Committee on Civil Liberties and Internal Affairs on the Setting up of Europol.* Strasbourg: European Parliament Session Documents, A3-0382/92.

Vassilaki. Irini. 1993. 'Transborder Flow of Personal Data'. *The Computer Law and Security Report 9.*

Woodward, Rachael. 1993. 'The Establishment of Europol: A Critique'. Paper presented before the Cyprus Police Academy International Seminar, 'Cooperation with the Police Forces of the Community and with Europol', Cyprus.

The Author

Peter Chalk, formerly Lecturer in International Relations at the University of Queensland, Australia, is now a policy analyst at RAND Corporation in Washington, United States of America. He is also contributing editor of the journal, *Studies in Conflict and Terrorism.*

7 The Fight against Terrorism in the Second and Third Pillars of the Maastricht Treaty: Complement or Overlap?

MONICA DEN BOER

Introduction

The core question addressed in this contribution is whether or not the current architecture of the Treaty on European Union (TEU) is adequate to deal with the reinforcement of European cooperation against terrorism. The subject of terrorism is primarily dealt with under the third pillar of the TEU (Title VI, Art. 29) and a special working party was created to discuss initiatives in this field. As we will find out, however, the member states have trouble in tackling the subject of terrorism in a homogeneous manner. There are a number of reasons for this. The first one is historical: terrorism was a subject of concern in the realm of European Political Cooperation, which was the forerunner of the second pillar on Common Foreign and Security Policy. Terrorism, which primarily used to be a matter of state security intelligence embedded in the international relations dynamics, has been ushered in the direction of international police cooperation, which is an issue on the Justice and Home Affairs agenda. The second reason for a lack of homogeneity in the anti-terrorist approach is therefore of a paradigmatic nature: there is an absence of a clear-cut conceptual grid that can impose a workable definition on the EU member states (see Chapter 8). Is terrorism primarily to be seen as an expression of anti-government or anti-state sentiments (in which case it is predominantly regarded as an internal security threat) or is it a form of imported activism employed in order to manipulate the foreign policies emanating from 'the West' (in which case the 'internal security threat' emanates from an external enemy)? Can terrorism, illegal immigration, drug trafficking and organized crime be lumped together without jeopardizing the distinction between the mandates of police and security services? (See Chapter 9.) Thirdly, defining strategies against terrorism is a challenging task in a multidimensional environment, where the interests of member states,[1] or those of the EU and external partners (Anderson, 1989: 127–47; Riley, 1993: 24),[2] may clash, further complicated by the competition between cooperative ventures (such as the European Union, the Council of Europe, Schengen and the Police Working Group on Terrorism).

These three reasons for the lack of a homogeneous approach to terrorism (Anderson *et al.*, 1995: 30) will be discussed below in the light of a number of observations about the progress of anti-terrorism efforts in the European Union.

Is History Repeating Itself?

Terrorism has not been put forward as the most prominent issue on the third pillar agenda. When studying the text of Title VI (Provisions on Police and Judicial Cooperation in Criminal Matters) of the TEU, the notion of terrorism emerges as a reason for police and judicial cooperation (Art. 29). Terrorism was included in Europol's mandate after ratification of the Convention.[3] Article 2.2 of the Convention states that, within two years at the latest, following the entry into force of the Convention, Europol shall also deal with crimes committed or likely to be committed in the course of terrorist activities against life, limb, personal freedom or property.

The reason why 'terrorism' was originally not included on Europol's agenda was primarily a political one. First, in the absence of a uniform definition of terrorism, it would be difficult for member states to establish whether or not action by Europol would be justified on the basis of the criterion that the interests of two or more member states had been affected (Art. 2.1, Europol Convention). Second, the inclusion of terrorism implies the handling of sensitive data which in some member states is a competence of the state security service; this, then, could result either in a sometimes undesirable exchange of data between ordinary police services and state security services or in lack of public accountability and transparency (see Chapter 9).

Therefore the fact that terrorism is 'only' mentioned in the context of police cooperation does not mean that the margins for expanding action against terrorism are small. A very important instrument is also provided by means of judicial cooperation in criminal matters (the former Art. K1(7), new Art. 31). Within this realm, negotiations between the member states have focused on ironing out the obstacles for extradition of terrorists. After pressure from the Spanish government, a convention[4] aiming at the improvement of extradition between EU member states was adopted in June 1996, after the controversial political offence exception had been partially watered down as a result of the insertion of an article that determines that conspiracy with or membership of a criminal organization that commits terrorist offences may no longer be defined as a (non-extraditable) political offence.[5] Although the row between Spain and Belgium,[6] the principle of double incrimination (for criminal conspiracy or membership of an armed group) and life sentences (which do not exist in Portugal) were a stumbling block in the negotiations,[7] the extradition convention was adopted 'by tacit approval' at the start of the Irish presidency.

Which are the other initiatives against terrorism that have been developed under the third pillar thus far? First, an attempt has been made at defining a common working terrain. On 25 October 1995,[8] the justice and home affairs ministers drafted the so-called Gomera Declaration, which seems to be based on a minimal consensus about reinforced cooperation against terrorism. Superficially, the Gomera Declaration does not do much more than repeat earlier terms of reference, such as those which were used in the context of Trevi. In the Gomera Declaration, the ministers of justice and home affairs establish that terrorism is a threat to democracy, the free exercise of human rights and the economic and social development of which no member state of the European Union can plead itself free; that terrorism has increased mainly as a consequence of activities based on fundamentalism; that terrorism has taken on such transnational proportions that it cannot be combated efficiently by each individual member state with its own means; that terrorism develops strategies and employs international organized crime models; and that terrorism could abuse possible judicial differences between the member states with a view to escaping punishment.

Following this Declaration, the member states argued that judicial and police cooperation should be improved by exchanging more operational information about terrorist organizations, with a view to mapping out their modus operandi, financing and money-laundering operations. The member states also wanted to improve coordination and collaboration between legal systems with a view to ruling out the possibility of terrorists escaping criminal penalties, and they sought to improve the extradition of those responsible for terrorist acts to competent judicial authorities, in accordance with international conventions, by having them tried and possibly having them sanctioned.

The wording in the Gomera Declaration makes it very plain that the definition of terrorism is moving closer to that of (international) organized crime. Not only does the Declaration actually mention that terrorism more frequently develops strategies and employs models of international organized crime (whatever these may be), it also refers to criminal activities ordinarily associated with international organized crime, such as money laundering. The similarity of the structure and activities of organized crime to those of terrorist organizations brings the formulation of a (semi-)identical law enforcement strategy very close. Key words that apply both to terrorism and to organized crime are 'organizations', 'transnational' and 'threat to economic and social stability'. Both crimes are regarded as phenomena that require a preventive, proactive approach, with the support of intelligence-gathering and/or covert policing strategies. Semantically, the gap between organized crime and terrorist activities is gradually becoming a very narrow one.

The Gomera Declaration also introduces another concept, which is that of fundamentalism. This move replaces the 'old' external threat, communism, with fundamentalism, and simultaneously signals the construction of a European identity through emphasizing the difference. The self – the European identity – is (re)-constituted by a confrontation with a new and unfamiliar culture (Behnke, 1996: 7) and this 'culturally defined differentiation' is expressed by alternately using the terms 'fundamentalism, Islamic fundamentalism, or islamism' (ibid.: 16). However, these politics of differentiation have failed to dominate the formulation of a security identity and, as we will see below, have not provided a unified strategy against threats of a terrorist nature.

Before dealing with the paradigmatic problem that the member states have encountered, some more items on the list of initiatives against terrorism ought to be discussed. Following an initiative of the United Kingdom, a proposal was laid down for a joint action for the introduction of a repertory of capacities in the field of anti-terrorism. On the basis of the adoption of the Gomera Declaration on 15 and 16 December 1995, the member states called for an intensive coordination for an efficient and preventive fight against terrorism, thereby paving the way for member states to be able to consult one another on specific capacities and expertise. The repertory is supposed to be kept up-to-date by one member state in

English, French and German.[9] At its meeting on 4 June 1996, the Justice and Home Affairs Council decided that the United Kingdom would be in charge for one year initially, after which the keeping of the repertory will be in the hands of the member state that holds the presidency. Every member state makes available special competences, knowledge or expertise in the field of anti-terrorism. The repertory also includes national contact points.[10] Furthermore, an activity under the third pillar concerns an annual evaluation of the internal and external threat posed to the European Union. The document, which is classified, compiles and analyses the terrorist events that have taken place on the territory of the member states, including the names of those who were (allegedly) responsible for these events. The document therefore constitutes a 'threat analysis', which is presented to the Council.[11]

Finding a Uniform Approach in a Pluriform Environment

One of the central ironies of European police cooperation is that the crimes most closely associated with internal security threats, such as terrorism, are those that stimulate transnational security cooperation (den Boer and Walker, 1993: 14). The EU member states are capable of demonstrating understanding and even solidarity when one of them is confronted with terrorist activities. A fitting illustration is the attitude of Schengen partners vis-à-vis France when, in 1995, it was subjected to a spate of Islamic fundamentalist bombings. France justified the continued closure of internal borders by having recourse to the provision in the Schengen Implementing Convention that a Schengen partner may unilaterally decide to close its borders when its internal security is at stake (Art. 2.2 of the Schengen Implementing Convention). However, the problem is that France did not take into account the condition that it should consult the other Schengen states before declaring, on 29 June 1995, that she wanted to have recourse to the internal security clause. During an informal meeting, the Executive Committee declared its solidarity. As a consequence of this event, work was undertaken to set up mobile patrols in a 20-kilometre zone on both sides of the internal borders. New criteria were also determined by the Executive Committee for the invocation of the internal security clause (Art. 2.2 of the Schengen Implementing Convention), namely that only the Executive Committee can decide that a Schengen partner is allowed to reinstall its internal border controls after a consultation procedure.

The definition of a joint strategy against terrorism can be substantiated by finding a common enemy, as is done in the Gomera Declaration (fundamentalism). What we find, however, is that this threat is still more strongly directed against the national governments of member states, rather than against the EU order. The internal 'securities' of the EU member states therefore do not simply add up to internal security of the EU. The levels of threat differ greatly, and the origin of the terrorist threat is still bound up with the idiosyncracies of the relevant member state (for example, colonial past or territorial division of power). The combination of the readiness of member states to help one another out when terrorism is concerned and a rather fragmented internal security situation leads to a paradoxical situation, namely that a sense of uniform anti-terrorist ideology fails to culminate in a harmonious and smooth combative mechanism. A perfect example of this is the above-mentioned controversy that erupted between the Spanish and Belgian government after the Belgian Council of State decided that two Basques who allegedly accommodated ETA terrorists were not to be extradited to Spain. The will to define a uniform strategy against terrorism stands therefore in marked contrast to the disharmony during the practical stage of cooperation between police and judicial authorities.

Apart from the configuration of member states, the involvement of different institutions at member state level complicates the formulation of a coherent strategy. Competences of secret security services differ between member states. In some member states, like The Netherlands, the dividing line between state security service and police is (at least formally) very sharp: the state security service (De Binnenlandse Veiligheidsdienst, or BVD) has for instance declared that it will not engage in investigations that traditionally fall under the heading of policing tasks, and that it does not seek to exchange information with the police about international organized crime.[12] This situation differs from that in Britain, where the Intelligence Service, MI6, first moved into the area of terrorism, which was not received with a great deal of enthusiasm by the Metropolitan Police Special Branch; thereafter, MI5 concerned itself increasingly with organized crime, again not to the satisfaction of the police services (Anderson et al., 1995: 173; Chapter 9 of the present volume). The reason why judicial and/or political authorities should become concerned about this is that secret security services can act without the necessity of public accountability and transparency of their actions (The Guardian, 1996; for observations about accountability in the third pillar of the Treaty on European Union, see Chapter 6). We should keep this in mind when, later, we discuss the 'Europeanization' of internal security. What indeed are the consequences of greater involvement of state security services in the third pillar policy-making process? How do turf battles between police and state security services 'at home' reflect on the representation of these institutions in the different working and steering groups within the third pillar?

The formulation of a coherent internal security agenda may be jeopardized by two further circumstances. The first is of an evolutionary nature, the second of an institutional nature. In terms of evolution, the state security services find themselves placed in a more competitive environment, as the decline of the external security threat from communist states has forced them to explore new security markets. These have been identified as (Islamic) fundamentalism, (organized) racism and xenophobia and, in some cases, as we have seen above, international organized crime (in particular drug trafficking, as undertaken by foreign heads of state, and nuclear smuggling). These security markets border upon those which have begun to be explored by police services (den Boer, 1999), certainly since international police cooperation has been given an official warrant in the context of Trevi and the third pillar of the TEU. Europol is at the crossroads of the security markets we have just identified. At the same time, the police services in the member states are also involved in increased competition with their neighbouring services: crime and victimization rates, crime clearance statistics, number of police officers per capita of population, efficiency of operations against drugs and organized crime, effectiveness of policing methods and innovative technology – all of these function as criteria for the comparative functioning of the police services. That which is most visible – not petty crime, but organized crime – is what is often most 'worthwhile' and 'rewarding' to police officers. It would not be an exaggeration to state that police effectiveness is an important catalyst in the credibility of state action. It shows what the development of the external security environment of EU member states can lead to, especially when we take into account that the collapse of the communist system is seen as one of the main causes of the growth of East European organized crime.

The formulation of a coherent security agenda within the third pillar is also made difficult because there is no long-term planning. Presidencies last only six months, which results in a change of agenda every half-year.[13] Every member state seeks to promote its own favourite internal security topic (its importance often measured against the background of national elections). Usually these items are not unrelated to the spectre of third pillar activities, but there is too little time to generate common knowledge and expertise in these areas.[14] Terrorism, with usually a requirement of immediate action, does not fit easily within long-term planning strategies, nor is there a hard-core common concern that consistently dominates the agenda.

Added to this is the effect of the sloppy architecture of the Maastricht and Amsterdam Treaties. Although the prevention and combating of terrorism is given a formal place in the context of the Union's objective of providing citizens with a high level of safety under Art. 29 of Title VI, it is also implicit in the provisions of the second pillar on Common Foreign and Security Policy: indeed, those external threats that are turned inward and that establish a threat to democracy and the state are Islamic fundamentalism and threats expressed by the Kurdish Liberation Party (PKK). The architecture of the TEU hides a thematic overlap between the pillars. The Intergovernmental Conference, during which the structure of the Maastricht Treaty was reviewed, has not offered a solution to this overlap. It will be up to the national institutions (state security services) to ensure feedback in two directions (ministries of justice and the interior on the one hand, and ministries of foreign affairs on the other) and they will have to look after the coordination of implementation strategies at the national level. As Neuwahl (1994: 227) says: 'the Member States continue to be present individually on the international plane. Since decision-making is getting more complex, it is hardly surprising that "consistency" is made into a guiding principle governing the relations between the various actors concerned.'

Consistency in anti-terrorist policy is thus put under pressure by a fragmented internal security, changing presidencies, short-term agendas and multiple actors. Aiming for consistency can therefore act as no more than a counterfactual to give direction to a permanent process of goal setting.

Borderlines and Security Identities

The dividing lines between 'home affairs' and 'foreign affairs' are thin, to say the least. The main reason for this is, as mentioned previously, that home affairs increasingly take on a European/international dimension (especially immigration, external border controls, organized crime, drug-trafficking and terrorism) and that foreign affairs have increasingly absorbed the diplomatic aspects of international cooperation as opposed to domestic affairs with an international potential. Under the system of European Political Cooperation (EPC), there could be categorical exclusion of matters such as the alleged telephone tapping of an anti-apartheid group in Britain, security in Northern Ireland and refugee status in the Community for Cypriots from Northern Cyprus (Neuwahl, 1994: 230–31). But under the TEU, the criteria of competence division between the second and third pillar are less clear. In this regard, Cremona (1994: 253–4) argues:

> The political dimension to the Community's external relations will also be affected by the co-operation envisaged within the Union in the field of Justice and Home Affairs, for example over immigration policy. ... It is not difficult to see how the Council of Ministers may wish to use the common policy on visas ... as an element in its relations with third states, whether within the context of the Community (an association agreement for example) or within the CFSP itself.

On the other hand, Title VI of the TEU links together a series of internal and external security matters. However, a bridge between the Common Foreign and Security Policy (CFSP) and the Justice and Home Affairs (JHA) Title is lacking. Anderson *et al.* (1995: 175) regard this as 'a retrograde step, since, between 1976 and 1993, there was such a bridge built into the framework of European Political Cooperation'. This fragmentation of linked policy issues may, however, be compensated by the 'communautarization' of issues such as immigration. But as terrorism and police cooperation in general are excluded from the possibility of being transferred to Community competence, there is little chance that a horizontal solution across the pillars will be found.[15]

As the borderline between 'home' and 'foreign', between 'internal' and 'external', is more and more difficult to draw, other principles could possibly be employed in order to define a satisfactory distribution of competence. The two candidates for further exploration are subsidiarity and security identity.

The principle of subsidiarity can roughly be paraphrased by the requirement that the Community shall only act if objectives pursued cannot be adequately attained by individual action of the member states. Applying this definition to crime and/or terrorism,

EU bodies (such as the Europol Drugs Unit) would not come into action unless two or more member states would be affected by it, if the crime/terrorist act would be of a serious nature, and if the national authorities would not be able to deal with the crime/terrorist act on their own. The problem with this requirement, however, is that, certainly in the context of enlargement, it may be hard to justify 15 member states having to take action when the interest of only two member states is at stake. The principle of subsidiarity should hence be weighed together with the principle of proportionality: everything that cannot be dealt with in a bilateral or multilateral context, and where Community action has a demonstrable advantage over small-scale or regional collaboration, could be dealt with at TEU level. Hence the member states should endeavour to define an inventory of items that should be dealt with at Community level (within either JHA or CFSP) or at bilateral/multilateral level (involvement of justice and home affairs ministries or of foreign ministries).

An additional criterion for the determination of whether or not the CFSP machinery should be involved is the extent to which the security of citizens living within the territory of the EU, or those based within external EU institutions, is under threat. In other words, not when the security of a nation state, but when the security of the European Union itself is jeopardized by a terrorist act, should the third pillar machinery be employed. However, as long as the 'referent object' (the state) (see Wæver, 1996: 105) is not replaced by another one (the Union), there is no such concept as a (common) security identity. This raises the question whether and to what extent the European Union can become a security community (Anderson et al., 1995: 176). The replacement of the 'state' constituent by a 'European Community' constituent requires a breaking away from the traditional and familiar forms of state action. However, Buzan (1991: 194) observes that, although West European states admit their inability to fulfil independently many economic and defence functions, they are reluctant to give up their sovereignty concerning security issues (Anderson et al., 1995: 176). In order to function as a security community, the European Union member states will have to tackle a number of fundamental questions concerning the conceptualization of security. The first question concerns the coherence of a criminal justice policy: should it have a predominantly repressive or preventive orientation (Walker, 1993: 113–17)? The second question concerns the interpretation of 'internal security dangers': what constitutes a sufficient reason to restore (internal) border checks, for instance? Finally, there is uncertainty about the extent to which enlargement will bear on the cohesiveness of the European Union as a security community (Anderson *et al.*, 1995: 177).

Moreover, there is only sporadic evidence of an immediate and vicious threat to the EU itself. Even angry farmers have not transformed their action into an international organized structure that threatens the EU with hostage taking and bombs. There is a justifiable need, however, for proactive consideration on this point, especially as the CFSP Title, according to den Boer and Walker (1993: 18–19),

> indicates a significant shift towards incorporation of the second pillar of the Hobbesian state, namely external coercive potential [and] this may begin to involve the Community in the types of antagonistic relationships where challenges to its internal security, in particular through espionage and terrorism, may emanate from external hostile powers. For the first time, terrorism and strategic intelligence associated with 'state security' may become bound up with the specific order of the EC rather than its Member States, so influencing the development of Community policing competence in these areas.

Even though there have been rhetorical attempts to frame external security threats by identifying post-bipolar enemies (illegal immigration, 'floods' of asylum seekers, East European organized crime), these have failed to spin off a genuine 'common' threat to the Union itself. Aggestam (1996: 20) blames the 'plurality of political cultures in the EU and the legacy of the member states', which 'seem to prevent the formation of a collective European identity that could give "meaning" to the words of "an ever closer union among the peoples of Europe"'. This explains, on the one hand, why EU member states have difficulty in showing a common response to terrorism and, on the other hand, terrorism seeming to have a less unifying force in terms of security threat than immigration and asylum.

Hence European security identity is still hugely fragmented. Its scattered nature is reinforced even further by the weakness of supranational government (intergovernmental cooperation) and the lack of public and social legitimacy. In one sense, enlargement of the European Union spells bad news for atttempts to define a common security identity: the absorption of the 'old' communist threat will be overshadowed by the difficulty of reaching a minimal consensus about the EU's external potential. Finally, it will not be an easy task to marry totally divergent conceptions of security: whereas West European states define security as a constellation of acts, actors and strategies against the loss of security, Central and East European states tend to define security as 'being secure'. Hence security becomes both the objective of European integration as well as the criterion by means of which the success of European integration is judged.

Conclusion

The third pillar does not seem the most appropriate machinery to deal with urgent matters of terrorism. The machinery is hierarchical: proposals and drafts are discussed at five different levels of decision making and agreement needs to be generated within the national administrations of the EU member states. The lack of a quick response to changing (internal and external) security situations, the emergence of new items on the agenda and the absence of joint emergency procedures hinder effective cooperation against terrorism at this level. Furthermore, initiatives under the third pillar are plagued by the rule of unanimity. Conventions have to be adopted and ratified by all member states. Owing to this 'double lock' procedure (O'Keeffe, 1995: 898), the tendency has been to switch to instruments that are not legally binding or that do not require ratification by the national parliaments (recommendations, declarations, resolutions). The introduction of 'lowest common denominator' agreements causes a political impasse. Member states always have the option to deviate from international agreements.

Finally, there is the problem of finding a common definition of terrorism, further complicated by the disorientation of the post-cold war era. Member states tend to move away from the tiresome exploration of common ground by focusing on practical means of cooperation. Three strategies stand out. First, EU member states endeavour to exchange more operational information and intelligence to improve the analysis of the modus operandi of terrorists (for instance, arms trade and money-laundering operations). The exchange of sensitive information on terrorism could well overlap with that on organized crime. Second, member states seek to improve the coordination between legal systems. An example is the creation of a formal framework for the exchange of liaison magistrates.[16] Third, there is increasing pressure for actually extraditing terrorists. There is an appeal to member states to be solidaristic and no longer have recourse to political exception clauses.[17]

In the meantime, however, the EU should contemplate a substantial framework that could enhance counterterrorism. Except for a review of the third pillar hierarchy and decision-making system, there is an urgent need for reflection on points of subsidiarity, proportionality and the definition of a European security identity.

Notes

1   See below for the discussion of the controversy between Spain and Belgium. Noteworthy historical examples include frustrations with the French government for not extraditing wanted terrorists from Spain and Italy (predominantly in the early 1980s) and a conflict between Belgium and Britain concerning Belgium's refusal to extradite Father Patrick Ryan to Britain (November 1988). See Riley (1993: 26).

2   See also *Volkskrant* (1996). The USA criticized the EU for refusing to introduce tough and effective sanctions against companies that invest in Libya and Iran.

3   Article 2.1 of the Convention based on article K3 of the TEU on the establishment of a European Police Office, 26 July 1995, OJC316. Anderson, chapter 8 in the present volume, observes that the need for cooperation in terrorist matters did not figure in early plans to develop Europol.

4   The convention on simplified extradition procedures between the member states of the European Union, OJC78: 1–2. *Agence Europe* (no. 6758, 27 June 1996) writes that the Executive Committee of the Schengen Agreement approved a declaration aiming at the implementation of transitional measures concerning extradition, pending the ratification of the EU convention that will govern the matter of extradition throughout the European Union.

5   *Agence Europe*, no. 6758, Thursday 27 June 1996.

6   This conflict was the result of a decision by the Belgian Council of State not to extradite a Basque couple who had allegedly offered accommodation to Basque terrorists (*NRC Handelsblad*, 10 February 1996).

7   Ontwerp-besluiten Unie-Verdrag, Brief van de Ministers van Justitie en van Binnenlandse Zaken, Staten Generaal, Vergaderjaar 1995–1996, Nrs. 90h and 47, 23 490: 9–10. See also below.

8   Déclaration de la Gomera sur le phénomène du terrorisme, Brussels, 25 October 1995, 10899/95.

9   Ontwerp-besluiten Unie-Verdrag, Brief van de Ministers van Justitie en van Binnenlandse Zaken, Staten Generaal, Vergaderjaar 1995–1996, Nrs. 90h en 47, 23 490: 4–5.

10   Mededeling aan de Pers, 1933e zitting van de Raad – Justitie en Binnenlandse Zaken, Luxembourg, 4 June 1996 (7813/96 (Presse 157)): 9.

11   Ontwerp-besluiten Unie-Verdrag, Brief van de Ministers van Justitie en van Binnenlandse Zaken, Staten Generaal, Vergaderjaar 1995–1996, Nrs. 90h en 47, 23 490: 5.

12   Inzake Opsporing, Enquêtecommissie Opsporingsmethoden, Eindrapport, Tweede Kamer der Staten-Generaal, Vergaderjaar 1995–1996, 24 072, no. 10, 350.

13   This shortcoming has been slightly compensated by the fact that no delegations were opposed to a draft resolution on the establishment of a biannual working programme, which lays down the priorities under the third pillar. This was discussed during the meeting of the Council of Justice and Home Affairs Ministers on 4 June 1996 (Mededeling aan de Pers, 1933e zitting van de Raad – Justitie en Binnenlandse Zaken, Luxembourg, 4 June 1996 (7813/96 (Presse 157)): 12 (and Annex II)). A multi-annual working programme however, cannot prevent, subjects of great topical value being added to the agenda.

14   The problem may also be situated within the national administrations. It is not uncommon for civil servants with a vast knowledge of the subject to move to different areas of expertise.

15   The new Art. 42 of Title VI TEU (replacing the old Art. K9, which is known as the 'passerelle') provides that the Council may, acting unanimously on the initiative of the Commission or a member state, and after consulting the European Parliament, decide to 'transfer' action in certain areas to the first pillar of the Treaty, in which Community instruments and a different decision-making system apply.

16   On 27 and 28 February 1997, the Third Pillar Coordinating Committee approved a joint action pertaining to the creation of a framework for the exchange of liaison magistrates in order to improve judicial cooperation between the EU member states.

17   During the IGC, the Spanish government insisted on the insertion

of a provision in the new TEU which would exclude EU nationals from demanding asylum in another EU member state. In the Treaty of Amsterdam, a protocol was inserted to this effect, determining the conditions under which an application for asylum made by a national of a member state may be taken into consideration or declared admissible for processing in another member state (Protocol to the Treaty establishing the European Community on asylum for nationals of EU member states).

References

Aggestam, Lisbeth. 1996. 'The "Role" of Security and Identity in the European Union'. Paper presented at the ECPR Joint Sessions of Workshops, Oslo, 29 March–3 April, Workshop 'Security and Identity in Europe'. Mimeo.

Anderson, Malcolm. 1989. *Policing the World. Interpol and the Politics of International Police Cooperation.* Oxford: Clarendon Press.

Anderson, Malcolm, Monica den Boer, Peter Cullen, William Gilmore, Charles Raab and Neil Walker. 1995. *Policing the European Union. Theory, Law and Practice.* Oxford: Clarendon Press.

Behnke, Andreas. 1996. 'Dialogues on Difference. Theoretical Remarks on a security political problematique'. Paper presented at the ECPR Joint Sessions of Workshops, Oslo, 29 March–3 April, Workshop 'Security and Identity in Europe'. Mimeo.

Boer, Monica den. 1999. 'Internationalisation: A Challenge to Police Organisations in Europe'. In *Policing Across the World: Issues for the Twenty First Century,* edited by Rob Mawby. London: UCL Press.

Boer, Monica den and Neil Walker. 1993. 'European Policing after 1992'. *Journal of Common Market Studies* 31: 3–28.

Buzan, Barry. 1991. *People, States and Fear. An Agenda for International Security Studies in the Post-Cold War Era.* Brighton: Wheatsheaf.

Cremona, Marise. 1994. 'The Common Foreign and Security Policy of the European Union and the External Relations Powers of the European Community'. In *Legal Issues of the Maastricht Treaty,* edited by David O'Keeffe and Patrick Twomey. London: Chancery.

Neuwahl, Nanette. 1994. 'Foreign and Security Policy and the Implementation of the Requirement of 'Consistency' under the Treaty on European Union'. In *Legal Issues of the Maastricht Treaty,* edited by David O'Keeffe and Patrick Twomey. London: Chancery.

O'Keeffe, David. 1995. 'Recasting the Third Pillar'. *Common Market Law Review* 3: 893–920.

Riley, Lisa. 1993. *Counterterrorism in Western Europe: Mechanisms for International Co-operation*. Working Paper X Series 'A System of European Police Cooperation after 1992'. University of Edinburgh.

The Guardian. 1996. 'On Her Majesty's Secret Service'. 29 January.

Volkskrant. 1996. 'VS ruziën met EU om terreurwet'. 6 August.

Wæver, Ole. 1996. 'European Security Identities'. *Journal of Common Market Studies* 34: 103–32.

Walker, Neil. 1993. 'The International Dimension'. In *Accountable Policing: Effectiveness, Empowerment and Equity*, edited by Robert Reiner and Sarah Spencer. London: IPPR.

The Author

Monica den Boer is Associate Professor in the Center for Law, Public Administration and Informatization at Tilburg University, The Netherlands. Previously, she was a Senior Lecturer at the European Institute of Public Administration in Maastricht.

8 Counterterrorism as an Objective of European Police Cooperation[1]

MALCOLM ANDERSON

Improved cooperation to counter terrorism has emerged as a high priority on the international agenda on several occasions in the last three decades. It has proved an elusive goal. The highly industrialized countries have repeatedly returned to the theme with repeated lack of success. For example, the Group of Seven (G7) leading economic nations meeting in the 1987 Tokyo meeting proposed a series of measures (reinforcing controls of suspect diplomatic missions, tighter immigration controls, quicker extradition procedures) and left the task of formulating specific measures to a specialist meeting of ministers the following year. The 1987 meeting produced no concrete results. In the June 1996 meeting of the G7 in Lyons, counterterrorism was again at the top of the agenda, with the USA proposing, inter alia, a 'no place to hide' extradition convention, and extraterritorial trade and investment sanctions against rogue nations. There was scepticism about the first and clear dissension about the second of these proposals and President Chirac's proposal to hold a special meeting to negotiate concrete solutions was accepted. The question, first raised in the 1980s (Anderson, 1989: 140), is whether these meetings are on a road which leads anywhere.

The main contention of this chapter is that effective and continuing cooperation in the field of counterterrorism is almost impossible to achieve because the basis of this cooperation must be agreement between governments on political rather than criminal law enforcement objectives. Even if broad agreement exists on political objectives, the use of criminal policing and of the instruments of mutual assistance in criminal law enforcement are complicated, inter alia, by the very diverse contexts in which political violence takes place, the difficulty of defining terrorism, the problematic legal basis of counterterrorist action, differing organization of antiterrorist agencies in different countries, and the reluctance of agencies and governments to share certain types of intelligence.

The Objectives and Ideology of Police Cooperation in the European Community/Union

Member states were agreed, from the 1970s, that improved police cooperation was desirable for certain specified law enforcement purposes. It has proved difficult to give precise definition to the objectives of this cooperation, which go beyond fighting certain broad categories of delinquency. Nonetheless, in some political milieux and law enforcement agencies, an internal security ideology has developed which makes systematic connections between these broad categories: terrorism, drug trafficking, organized crime, trans-frontier crime, illegal immigration, asylum seekers, minority ethnic groups and so on (Bigo and Leveau, 1992; Bigo, 1994, 1996). This ideology conceives diverse problems as being elements of one generalized security threat, in an international political context in which there has been a blurring of the distinction between internal and external security. The security ideology is associated with new attitudes towards the surveillance of populations and the internationalization of the outlook of ministries of justice and the interior.

This ideology has sometimes informed proposals made by governments. For example, French Minister of Justice Toubon proposed, in April 1996, to add to the list of offences defined as terrorism by French legislation 'assistance to entry [into the country], to the movement and to the unauthorised residence [in France] of a foreigner'. In this case illegal immigration and terrorism were intimately linked. However, within the security spectrum suggested by this ideology, changes in the environment have influenced the priority placed on different objectives and justifications of police cooperation. In broad terms, over the last 25 years, emphasis has changed from terrorism, to drugs, to illegal immigration, to organized crime, and varying connections have sometimes been assumed between these forms of criminality. Progress in cooperation has not been smooth but has gone in fits and starts. Specific criminal events, such as the killing of athletes at the 1972 Munich Olympics, the Brighton bombing in 1984 and the wave of bombings in Paris in 1986, were triggers for government action. Such events create an overwhelming pressure on governments, aptly described as the 'politics of the latest outrage'. The arguments for promoting cooperation are therefore seldom carefully thought through, but are usually limited to statements that collective action is essential to combat obvious social evils. But the various objectives set and justifications advanced are not as self-evident as they seem when first suggested.

Behind the shifting priorities and changing problems, certain continuities in attitudes, especially towards terrorism, may be found. In European and, more generally, Western government appreciations of terrorism, six characteristics are commonly found (Herman and O'Sullivan, 1991: 43–4). First, the West, which stands for decency and the rule of law, is an innocent target and victim of terrorism. Second, the West responds only to other people's use of force. Third, in contrast to the West, terrorists do not adhere to 'civilized norms of conduct'. Fourth, in those cases where the West supports insurgents who use force, this is done on behalf of democracy against repressive regimes. Fifth, democracies are hated by and vulnerable to terrorists, and the aim of terrorists is to undermine democratic institutions. Sixth, during the cold war, the efforts to undermine democracies had Soviet support. The link between international socialism and international terrorism was seen as not simply fortuitous. An analogous link is now being made between Islam and terrorism.

The General Problems of Counterterrorism as an Objective

The initial impetus towards specifically European police cooperation was the growth of 'terrorist' incidents perpetrated by indigenous and Middle Eastern groups in the late 1960s and early 1970s. The failure of the German authorities to imprison effectively those responsible for the 1972 massacre of Israeli athletes at the Munich Olympic Games was the most conspicuous of a number of incidents which led to the 1975 establishment of the Trevi Group for counterterrorist cooperation among the EC member states. It stimulated, in the late 1970s, the most far-reaching proposal to date for European criminal law enforcement – 'the European judicial space' proposed by President Giscard d'Estaing of France – in order that individual states should not be blackmailed by terrorist (particularly Middle Eastern) groups. Countering terrorism tended to be the main rhetorical justification for international police cooperation for over a decade, until the effects of the 1986 wave of bombings in Paris began to wane. It produced a great number of affirmations of faith in transnational solutions such as that of President Mitterrand in 1987: 'Since terrorism is international, investigation, prevention, repression and sanctions should also be international.' The practical achievements of cooperation did not live up to the political rhetoric associated with counterterrorism. As Interior Minister

Scalfaro of Italy said, in 1986: 'If good cooperation between states was already normal practice, no one would feel the necessity of constantly referring to it.'

Anti-terrorist action is a dubious basis for institutionalized transnational police cooperation, for a variety of reasons. The first is that terrorism is usually directed towards influencing state policy. It is therefore par excellence an issue of state security. No state is willing to give up exclusive control over information about its own security unless compelled to do so, or if it can engage in useful trade of intelligence with another government. Second, since political causes and interests are involved, governments usually have widely differing perspectives on the implications and importance of particular terrorist incidents. Third, a wide variety of agencies – both police and intelligence services – are involved in countering terrorism and coordination between them within states is highly problematic: different agencies often have different interests in international cooperation. Fourth, political violence linked to broadly based political movements cannot be repressed by police action alone but requires coordinated government policies aimed at removing the underlying conditions which provoke violence. Fifth, although acts of terror have a dramatic impact on public opinion, these are relatively rare compared with ordinary criminality, and long periods can pass without countries experiencing any incident; this weakens the day-to-day commitment of police agencies to international cooperation.

Giving a high profile to counterterrorism has been part of a general shift in patterns of policing in some of the major countries of Western Europe. Some police services have begun to shift their focus from local crime to regional, national and transnational crime. Crime with more than local ramifications includes serious crimes of fraud, violence, such as bank robbery and kidnapping, the various activities of organized crime, including illegal trading enterprises, environmental crime, organized prostitution, human smuggling, counterfeiting of currency and identity documents, and political crime, such as subversion and terrorism. The shift of emphasis from local crime runs parallel with the creation of specialized central police units and the increased employment of controversial proactive policing techniques and instruments, such as wire-tapping, covert surveillance, entrapment and the use of paid informants. 'High policing' together with the techniques traditionally associated with its practice, is therefore increasingly entering the realm of 'ordinary policing'. This is especially the case since organized crime has recently become the target of police organizations throughout Europe.

What is Terrorism?

There is a preliminary problem which bedevils international cooperation in counterterrorism – arriving at a common understanding of what the term 'terrorism' means. The absence of this understanding can seriously inhibit practical trans-frontier cooperation.

The problems of definition of terrorism are well known. One problem is how to differentiate political terrorism from other forms of activity which may attract the terrorist label. Wilkinson, for example, seeks to distinguish political terrorism from criminal, psychic and war terrorism (Wilkinson, 1974). In principle, this is a worthwhile attempt at sub-categorization, since most political theorists and some politicians agree that the manner in which terrorists acts or threats ought to be evaluated and tackled may differ according to whether such behaviour is politically motivated. In practice, however, the various sub-categories shade into one another. Criminal terrorism, defined as the systematic use of terror for material ends, may be linked to political terrorism: for example, where the proceeds of the terrorist act are used in support of a wider political struggle. Psychic terrorism has mystical, religious or magical objectives. But who is to say where these categories end and the category of politics begins? If anything, the distinction between war terrorism and political terrorism is even more difficult to sustain. War terrorism may be defined in terms of a commitment to destroy the enemy through a military campaign, but this focuses on means rather than ends. Groups who use the methods of war may do so in pursuit of objectives which are just as 'political' as those sought by other groups using less intensive methods of armed struggle; indeed, in many cases the objectives of rival 'terrorist' groups may be very similar, their main disagreement being over means.

Most legal definitions of political terrorism venture little beyond the stock formula of 'the use of violence for political ends',[2] but this leaves a number of questions unanswered. Following a rigorous analysis of the shortcomings of earlier efforts, Wardlaw settles upon the much-quoted formula:

> political terrorism is the use, or threat of use, of violence by an individual or group, whether acting for or in opposition to established authority, when such action is designed to create extreme anxiety and/ or fear-inducing effects in a target group larger than the immediate victims with the purpose of coercing that group into acceding to the political demands of the perpetrators. (Wardlaw, 1989: 16)

Some would object to Wardlaw's inclusion of isolated individuals, insisting that terrorism presupposes the existence of a terrorist *organization*. Others would ponder the use of words such as 'designed' and 'purpose', debating the extent to which terrorism need involve the pursuit of a systematic and internally coherent strategy. However, perhaps the most intractable issue raised by this definition concerns the circumstances under which actions either 'for or in opposition to' the 'established authority' of the state fall within the ambit of terrorism.

The answer to this question rests upon a value judgment which seeks to distinguish legitimate violence from illegitimate violence of the terrorist. The legitimacy of the state's use of force cannot depend merely upon the lawfulness of its activities, as this would entail the unacceptable consequence that, if the police or armed forces stray beyond their legal powers, they then automatically become terrorists (Finney, 1990: 3). The justification for official violence must, therefore, rest upon the broader legitimacy of the incumbent regimes, measured by tests such as commitment to democratic values, a minimum framework of individual and minority rights, and the general adherence of state authorities to the rule of law.[3] In turn this raises the converse question of the justification of violence perpetrated by insurgents against an illegitimate regime, however defined. From this wider perspective, the ethical boundary between state and not-state violence becomes extremely hazy. Hence the moral relativism implicit in Yasser Arafat's aphorism delivered to the General Assembly of the United Nations: 'one man's terrorist is another man's freedom fighter'.

The term 'terrorism' has entered into ordinary language, political discourse and legal instruments. Its use cannot, therefore, be avoided. But it is desirable to specify exactly the context and the form of political violence which is the subject of repressive measures (and of international cooperation) and not group every act of political violence into a catch-all category. It matters a great deal whether acts of political violence are committed by an autonomist movement which is indigenous to a West European country rather than a Japanese or Middle Eastern organization making a sortie into Western Europe. In the case of the former, a movement like ETA or the PIRA is certain to have support among sections of the population within the countries: the PIRA sympathizers in the Republic of Ireland and the cases brought to trial in France of Bretons harbouring Basques are examples. The policing and criminal policy implications tend to vary when this situation arises. Difficult foreign policy issues have arisen in the control of Middle Eastern and 'Islamic' terrorism, resulting in tensions between West European partners.

The Slow Development of International Police Cooperation

Faced with a conceptual and normative quagmire, international attempts to cooperate against terrorism developed slowly and hesitantly. For example, international terrorism has posed difficult problems for Interpol. Its 1956 statutes excluded the communication of information on cases of a political, religious or ethnic character. This ban was dropped at the 1984 Interpol General Assembly, when policy on 'acts of violence commonly called terrorism' was debated and the doctrine of 'preponderance' adopted. According to this doctrine, actions may be more or less criminal for Interpol to transmit messages about them. This approach has ended the controversy caused by Interpol's previously non-interventionist stance, while retaining an awareness of the complexity of the problem. With a worldwide membership, Interpol is bound to proceed cautiously, and could not adopt a definition of terrorism favoured by Western democracies, or, indeed, by any other regional bloc.

A number of overlapping mechanisms were created through which European governments cooperate to combat terrorism, including the Club of Berne, the Club of Vienna, the Trevi Group and the European Convention on the Suppression of Terrorism (Anderson, 1989: 127–47; Riley, 1993) and now Europol, which became operational in 1996 after the ratification of the Europol Convention. Although there were hesitations, combatting terrorism was included in Europol's remit.[4] Despite their common perception of the general nature of the terrorist problem, the use made of these cooperative fora has remained limited. West European governments have often been unwilling to give unequivocal backing to one another because of different analyses of the specific problem and different political interests (Clutterbuck, 1990: 119–23; Martin and Romano, 1992: 30ff). This has been apparent in cases such as the Red Brigades, ETA and the PIRA. The general desire to cooperate has not always been sufficient to overcome reservations in particular cases, and the open-textured quality of the concept of terrorism has provided ample scope for divergent positions to be articulated.

Striking examples exist of reticence and non-cooperation between West European governments on terrorist issues. Until 1985, the French authorities were reluctant to extradite Basque terrorists; between 1986 and 1988, they seemed willing to bargain with Middle Eastern terrorist groups in return for the release of hostages; and in January 1994 they refused to extradite Iranians wanted for murder in Switzerland on grounds of national interest, despite the vigorous protest of the Swiss authorities. In 1988, Belgium and Ireland refused to cooperate with the United Kingdom in extraditing Father Ryan, suspected of arms trafficking for the PIRA. In 1996, the Belgian government refused to extradite to Spain two Basques wanted by the Spanish authorities. In August 1994, Charles Pasqua, French Minister of the Interior, criticized the UK and other West European states for their tolerant attitude to Islamic fundamentalism in the wake of concern that violence would spread from Algeria to France.

Redefinition of the Security Interest of West European States

The linkage between security fields lies at the core of the redefinition of the West European security situation following the collapse of the Soviet Union. Integration of the tasks and functions of police services, immigration services, customs and intelligence services (den Boer, 1994: 7; Walker, 1995), is supported within high policing discourse by the gradual shaping of an 'internal security continuum' referred to in the first section of this chapter, connecting terrorism, drugs trafficking, organized crime, immigration and asylum seeking. Indeed, a crucial factor behind the merging of internal and external security has been the definition of immigration and asylum seeking as problems for the internal security of West European states. This linking process operates at the level of cultural meaning and is associated with a variety of discursive techniques (Bigo, 1994; den Boer, 1994; Brion et al., 1994: 38; Solomos, 1993). The image of migratory flows jeopardizing internal security is often integrated into the vocabulary of law and order (Bigo and Leveau, 1992: 9, 29).

There are three modes in which internal security concerns have become amalgamated with immigration and asylum. The first of these is ideological merging: law enforcement agencies in Europe started to redefine internal security threats. The old external threat of communism was replaced by an external threat established by mass immigration, organized crime and imported terrorism, the penetration of which would, like the old threat, lead to the destabilization of 'well-balanced' Western societies. This form of threat analysis has led to the growing importance attributed to the collection of strategic intelligence, the increased role of certain national police agencies, the intrusion of intelligence services into domains previously regarded as the preserve of the 'police', and problems of definition of roles and coordination of police agencies.

Police Organization and Counterterrorism

In Western Europe, political terrorism is a relatively rare form of crime compared with other forms of serious crime. Very diverse groups are accused of this kind of crime. For these reasons it is not feasible to concentrate all police action against political terrorism in one specialized national unit. The consequence is that at least two agencies, and potentially more in some countries, are involved whenever there is a politically motivated offence.

France provides a striking example of the multiplicity of agencies potentially involved in a major incident. These include the external security service, the Direction Générale de la Sécurité Extérieure (DGSE), in the ministry of defence; the internal security service, the Direction de la Surveillance du Territoire (DST), in the ministry of the interior; the general intelligence service of the police, the Renseignements Généraux (RG); the criminal investigation police, the Police Judiciaire, in the ministry of the interior, but acting under the authority of the magistrature; the specialist police anti-terrorist squad, the Service de Recherche, d'Assistance, d'Intervention et de Dissuassion (RAID); and the specialist anti-terrorist squad of the Gendarmerie Nationale (in the ministry of defence), the Groupement d'Intervention de la Gendarmerie Nationale (GIGN). At various times, each of these agencies has taken the lead, sometimes trying to establish an exclusive control, in policing particular terrorist incidents. Sometimes operations were badly mismanaged, as with the intervention of the GIGN against three suspected Irish members of the INLA in Vincennes in 1983. Although the Irish were undoubtedly members of the INLA, it was members of the GIGN who ended in the dock, accused of attempting to pervert the course of justice. Legal proceedings arising from this case only concluded in 1999.

In an attempt to bring order into a potentially chaotic situation, the Unité de Coordination de la Lutte Anti-Terroriste (UCLAT) was set up in 1984 in order to provide central coordination of intelligence and operations; all the relevant agencies are represented on it.

This has gone some way towards the goals of preventing intelligence hoarding and independent, possibly conflicting, action taken by different agencies. But neither of these two objectives can be completely achieved. Intelligence may not be passed on, particularly by security services, for a range of good and bad reasons. One of these is that intelligence may consist of highly sensitive and uncorroborated suspicion. Circulation of this within national agencies can cause problems; transferring such information across national boundaries may be strongly resisted. Coordinated anti-terrorist action may be rendered impossible by the necessity of reacting very quickly to a particular incident and this has the potential to cut across investigations and operations already in hand by other agencies. This problem is magnified if terrorist incidents have trans-frontier ramifications because police officers are likely to be less well informed about what is going on in other jurisdictions.

The Problematic Legal Framework of Counterterrorism Cooperation

Exceptional legal powers are regarded as essential for police action against terrorism – and now against organized crime. There is currently a second wave of legislation in various EU member states aimed at enlarging police powers in the sphere of pro-active criminal investigation. During the late 1970s, there was a spate of anti-terrorist laws in several European countries; in the 1990s, the fight against organized crime has provided political support for the introduction of new legislation. The first wave in the 1970s was marked by the introduction of legislation in Italy, Germany, the United Kingdom and, to a lesser extent, France, aimed at both domestic and 'imported' terrorism. Italy provides an extreme example. The Italian *Reale* laws of 1975 (extended in 1977) increased police powers of search, arrest, detention on suspicion and the tapping of telephones, which required the written consent of a magistrate. The law of 18 May 1978 went further and permitted magistrates to approve telephone taps verbally, so that police could act immediately. The notorious Cossiga law (Law 15 of 6 February 1980) authorized police to search houses or apartment blocks without prior authorization of a magistrate, if there were reasonable grounds for believing they harboured someone wanted for a terrorist crime. Other legislation facilitated intelligence gathering by approving the establishment of a computerized database within the ministry of the interior (Clutterbuck, 1990: 37–9, 154, 186).

After the kidnap and murder of Dr Schleyer in 1976, German laws strengthened police powers in dealing with terrorist suspects. Police were permitted to search all apartments in a block if they suspected that terrorists and hostages were there, and they were empowered to set up roadblocks to establish the identity of people passing through neighbourhoods in the vicinity of terrorist incidents. In addition, a powerful computerized data-bank was set up within the Bundeskriminalamt (BKA) (ibid.: 58). The 1974 Prevention of Terrorism Act in the United Kingdom authorized police to demand evidence of identity and to arrest people without warrant if they were suspected of any of the offences covered by the Act, such as membership of the PIRA or involvement in the commission, preparation or instigation of acts of terrorism. When the Act was reviewed in 1989, police were given extended access to bank accounts and business records anywhere in the United Kingdom: they were empowered to share information with each other and with the social security authorities, and the onus was placed on suspected racketeers 'to prove that there was a legitimate source of their funds' (ibid.: 93). The 1989 Act also differs from its predecessors in that it does not automatically expire after five years, so conveying the sombre message that the problem of terrorism is no longer considered a temporary one. In France, police powers were increased in 1986 to permit police officers to prevent people leaving the scene of the crime if they required information (ibid.: 78).

These piecemeal national measures to strengthen law enforcement (in which civil liberties are curtailed) when terrorist acts were committed were flanked by attempts to improve international mutual legal assistance. The main problem was considered to be the difficulty of extraditing individuals accused of offences. The effect of the political offence exception in the European Convention on Extradition was an impediment to bringing those responsible for terrorist acts to justice (Council of Europe, 1979: 5–6). This initiated a review culminating in the drafting of the 1977 European Convention on the Suppression of Terrorism (Vercher, 1992: 350–52). This Convention quickly gained the necessary degree of support and entered into force in September 1978. Among others, all 12 members of the EU prior to the 1995 expansion, as well as the three new EU members, Austria, Finland, Sweden and Norway, have ratified it.

The effect of the 1977 Convention is that the political offence exception is withdrawn in relation to serious offences, but the accused may be afforded another kind of protection, by Art. 5, in the form of of an 'asylum' or 'non-discrimination' clause. Furthermore, while the Convention is designed to facilitate extradition, it does not require it. However, where extradition is not possible, owing to the nationality of the accused or other factors, Art. 7 resorts to an extradite or prosecute obligation. Article 6 imposes certain obligations to create extraterritorial jurisdiction serious offences in order to ensure that prosecutions can, in fact, be launched in these circumstances.

It is often claimed that the conclusion of this Convention is evidence of the closer cooperation in the fight against serious transnational criminality. This cooperation is made possible by 'the special climate of mutual confidence' which exists among members of the organization, 'based on their collective recognition of the rule of law and the protection of human rights' (Council of Europe, 1979: 10). While there may be some truth in such assertions, real limits to mutual confidence continue to exist. This is demonstrated by the facility, provided in Art. 13 of the 1977 Convention, to place extensive reservations on the obligations contained in Art. 1 to extradite for specified offences (Lowe and Young, 1978: 318; van den Wyngaert, 1991: 301). When extradition is refused because of an Art. 13 reservation, the obligation to submit the case to the domestic prosecutorial authorities for the purpose of instituting criminal proceedings, contained in Art. 7, should be triggered but, in practice, has sometimes been ignored.

The reservations procedure has been heavily used by participating states: of the 12 members of the EU prior to the 1995 enlargement, only five (Germany, Ireland, Luxembourg, Spain and the United Kingdom) declined to take advantage of Art. 13, facilitating requests for seizure of assets. A further five (Denmark, France, Greece, Italy and the Netherlands) reserved the right to refuse extradition in respect of all Art. 1 offences. Portugal, in an action with much the same effect, made its participation in the Convention subject to its constitutional provisions relating to non-extradition on political grounds. Belgium reserved its right to decline to extradite in respect of offences which it considers political, excepting those 'committed upon the taking of hostages'. Commentators have, unsurprisingly, generally concluded that the 1977 Convention has not had a significant practical impact on European extradition practice (van den Wyngaert, 1991; Bartsch, 1991: 504; Gilbert, 1991: 142).

European Political Cooperation concern with terrorism was contemporaneous with progress on the 1977 Council of Europe

Convention on the Suppression of Terrorism and the relationship between the two became central to the debate on extradition. Belgium proposed that the EU members should formally agree to apply the Convention *inter se* without reservations. As has been noted, 'This work was already underway when President Giscard d'Estaing took a much bolder initiative, which for a time monopolized the attention of the Nine and delayed progress on the Belgian proposal' (Nuttall, 1992: 294). This was the proposal for a common European Judicial Space which envisaged a more extensive set of EC arrangements in the extradition field. The Belgian proposal was opened for signature at the Dublin European Council on 4 December 1979, while the wider French initiative was still being drawn up. But the French proposal failed to attract the support of the Netherlands and was not adopted. This had a negative impact on French support for the 1979 Dublin Agreement, which never received sufficient ratifications to permit its entry into force.

The fiasco over the 1979 Dublin Agreement diminished enthusiasm for judicial cooperation among the member states. The Judicial Cooperation Working Group (JCWG) was reconstituted only in the mid-1980s, with its work divided between a group dealing with criminal matters and another with civil judicial cooperation. Since that time, extradition has remained at the top of the JCWG agenda without much progress being made. Improved extradition arrangements were given a high priority by European interior and justice ministers at the meeting in Athens in December 1988, following severe political strain over two highly publicized cases. One of these, which greatly soured relations between the United Kingdom, Belgium and Ireland, arose out of the Father Patrick Ryan controversy. The other related to the equally contentious Abdel Osama Al Zomar case, in which a Palestinian wanted by the Italian authorities for alleged involvement in the bombing of a Rome synagogue was deported by the Greek government to Libya, rather than being extradited to Italy. The continuing suspicions of other jurisdictions and of other governments' motives in terrorist cases prevent a basic agreement being reached on the automatic transfer of suspected terrorists between jurisdictions.

Conclusion

Terrorism has been the subject of a vast amount of writing which often uncritically accepts the official definitions and ways of categorizing the problem. Most governments wish to treat political violence aimed at them as a straightforwardly criminal act which should be the subject of the cooperation of other governments without hesitation, delay or reservation. This cannot be done because political violence is triggered in a wide variety of situations and is associated with very diverse political causes.

Terrorism, particularly 'international terrorism', is not a homogeneous criminal threat which governments invariably have a common interest in repressing. This lack of common interest and outlook is the product of a variety of factors, and usually several factors at the same time: divergent colonial histories, regional problems, struggles for autonomy, the inability of states to guarantee internal security, extreme social tensions, cultural and linguistic cleavages – the complex origins of terrorism seldom reach the surface of public or political discourse (Bourdieu, 1992: 132). Lack of convergence between otherwise friendly governments may also have to do with calculations of interest in international relations or raisons d'état which allege that there are more important national interests at stake than the imprisonment of individual terrorists. The lack of a common approach also reflects and reinforces the various unresolved tensions in the very definition of terrorism. No legal framework has yet been agreed which allows similar treatment of suspects in all West European jurisdictions; no international legal instrument yet exists which ensures automatic extradition of suspects. The degree of practical police cooperation is also inhibited by different police and intelligence service organizations in different countries and a widespread hesitation about transfer of certain kinds of intelligence to foreign administrations.

It is a central paradox of police cooperation that many areas in which demand for collaboration on functional grounds is most persuasive are also those which bear most intimately upon state-specific interests. Terrorism is the most obvious example. The organizational sophistication, contact network and scope of activities of many terrorist organizations, whether 'international' or 'transnational' (Riley, 1993: 12; Anderson et al., 1996: 26–30) are such that international cooperation is required if they are to be effectively combated. However, these organizations offer such direct and profound threats to state interests that target states will jealously guard the right to control the purpose and scope of such operations (Riley, 1993: 9). Although the need for cooperation in terrorist matters supplied the initial impetus for the development of Trevi and remained a priority in the Maastricht Treaty, it did not figure in early plans to develop Europol, and opposing perspectives on anti-terrorism continue to be evident in the debate over the final text of the Europol Convention.

Notes

1   This chapter is based on research conducted by a team in the University of Edinburgh. The main findings of the research are published in Anderson, den Boer and others (1996).

2   As consistently used in the British Prevention of Terrorism Acts, 1974–89. See Finnie (1990: 2).

3   Some commentators have argued for a wider definition of state terrorism than that flowing from failure to adhere to basic democratic and rule-of-law standards. For an imaginative attempt to develop a broader approach concentrating on the themes of 'systems terror' and 'terror as effacement', see Christodoulidis and Veitch (1994).

4   Europol created in 1998 a counterterrorism group and this group identified various functions which Europol should perform in relation to counterterrorism. No operational involvement of Europol has yet been reported.

References

Anderson, Malcolm. 1989. *Policing the World. Interpol and the Politics of International Police Cooperation*. Oxford: Clarendon Press.

Anderson, Malcolm and Monica den Boer, eds. 1994. *Policing Across National Boundaries*. London: Pinter.

Anderson, Malcolm, Monica den Boer *et al*. 1996. *Policing the European Union: Theory, Law and Practice*. Oxford: Clarendon Press.

Bartsch, Hans-Jurgen. 1991. 'The Western European Approach'. *Revue Internationale de Droit Pénal* 62: 499–510.

Bigo, Didier. 1994. 'The European Internal Security Field: Stakes and Rivalries in a Newly Developing Area of Police Intervention'. In *Policing Across National Boundaries*, edited by Malcolm Anderson and Monica den Boer. London: Pinter.

Bigo, Didier. 1996. *Les Polices en réseaux*. Paris: Presses de la Fondation Nationale des Sciences Politiques.

Bigo, Didier and Rémy Leveau. 1992. *L'Europe de la Sécurité Intérieure*. Report for the Institut des Hautes Etudes de la Sécurité Intérieure, Paris.

Boer, Monica den. 1994. 'Rhetorics of Crime and Ethnicity in the Construction of Europe'. Paper presented before the 'Police and Immigration:

Towards a Europe of Internal Security' Workshop, European Consortium for Political Research Joint Sessions of Workshops. Madrid.

Bourdieu, Pierre. 1992. *Language and Symbolic Power*. Oxford: Blackwell.

Brion, Fabienne, Luc Verheyen and Greet Spiessens. 1994. *Études de l'Immigration. L'Inégalité Pénale; Immigration, criminalité et système d'administration de la justice pénale.* Brussels: Centre d'Information d'INBEL.

Christodoulidis, Emilios and T. Scott Veitch. 1994. 'Terrorism and Systems Terror'. *Economy and Society* 23: 459–83.

Clutterbuck, Richard. 1990. *Terrorism, Drugs and Crime in Europe after 1992*. London: Routledge.

Council of Europe. 1979. *Explanatory Report on the European Convention on the Suppression of Terrorism*. Strasbourg: Council of Europe.

Finnie, Wilson. 1990. 'Old Wine in New Bottles? The Evolution of Anti-Terrorist Legislation'. *Judicial Review* 35: 1–22.

Gilbert, Geoff. 1991. *Aspects of Extradition Law*. Dordrecht: Nijhoff.

Herman, E.S. and G. O'Sullivan. 1991. '"Terrorism" as Ideology and Cultural Industry'. In *Western State Terrorism*, edited by G. Alexander. Cambridge: Polity.

Lowe, A. and J. Young. 1978. 'Suppressing Terrorism under the European Convention: A British Perspective'. *Netherlands International Law Review* 25: 305–33.

Martin, John M. and Anne T. Romano. 1992. *Multinational Crime. Terrorism, Espionage, Drug and Arms Trafficking*. London: Sage.

Nuttall, Simon. 1992. *European Political Co-operation*. Oxford: Oxford University Press.

Riley, Lisa. 1993. *Counterterrorism in Western Europe: Mechanisms for International Cooperation*. Working Paper X Series, 'A System of European Police Cooperation after 1992.' University of Edinburgh.

Solomos, J. 1993. 'Constructions of Black Criminality: Racialisation and Criminalisation in Perspective'. In *Racism and Criminology*, edited by Dee Cook and Barbara Hudson. London: Sage.

Vercher, Antonio. 1992. *Terrorism in Europe. An International Comparative Legal Analysis*. Oxford: Clarendon Press.

Walker, Neil. 1995. 'Policing the European Union: The Politics of Transition'. In *Policing Change, Changing Police*, edited by O. Marenin. New York: Garland Press.

Wardlaw, Grant. 1989. *Political Terrorism: Theory, Tactics and Counter-Measures*, 2nd edition. Cambridge: Cambridge University Press.

Wilkinson, Paul. 1974. *Political Terrorism*. London: Macmillan.

Wyngaert, Christine van den. 1991. 'The political Offence Exception to Extradition: How to plug the "Terrorist Loophole" Without Departing

from Fundamental Human Rights'. *Revue Internationale de Droit Pénal.*
62: 291–310.

The Author
Malcolm Anderson is Emeritus Professor of Politics and former Director
of the International Social Science Institute at the University of Edinburgh,
Scotland.

9 Counterterrorism Policy in Fortress Europe: Implications for Human Rights

RONALD D. CRELINSTEN AND IFFET ÖZKUT

Introduction

Since the end of the cold war, there has been a progressive assimilation of 'serious' criminal concerns such as drug trafficking and organized crime into the national security mandate of an increasingly integrated Europe. The relaxing of internal borders and the need to enhance security at external borders has led to increased attention to immigrant and refugee flows as well. This transformation in the definition of national security threats has led, in turn, to a broader operational mandate for agencies responsible for counterterrorism. In this chapter we explore the implications of these changes for the development of counterterrorism policy within the European Union. In particular, we argue that they have serious negative consequences for the protection of the individual rights of many European citizens and residents.

First, we examine two contrasting approaches within the criminological tradition regarding the justification of punishment in liberal democracies, one of which seems to lend itself more readily to human rights abuses, particularly in the area of policing. Next, we examine how these definitional and operational changes in the area of counterterrorism relate to the rights of immigrants, refugees and asylum seekers in a Europe increasingly concerned about security. The politicization of social problems engendered by the movements of people into the European Union will be explored with a view to identifying an alternative to the security model of counterterrorism that is at present dominating policy discourse within the EU, with particular emphasis on education at all levels of European society and officialdom. Finally, we discuss the feasibility of implementing this alternative model in the fiscally conscious atmosphere that is prevalent in the industrialized world.

Two Kinds of Justice

In liberal democracies, there are two primary justifications for subjecting any citizen to the violence inherent in criminal justice, whether it be arrest, detention or punishment. The first derives from a classical tradition of punishment originating from the Enlightenment and such thinkers as Cesare Beccaria and Montesquieu. The idea is that the state has the right to protect its citizens from dangerous acts; that is, those acts that contravene the law of the land. Hence the idea of proportionality of punishment (the punishment must fit the crime), the non-retroactivity of the law (one cannot punish someone for doing something which was not proscribed at the time) and, most importantly, deterrence (the idea that punishment has a moral educative function whereby, when an offender is punished, others are taught what is right and what is wrong and, in the process, are deterred from acting likewise). What differentiates the state's use of violence from that of the average citizen is the rule of law and the imperatives of due process. The rights of the accused are protected and the powers of the police are limited by such concepts as reasonable suspicion. Redress is supposed to be available to those wrongly accused or imprisoned. Because of these safeguards, the state's use of violence in the exercise of criminal justice is legitimized.

The second idea derives from a positivist tradition of punishment that tailored its goals to a classification of criminal types. The central idea of this school of thought is that the state has the right to protect its citizens from dangerous people; that is, those identified as incorrigible or inherently criminal. Hence the idea of rehabilitation as a valid goal of punishment for those who are redeemable, and neutralization (exile, deportation, death or life imprisonment) for those who are not. It was up to science to identify those variables that would help law enforcement and criminal justice agents to determine who was who. Central to this approach is the idea that criminals differ in some fundamental way, be it biological, psychological, social or cultural, from the law-abiding citizen. It is this splitting off of the criminal from the non-criminal that is the progenitor of the notion that the criminal is an 'outsider', a stranger, an alien, different from the rest of us, especially in the case of those considered to be unredeemable, incorrigible or untreatable. It is no coincidence that many theories of criminal behaviour within this tradition have had racist overtones and have singled out immigrants or racial and ethnic minorities as the source of crime and disorder in societies undergoing rapid change (Gould, 1981).[1]

Kelman and Hamilton (1989), in their study of sanctioned massacres, identify dehumanization as one of the primary factors that facilitates the commission of gross human rights violations. (For an application of this concept to the phenomenon of torture, see Kelman, 1995; Crelinsten, 1995.) Whether committed by terrorists against innocent victims or by law enforcement agents against suspected terrorists or criminals, it is far easier to mistreat, torture or kill an enemy, an alien other, than a fellow human being. For this reason, definitional or conceptual issues can have very real consequences when applied to the real world. In the next section, we examine some of the implications of these more abstract issues in the area of police and security operations. It will be seen that it is an easy step from the development of a criminological enterprise to identify criminal classes – an essentially scientific exercise – to the construction of a dangerous class for selective attention from control agencies – an essentially ideological or political exercise.

From the Identification of Criminals to the Selective Targeting of Outsiders

In societies where the gap between social, ethnic, cultural or economic groups widens or the politics of hate selects certain groups for vilification and scapegoating, a criminal justice policy that is based on selective targeting of dangerous classes can too easily become fertile ground for enemy construction and the kinds of simplifying myths of good versus evil that were so prevalent during the cold war. In an article in *The Guardian*, Martin Woolacott (1996) argues that

> solving individual crimes may now be neglected so that police forces can identify, isolate and suppress the criminal 'class'. These people – most of them young men – will be constantly picked up, searched and prosecuted for loitering, drinking or carrying weapons. Offences will often be generated in this way, and the offenders will be imprisoned in large numbers.

Here is the operational consequence of a crime control policy based on enemy creation: large numbers of a select group of citizens being processed by the criminal justice system and ending up overrepresented in the prisons. While typical of the American prison system, the same trend seems to be true of European prisons as well. Chalk (1994: 143), for example, points to 'numerous studies

... conducted in Western Europe which focus on the relative overrepresentation of ethnic minorities in West European prisons'.

Woolacott (1996) goes on to argue that 'crime is beginning to be dealt with as if it were an insurgency, a thesis that is supported by moves in a number of countries to bring their espionage services into the crime fight'. This shift from a more law-based model of crime control to a counterinsurgency model in the fight against ordinary crime parallels a similar shift that occurred in counter-terrorism, especially during the 1980s, from a criminal justice model to a war model. (For more on this shift, see Crelinsten, 1989.) Within Europe, it has primarily been via deformations of the criminal justice model that states have moved away from the rule of law and democratic acceptability in their fight against terrorism (see Crelinsten and Schmid, 1993: 333–4). In the 1994 Report of the Committee on Foreign Affairs and Security on terrorism and its effects on security in Europe, the rapporteur (Lacaze, 1994: 11) highlights some of the best known examples: 'France used a Court for State Security, Spain established a Special Court, the United Kingdom used Internment without Trial in Northern Ireland, and Germany restricted the rights of the defence in certain legal proceedings'.

Within the war model of counterterrorism, excessive use of force has been the primary problem, particularly in the case of political killings where a suspect is shot rather than arrested. Ordinary policing is fraught with the same difficulty: suspects identified (often mistakenly) as armed and dangerous are shot (often without provocation) rather than arrested. In subsequent inquiries, police argue that the suspect resisted arrest or tried to flee. The similarity between such cases and the alleged cases of shoot-to-kill incidents in counterterrorism are striking. The assimilation of criminal phenomena and illegal immigration into the counterterrorism mandate has the potential to reinforce a counterinsurgency approach to counterterrorism by importing this militarization of crime control along with the definitional shift. If, in the process, the identification and selective targeting of dangerous classes of persons becomes the central strategy of counterterrorism within a united Europe, such cases of excessive use of force can only be expected to increase.

A (Selective) Merging of Mandates

A central element of a war model or counterinsurgency model is the importance of intelligence about the enemy. After all, terrorists, as well as drug traffickers and criminal organizations, operate in secret and so special investigative techniques are required to obtain information on their activities (Crelinsten, 1989). Once one begins to approach crime control from a counterinsurgency perspective (a war model), it is a natural step to bring one's security services into the fight against crime, a trend already identified by Woolacott (1996). Indeed, from MI5 in Great Britain to the CSIS (Canadian Security and Intelligence Service) in Canada, security services are turning their attention to more purely criminal phenomena that were formerly handled by police, albeit by special units in many cases. It is also natural that those police forces or units that specialize in the fight against organized crime will become more involved in counterterrorism, either directly or via increased cooperation with security agencies. In an October 1995 speech to the English-speaking Union, Stella Rimmington, then Director-General of MI5, spoke of the rise of organized crime in just such terms:

> countering the threat successfully will require those same methods which have been developed to deal with the more familiar threats such as terrorism. This means the same strategic approach, the same investigative techniques. But, above all, it means the same close national and international cooperation between security-intelligence and law enforcement agencies in the context of wider political cooperation between governments. (Rimmington, 1995)

It is precisely because, at an operational level, security intelligence so closely resembles proactive policing (see Crelinsten, 1989) that there is this trend towards increasing cooperation between police and security agencies in the area of combating both criminal activity and terrorism. It is also the reason that the counterterrorism mandate has been widened to include non-political phenomena of a criminal nature, as well as illegal immigration. The end of the cold war has played a role here as well, as security intelligence agencies search for new mandates to justify their continued existence in a post-cold war era (see Rimmington, 1995).

It is ironic that, despite this trend towards militarizing the policing of ordinary crime, and its concomitant trend towards identifying a criminal class for selective surveillance by police, security agencies, in turn, tend to resist incorporating some forms of domestic violence[2] into their counterterrorism mandates that arguably have a political dimension. Lustgarten and Leigh (1994: 383), for example, describe how an informant from the British Security Service replied to 'our query about whether the Service would treat the growing number of racist attacks ... as falling within their mandate'.

> The answer was no; for the reason that 'There is no evidence of systematic organised racial violence by any political group, and in the vast majority of cases of racial harassment reported to the police there is no evidence of the involvement of any political group' (ibid.).

A similar argument was used in the 1980s by the FBI to exclude bombing attacks against abortion clinics in the USA from their counterterrorism mandate. It was only in the 1990s that the FBI recognized such attacks as the work of organized groups and began investigating them. Here we see how definitional issues find their way into the policy arena in very concrete ways that have an impact on police and security mandates. Lustgarten and Leigh (ibid.: 384–5), for their part, categorically reject the exclusion of racist violence from the counterterrorism mandate as 'a discretionary policy choice adopted with no compelling justification. Indeed on policy grounds it seems quite wrong'. They continue:

> Violence targeted at a section of the public which may be socially isolated or unpopular and large enough to constitute a distinct group demands to be treated as terrorism if the underlying purpose is 'political'. And there is no room for doubt that violence directed at making ethnic minorities feel psychologically insecure and not at home in Britain is political: it is part of a conflict about who counts as British – about citizenship and national identity. Few questions are more quintessentially political.

The reluctance of security services to view some forms of domestic violence as terrorism has usually been coupled with a tendency to localize the terrorist threat externally, as an international phenomenon rather than a domestic one. It is therefore no surprise that the hate-generated anti-foreigner violence that is sweeping Europe can be excluded from the counterterrorist mandate. This is troubling to those concerned about civil liberties. In 1994, the Committee on Civil Liberties and Internal Affairs of the European Parliament called terrorism 'a European problem'. It also expressed concern 'about the development of racism and xenophobia in the European Community' and singled out anti-foreigner violence in Germany 'as *terrorist* attacks influenced by extreme right-wing groups' (see Salisch, 1994: 16–17, emphasis added). It would appear that the body responsible for civil liberties in the European Parliament was attempting to refute or to counter the trend to internationalize the terrorist threat and to ignore internal problems such as hate-motivated violence and terrorism, recognizing the inherent dangers in such an approach to the protection of the rights of those who are the object of hate-motivated violence.

Things may be changing, however. The provisional agendas for the March and June 1996 meetings of the Justice and Home Affairs Council under the Italian presidency included a set of regulations on Europol dealing with 'Terrorism: statistics on racism and xenophobia, and extremist religious cults' (*Statewatch*, 1996a: 2). While the latter reflects a new kind of enemy, based no doubt on the Aum Shinrikyo in Japan and, perhaps, the Order of the Solar Temple in Switzerland and Canada, the former does at least address the problem of racism directly. At that same Council, a Joint Action on racism and xenophobia was also adopted. However, according to *Statewatch* (1996b), 'it is *not* expected that the Joint Action will be applied to racist actions or practices emanating from state agencies like the police, courts or prisons' (emphasis added).

More recently, 1997 was declared the European Year against Racism and Xenophobia and, at the June 1997 Amsterdam European Council, an agreement was made on a European Monitoring Centre on Racism and Xenophobia, to be established in Vienna. Appropriately, the official opening of this Centre in April 2000 was one of the few events not boycotted by top EU officials, who refused to attend many official events in Austria to protest the inclusion of the far right Freedom Party in the government. Article F of the Treaty on European Union (TEU) was also amended in 1997 to underscore respect for human rights and fundamental freedoms (paragraphs 1 and 2) and a new non-discrimination principle was added to the Treaty establishing the European Community (TEC).[3] In addition, a new article (K1) was added to Title VI of the TEU dealing with police and judicial cooperation in criminal matters, the first paragraph of which highlights the prevention and control of racism and xenophobia.[4] It remains to be seen how the Schoessel government in Austria can adhere to such principles when one of its coalition partners espouses the kind of xenophobic immigration policies that might conceivably fall within the mandate of the Vienna-based monitoring centre.

Security Intelligence and the Problem of Accountability

From a policing point of view, the two approaches to criminal justice and law enforcement described above can be translated into the idea of (a) a criminal investigation aimed at solving particular crimes (acts) via the determination of guilt or innocence of a suspect, and (b) the identification and selective surveillance of a particular class of individuals considered most prone to commit crimes in the first place. Viewed in this way, it becomes clear that the second approach is much more conducive to human rights violations than the first, particularly because of the inherently dehumanizing episte-mology underlying its depiction of the objects of control, whether 'criminals', 'terrorists' or 'illegal aliens'. The militarization of ordi-nary crime control has alerted critics to the danger of human rights abuses, typified by the disproportionate representation of blacks in American prisons, on death row, or subject to police checks. Simi-larly, the increasing militarization of the terrorist problem, when coupled with a widening of the security mandate to include criminal phenomena, should alert us to the possibility of comparable human rights concerns in the counterterrorism field.

Another way of characterizing this transformation is to say that *reactive* policing or crime *solving* has given way more and more to *proactive* policing or crime *detection*. It is no coincidence that proactive policing quite closely resembles security intelligence, par-ticularly in terms of the investigative techniques used (Crelinsten, 1989: 254–5). In both cases, the kinds of concerns related to the determination of the guilt or innocence of a suspect, subsumed under the notion of the rule of law, are less important than the gathering of information per se. In reactive policing, information is gathered for evidentiary purposes, for use in a court of law, and the way in which it is gathered and the opportunities given to the suspects to defend themselves are crucial to whether this evidence is admissible during a trial. In proactive policing and also in security intelligence, information is gathered so as to enable control agen-cies to counter the activities of those being watched. The information, collected by a variety of methods, is transformed by analysis into intelligence. Countering does not necessarily imply criminal pros-ecution: in fact, many 'suspects' are allowed to bargain away charges for continued cooperation as informers.

The imperatives of information gathering often conflict with those of criminal investigation and due process. Criminal charges can be dropped if successful prosecution could mean the revealing of sources. In the United Kingdom, the doctrine of public interest immunity has been used to try and protect vulnerable sources and techniques used by MI5 from being revealed during a trial. 'In each case, the decision on disclosure rests with the judge. The aim is to ensure that the defence may obtain as much material information as possible within the constraints of the requirements of national security' (*Statewatch*, 1994). Some defendants and their lawyers try and take advantage of this, demanding secret information from the prosecution in the hope that they will drop charges rather than reveal the information. Lustgarten and Leigh (1994: 292) call this practice 'greymail' (a lighter shade of blackmail).

In the area of counterterrorism, this inherent conflict between prosecution goals and intelligence goals has led to compromises which tend to undermine strict adherence to the rule of law. One example is the videotaping of intelligence sources' testimony, which protects the identity of the source but also deprives the defence of the opportunity for cross-examination. The end result has been a trend to circumvent the controls built into the criminal justice system by the classical (deterrent) approach to punishment and an increasing reliance on certain kinds of expertise that are tailored to the identification and neutralization of dangerous 'enemies'. In the worst cases, those identified as extremely dangerous have been killed rather than brought to trial.

A switch from a criminal justice, law-oriented approach to a military or counterinsurgency approach leads to certain assumptions about the behaviour of innocent and guilty persons. For example, in proposing that more powers be given to police and security agencies for identity checks and other forms of surveillance, Clutterbuck (1994: 220) has suggested that 'only the guilty have anything to fear'. He also argues that, 'in a free society, people do not need to conceal their identity from a police officer unless they have done or mean to do something illegal' (ibid.: 78). This assumes that 'only the guilty' have anything to hide and that any concerns of privacy are a luxury at best, given the degree of threat that terrorism and international crime pose to society. At worst, a concern for privacy can be interpreted as a symptom of guilt. The same logic underlies Clutterbuck's call for a reinterpretation of the right to remain silent, whereby the court can interpret a refusal to answer questions in any way it deems fit: 'Again, only the guilty have anything to fear from this' (ibid.: 213).

Contrast this position with that of Lustgarten and Leigh (1994: 40), who argue that 'it is imperative to create a legal regime and a moral climate in which the powers of agents of the state to intrude upon its citizens' privacy are rigorously restricted'. Concerning clandestine interception of communications or eavesdropping, these authors point to 'a belief in some official circles that we should simply accustom ourselves to the fact that our conversations may be monitored by agents of the state' (ibid.). They reject this outright, arguing that silence, withdrawal, mistrust and 'existential insecurity' (ibid.: 41) will replace the sociability, friendship and trust that characterize social life. 'No more odious a society can be imagined than one in which no one dares to speak his or her true thoughts, even in private, for fear that state officials will learn of them' (ibid.).

By arguing that 'only the guilty have anything to fear', Clutterbuck implies that anyone who wishes to remain silent or who objects to identity checks or resists arrest must be guilty of something, otherwise they would readily acquiesce. But this is true only if the innocent citizen is convinced that agents of the state are subject to strict controls and that redress is available in the case of abuse. Unfortunately, this is far from the case in many liberal democracies. One has only to read the cases documented by Amnesty International (1994a; 1994b; 1994c; 1994d; 1995a; 1995b) and other human rights agencies to know that simply objecting to or questioning police checks can too easily lead to ill-treatment, sometimes akin to torture, and that official complaints rarely result in prosecution, let alone conviction, of the offending officers. The situation is even more problematic for security services, which must operate in secret and often must protect their sources at the expense of successful prosecution. As a result, accountability becomes 'inward and self-directed' (Franks, 1989: 20).

Brodeur (1983: 512) has remarked that 'striving to prevent political policing from hampering the right to dissent is as hopeless as trying to keep a stake from casting its shadow'. If it is inevitable that security intelligence will impinge on the civil liberties of those who are targets simply because of the secret nature of its operations and the resulting lack of public scrutiny and accountability, it is incumbent upon parliaments and legislatures to develop oversight procedures that will redress those infringements when they occur. In view of this, it can only be extremely troubling that the draft Europol Convention was stalled precisely over the role of the European Court of Justice as a possible avenue of redress in the case of police abuses (*Statewatch*, 1995b). The Europol Convention was finally ratified by all member states in June 1998, came into force on 1 October 1998, and actually began working on 1 July 1999. While Europol is accountable only to the EU Council of Justice and Home Affairs Ministers, Art. 40(2) of the Convention allows member states to opt into the jurisdiction of the European Court of Justice if disputes are not settled within six months.[5] All member states except the United Kingdom have done so, leaving the degree of judicial control for UK citizens lower than that for all other EU citizens.[6]

Equally problematic is the fact that 'cooperation in the fields of justice and internal affairs has largely remained an intergovernmental matter in the Union Treaty, with all the disadvantages this implies for the legal protection of individuals and democratic supervision by the national parliaments and the European Parliament' (Robles Piquer, 1993: 5). Only 'effective and continual parliamentary and judicial oversight' (Chalk, 1994: 133) can provide the degree of accountability required when the very nature of the state activity under scrutiny renders probable the likelihood of abuse. To leave oversight to intergovernmental cooperation is to create a climate in which impunity for police excesses can only flourish.

The Amsterdam Treaty of June 1997 does not rectify either of these concerns. While a new Art. K7 of the TEU does give the European Court of Justice (ECJ) jurisdiction to rule on certain decisions and interpretations made under Title VI dealing with provisions on police and judicial cooperation in criminal matters, paragraph 5 of that article explicitly excludes any decisions or measures dealing with 'the maintenance of law and order and the safeguarding of internal security'.[7] As such, the ECJ has no jurisdiction over exactly those areas that concern us here. As for the reliance on intergovernmental cooperation in the fields of justice and home affairs (namely, third pillar issues), while some areas of cooperation are now subject to legal review of the ECJ,[8] police cooperation – either direct or through Europol – is not. In short, all areas of cooperation pertaining to criminal matters as defined in Title VI of the new TEU remain at the intergovernmental level, without judicial or parliamentary oversight. Article K1 lists these matters as 'crime, organized or otherwise, in particular terrorism, trafficking in persons and offences against children, illicit drug trafficking and illicit arms trafficking, corruption and fraud'.

A Borderless Europe: a Focus on Movement of Persons

The relaxing of internal borders within the Schengen countries and the move to broaden this to the whole European Union (EU) has highlighted the need to enhance security at external borders surrounding the EU since, once inside, there would be free movement of goods and people within and between member states. This has led to increased attention to the movement of people from outside Europe to within. The increased flows of immigrants, refugees and asylum seekers from the East in the wake of the collapse of the Soviet Empire crystallized these concerns (see Chalk, 1994: 121–4). The result has been a concerted move to increase cooperation among police and security forces and customs agencies. Suddenly, illegal immigration and such issues as deportation and expulsion have become much more germane to the counterterrorism mandate. As Chalk (ibid.: 122) notes:

> The inclusion of the fight against terrorism (and other forms of serious crime) and illegal immigration in one single framework of internal security cooperation has been interpreted by numerous commentators as an internationalization of the national police agenda which routinely targets 'aliens' as a potential 'high-risk' category.

The term 'Fortress Europe' has arisen to describe this heightened concern to strengthen external borders and entry points leading into the EU.

Chapter 2 of the June 1997 Amsterdam Treaty reflects these interlocking concerns with its emphasis on the 'progressive establishment of an area of freedom, security and justice'. While the first concept, freedom, reflects a concern with fundamental rights, as described previously, it is coupled with those of security and justice. It is this consistent coupling that concerns us here. In this same chapter, an amendment to Art. B, fourth indent, in the TEU captures the mix well:

> to maintain and develop the Union as an area of freedom, security and justice, in which the free movement of persons is assured in conjunction with appropriate measures with respect to external borders, immigration, asylum and the prevention and combating of crime.

This list of areas where measures are to be taken is consistent with the expanded terms of reference that were given to the Europol

Drugs Unit, established in January 1994. As its name suggests, the Unit's prime objective was initially to combat drug trafficking, as well as associated money laundering. These were later extended to include measures to combat trafficking in radioactive and nuclear substances – a prime concern of many in the counterterrorism field – *clandestine immigration networks*, vehicle trafficking and money laundering associated with these criminal activities. The mandate was later expanded to include combating trade in human beings. The phrase 'trafficking in persons and offences against children' in Art. K1 clearly addresses the issue of illegal immigration, particularly as it relates to organized crime networks which transport illegal aliens across borders, as much as it addresses any alleged slave trade or child pornography rings.

The routine identification of aliens as a potential high-risk category is consistent with what has already been described as a militarizing or counterinsurgency trend in ordinary policing, with its concentration on an identifiable class or type of criminal. It is no coincidence that Chalk (1994: 123) refers to Amnesty International's 1993 annual report, which cites the previous year, 1992, as 'an appalling year for human rights in Europe'. The primary problem identified was police racism against immigrants. Here we see the process of enemy identification, inherent in both the positivist tradition and proactive policing, combining with a process of internationalization, whereby the targets of policing are sought in the most obvious 'outsiders', that is, immigrants, refugees, asylum seekers and the communities in which they live – in a word, non-EC nationals. According to Chalk (ibid.: 124), given that the EU has not yet acceded to the European Convention on Human Rights and Fundamental Freedoms (ECHR), 'it is not at all clear whether non-EC nationals would have access to any effective forum to which they could appeal against unjust police and judicial actions/decisions'. Article K7, para. 5 of the new TEU, which we have seen excludes the European Court of Justice from ruling on such actions, would suggest not (see note 7).

While Art. F of the TEU was amended in June 1997 to emphasize respect for human rights,[9] the EU has still not acceded to the ECHR, though all member states are parties to it. Nor has a list of fundamental rights of the European citizen been added to the Treaty, although the Cologne European Council of 3–4 June 1999 did call for the drafting of a Charter of Fundamental Rights. The Tampere European Council of 15–16 October 1999 determined the composition, method of work and practical arrangements for the body that will draft such a Charter. It is hoped that a Draft Charter will be ready for the European Council of December 2000.[10] Of course, it is not certain that any Draft Charter will then automatically be incorporated into any Treaties, since some member states may object or require changes. The process will likely drag on for some time. All this suggests that police and security agents selectively focusing on an easily identifiable class of people will inevitably lead to incidents of abuse and that any complaints by the victims of such abuse will likely not result in any kind of speedy redress.

There is mounting evidence that this has indeed been the case in several European countries. In many of the individual cases reported by Amnesty International, arrests seem to have occurred in the context of police asking a foreigner or a person from a visible minority for his or her identity papers and then using force to arrest them when the person asked why they were being singled out. Similarly, in cases where an individual has been arrested on suspicion of having committed a particular offence, they are beaten or ill-treated during the arrest process or on the way to the police station. Many are ill-treated during the period of detention (usually within 24 hours) before they are brought before a judge or other judicial authority. Typically, if they state that they intend to lodge a formal complaint, they are either beaten even more or charged with resisting arrest or assaulting or insulting an officer. Clearly, the assimilation of illegal immigration into the security mandate has the potential of increasing dramatically the possibility of selectively focusing on foreigners or those who appear to be foreign. Given the problems inherent in security intelligence and its accountability, this, in turn, could increase the likelihood of human rights abuses.

A Security Model of Counterterrorism

This European focus on immigration and asylum has dovetailed with the emergence of a 'security model' of counterterrorism that emphasizes technological surveillance, militaristic border controls and stereotypic profiling of non-EC nationals as the sea in which the terrorist fish swim. Within political and police circles at least, this development appears to be at the expense of any deep concern for harmonizing social policies concerning immigration, refugees and asylum seekers, drug use and other more purely social issues. What should be considered purely social problems to be addressed by social agencies and social policies, such as education, welfare, job creation and health care, are becoming the province of policing, security intelligence, criminal justice and border control. Given the post-cold war impetus to find new mandates for the security services and, in the process, new targets for investigation, the police and security community has begun to play a central role in the realignment of counterterrorism policy in the direction of this security model. Because it has such an impact on all levels of European society – social, economic and political – the influx of immigrants, asylum seekers and refugees into the EU has become a focal point for many of the concerns expressed about counter-terrorism in a unified European Community.

It is in the grey area separating strictly social concerns and more political ones that many of the issues surrounding immigrants, refugees and asylum seekers can have an impact on security threat analysis. It is true that immigrants, migrant workers, refugees and asylum seekers often import their conflicts – along with their customs and values – into the European nations where they seek residence or work. The communities in which they live can harbour sympathizers or supporters of groups who promote or use violence against the states from which they came. Fund raising for such groups can often be disguised as collecting money for cultural or social events, or it can take the uglier form of extortion and intimidation. Terrorist groups, unscrupulous gangs or racketeers, can prey on the outsider status of the residents or, as in the case of illegal aliens, their fear of the authorities, to force them to carry out 'dirty work' for them. Such communities can also serve as safe havens or sanctuaries for terrorists or criminals engaged in covert planning of future attacks or operations. As a result, immigrant and refugee communities can easily become focal points for security intelligence and political policing, either as a source of potential security threats or as a pool of informers or recruits.

Consequences of Selective Targeting

The fact that many of the abuses reported by Amnesty International occurred within the context of identity checks belies Clutterbuck's assurance that only the guilty have anything to fear from enhanced powers of surveillance and identification by law enforcement and security agents. If security policing becomes based more and more on typologies and profiles of likely classes of targets, there is little a potential target can do once he or she has been selected by an agent because they fit that profile or belong to that category in the typology. In fact, protestations or resistance may only lead to victimization and abuse. To avoid being selected for policing of any kind, whether it be an identity check or an arrest on suspicion of having committed an offence, members of groups which are frequent targets can try and change their appearance, demeanour or behaviour to reduce the likelihood of being selected. For example, many middle-class black Americans have learned not to look or act conspicuous, especially when driving luxury cars, in order not to attract the attention of police. They have also learned to be extremely passive and cooperative when dealing with police checks and requests for identification in order not to provoke the police into any kind of forceful or violent action. This is because experience has taught them that to protest or to question the police action in any way can easily result in just the kind of ill-treatment and criminal charges described in the European cases. What does this mean for the civil liberties of those who must adjust their lifestyle to avoid being the targets of police or security agents? It would appear that a kind of policing that relies on the identification of dangerous classes of people has a great potential for impinging on the rights of large numbers of completely innocent people.

Blanket assumptions about who constitutes a security threat can have particularly serious consequences for asylum seekers and refugees, both of whom would likely fall into any kind of 'foreigner' profile. Amnesty International points out that many asylum seekers fail to report abuse or ill-treatment at the hands of police for fear that their requests for asylum will be refused as a result (Amnesty International, 1994c). An asylum seeker's status is a precarious one, since anything that might cast the individual in a negative light can lessen their chances of getting refugee status. Clearly, this self-imposed silence can open the door to further problems if, for example, a police report that fails to mention the abuse or even charges the individual with assault or resisting arrest ultimately results in deportation. In other cases, immigrants, refugees or asylum seekers who have been tortured in their home countries react apprehensively and even violently to any approach by a uniformed officer. This could easily lead an individual to panic if asked by police for identity papers or to resist any attempt to be taken to a police station. In the case of actual deportation, the chances of ill-treatment or abuse can only be heightened by such violent reactions. In most cases, agents responsible for deporting people lack training about the particular sensitivities of torture victims and refugee claimants. Such knowledge might help them in what is clearly a difficult and distasteful task. However, if deportees are viewed as an underclass or as potential terrorists or some kind of subhuman lowlife, ill-treatment during deportation is all the more likely to occur. The fact that the person's refugee claim has been refused can only serve to strengthen any prejudice towards the individual that an agent might hold and confirm his or her suspicion that the claim was a bogus one in the first place. Recent figures suggest that there has been an exponential increase in the number of people being deported across the European Union (*Statewatch*, 1996a: 18): 'From 15,000 in 1990 De Stoop estimates that over 100,000 people were deported in 1993 and the figure doubled again to 200,000 in 1994.'[11]

Finally, there is the question of self-fulfilling prophecy. One of the French presidency's proposals for joint action by EU member states in the first six months of 1995 was to commit member states to imposing requirements on foreign nationals to carry and produce on demand residence and identity documents. According to *Statewatch* (1995a),

> systematic ID and status checks and computerised files on all immigrants will provide the means of effective police control of Europe's immigrant and black communities. Their combination with employer sanctions and the barring of those unable to produce the right documents from all welfare benefits, will drive desperate migrant workers and de facto (but unrecognised) refugees deeper into illegality and modern slavery.

In other words, fears of an influx of illegals and criminals into Europe will generate policies that increase the likelihood of illegality and criminal activity, including that of criminal exploitation by organized crime of illegal aliens (for example, 'trafficking in persons'). In similar fashion, repressive security policies may serve to alienate immigrant and refugee communities to the point of increasing the possibility of successful fund raising or recruitment by terrorist or extremist groups and decreasing community cooperation with security operations.

Counterterrorism Policy and Human Rights

Crelinsten and Schmid (1993: 309–13) attempt to classify the various kinds of policy models that have been used by liberal democracies in the fight against terrorism. Some have been reactive, others proactive or preventive. Some have been short-term, others long-term. Some have been coercive, others conciliatory. Some address the coercive capabilities of the terrorist, such as target-hardening, criminal justice and the military aspects of a counterinsurgency model, while others address the terrorist's political capabilities. The latter approach would include the hearts-and-minds aspect of a counterinsurgency model, including addressing some of the grievances that the terrorist exploits to gain supporters and sympathizers. It also includes the broader issue of trying to influence the perceptions of the many audiences involved in the terrorist communicational nexus. As Crelinsten and Schmid (ibid.: 311) put it:

> Counter-terrorism policies that recognize the multiple audiences that are addressed – intentionally or unintentionally – by terrorist violence and that develop strategies and tactics to counteract and influence the perceptions of these audiences could ultimately reduce the political credibility or legitimacy of the terrorist. In doing so, *such policies might obviate the necessity to resort to repressive violence* in dealing with terrorists and their supporters or sponsors. (emphasis added)

In the context of counterterrorism, elements of such an approach include educating the public about democratic values and terrorist values, and distinguishing carefully between legitimate armed resistance against non-democratic regimes and clandestine armed attacks by tiny groups on unarmed civilians. This would help to avoid the moral relativism implied by the cliché: 'one man's terrorist is another man's freedom fighter'. A sound human rights policy and a respect for the rule of law are essential elements in such an educational programme. It also includes educating the public about what is possible and what is impossible for a government to do during a crisis – what might be called 'the realm of the possible'. Again, adherence to the rule of law and respect for human rights are central to this kind of understanding.

There are concrete benefits that accrue from such an approach. The first is the promotion of public trust in government, a core value of any true democracy. A corollary of this is the prevention of unrealistic public expectations concerning a government's capabilities in dealing with terrorism or a specific crisis. This might also serve to inoculate the public against the kinds of media sensationalism that break out during a real crisis, so that they are less prone to panic or demand quick solutions that, in the long run, create more problems than they solve. (For more on the impact of the media, particularly television, on terrorist crises, see Crelinsten, 1994 and Crelinsten, 1997.)

Another element involves addressing the constituents of terrorist groups and other groups that may share their political goals while averring or condemning violence themselves. One important element would be to counter the Manichaean arguments of terrorists who tend to depict the world in black and white terms of good versus evil (if you're not for us, you're against us) and to promote the middle ground. It would also include creating a social climate that might allow individuals to leave terrorist groups, by offering what Wilkinson (1987) has called, in a different context, 'pathways out of terrorism'. By preventing the maintenance of beliefs that bind an individual to a clandestine group and providing positive incentives to re-enter society, governments can sometimes achieve results that coercion or repression cannot (Crelinsten and Schmid, 1993: 328–9).

Promoting Human Rights and Anti-racist Education

Policies that address the perceptions of multiple audiences can also be applied to many of the problematic areas arising from the widening of the counterterrorism mandate, in particular those related to victimization of so-called 'illegals', whether guest workers (*gastarbeiters*), refugees or immigrants. Public policy that favours the development of anti-racist education and fosters the dissemination of human rights training to social control agents could provide a sociopolitical climate conducive to long-term prevention rather than the quick fixes that more coercive policies offer. Among the most important values or skills that might be included in such programmes are the following:

- tolerance and mutual understanding of differences between racial, ethnic and religious groups;
- the ability to formulate or discuss misunderstandings and to maintain communication;
- acceptance of unusual or different behaviour with regard to language, non-verbal communication and social rules;
- knowledge and recognition of different concepts, viewpoints, ways of life;
- focusing on common work and interests and on cooperation;
- the ability to combat racist behaviour and prejudice;
- building awareness of racism and racist propaganda via critical thinking, media literacy and content analysis.

Many international conventions on human rights single out education as a fundamental right and emphasize education as a vehicle for promoting democratic, pluralistic and anti-racist values. For example, both the Universal Declaration of Human Rights (Art. 26) and the International Covenant on Economic, Social and Cultural Rights (Art. 13) refer to the right to education, the access to various levels of education and the purposes of education. The purposes of education are also referred to in the UN Declaration on the Elimination of All Forms of Racial Discrimination (Art. 8), the International Convention on the Elimination of All Forms of Racial Discrimination (Art. 7), the Declaration on the Elimination of All Forms of Intolerance and of Discrimination Based on Religion or Belief (Art. 5, para. 3) and the UNESCO Declaration on Race and Racial Prejudice (Art. 5, para. 2 and Art. 6, para. 2). The purposes of education include strengthening respect for human rights; promoting understanding, tolerance and friendship among all nations and racial, ethnic or religious groups; furthering the maintenance of peace; enabling people to participate effectively in a free society; combating prejudices and racist attitudes which lead to racial discrimination; and the prevention and eradication of racism and racist propaganda (Van Boven, 1993).

There are three areas in which the inculcation of values such as these is most pressing: the schools (both students and teachers); social control agencies that deal with immigrants, refugees and asylum seekers; and police colleges and military academies. Each can be viewed as an important link in a broad, long-range and preventive approach to counterterrorism that addresses the wider sociopolitical context in which terrorism waxes and wanes.

First, there are the schools. Albert Einstein once suggested that the spell of nationalism can be broken by teaching history in such a way as to avoid instilling in students 'an obsession with the past'. He also felt that the teaching of geography and history could promote pacifism if it were able to foster sympathetic understanding for the national characteristics of the different countries in the world, 'especially of those whom we are in the habit of describing as "backward"' (cited in Crelinsten, 1980: 211). Einstein's emphasis on the teaching of history and geography and on habits of description suggests a concrete way that the values and skills listed above might be incorporated into school curricula. Too often we are taught lessons that obscure understanding of other cultures, that mystify the practices and beliefs of other civilizations and that pathologize or demonize the behaviour of historical or political enemies. It is an 'obsession with the past' that often lies at the root of intractable conflicts, particularly of an ethnic nature. Rather than focusing on the present and attempting to foster harmonious relations in the conduct of everyday life, many people dwell on real or perceived injustices from the past. In doing so, they expend much energy and talent in perpetuating enmity, suspicion, misunderstanding and, ultimately, injustices of their own (see Rogers, 1990). Teaching methods that foster an understanding of the interdependence of human beings and an appreciation of ethnic, linguistic, cultural and historical diversity can contribute to reducing the fear and cultivated ignorance that lie at the root of much hatred and violence. Such ways of thinking can also diminish the attractiveness of hate rhetoric and 'us–them' thinking. Recruitment would become more difficult and support for extremist and terrorist groups would become harder to sustain.

If terrorism occurs in a broader context, so too does counterterrorism. While this chapter has focused primarily on police and security agencies, given the primacy of coercive, repressive models of counterterrorism, there are many other forms of social control that are involved in the wider context within which counterterrorist policies operate. Control agents who deal on a daily basis with the very people who are at present perceived as most likely to be involved in terrorism must receive training that will help them see beyond the stereotypes and the demonology. These include social workers, hiring or job placement agents, employers, members of refugee or immigration boards, customs officials, government bureaucrats, medical professionals, and school and adult education officials. Because the post-cold war mandate has broadened and because a moral panic about organized crime networks, drug traffickers, illegal immigrants and refugees is in full swing, governments should work all the more diligently to ensure that agents of the state, at all levels, are able to deal with their clients as human beings, not potential menaces to society. The non-discrimination clause of the TEC (Art. 6a) that was added in June 1997 clearly attempts to foster such thinking (see note 3).

Finally, it is those control agents who are imbued with the right to exercise the state's monopoly on violence that are most in need of special training in the area of human rights and the rule of law. Here we would include police, security intelligence agents, private security professionals, prosecutors, public defenders, judges, correctional officers, prison guards and parole officers, as well as military personnel. Many police academies do include courses on the rights of the accused and the nature of police powers and their judicial controls, while military academies sometimes include courses on human rights. The question is how such training relates to actual practice. It is one thing to teach these things at the academy and quite another to ensure that the lessons are followed in the field.

Conclusion

Cohen and Golan (1991: 110) identify two sets of conditions that are conducive to the violation of human rights: a set of social and political conditions and a set of legal conditions. The legal conditions include extended periods of incommunicado detention, the inability to identify interrogators, trials under military law or other similar procedures, the absence of independent checks on the detainees' medical condition, rules of evidence that do not automatically rule out confessions obtained under torture, and some degree of immunity enjoyed by interrogators from legal prosecution. Most of these conditions fall along what Crelinsten and Schmid (1993: 333–4) call the 'criminal justice route' towards democratic unacceptability.

The social and political conditions identified by Cohen and Golan (1991) include a national emergency or other perceived threat to security, the need to process large numbers of suspects, the dehumanization of an out-group, a high level of authorization to violate accepted moral principles and the presence of a 'sacred mission' which justifies anything. Here we see many of the features that characterize the post-cold war era in Europe. While short of a declared state of emergency, the moral panic about criminals and aliens running rampant in a borderless Europe is consistent with an aura of emergency, while the huge numbers of deportations cited previously suggest that large numbers of individuals need to be processed. A model of counterterrorism that seeks to identify a dangerous class for selective attention can very easily lead to a set of social and political conditions described by Cohen and Golan.

We have argued that it is at the level of social policies pertaining to the promotion of human rights that prevention of such an eventuality must be sought. In an era where government cutbacks on social programmes have become the norm in liberal democracies, it is admittedly difficult to suggest large-scale expenditures on ambitious educational projects. In addition, given the mass media's propensity to promote public fear and loathing of the dangerous outsider via a steady supply of human interest stories focusing on victims of terrorism and bombing, it is likely that the social climate is not even ripe for such an approach. Yet it is exactly at such times of public anxiety and precisely when sociopolitical change is acute that political leaders must seek innovative ways to deal with pressing problems such as terrorism, whatever its form. It is our fervent hope that European counterterrorism policy at the beginning of this new millennium can avoid the kind of unintended consequences that are too easily overlooked when technocrats and ideologues prevail.

Notes

1   A new edition of this classic exploration of racism within the positivist tradition was published in 1996. It includes a new introduction that addresses some of the latest manifestations of the same phenomenon.

2   By 'domestic violence', we mean public violence within a state, rather than violence in the home or interpersonal violence such as spousal abuse.

3   The new Art. 6a in the TEC reads: 'Without prejudice to the other provisions of this Treaty and within the limits of the powers conferred by it upon the Community, the Council, acting unanimously on a proposal from the Commission and after consulting the European Parliament, may take appropriate action to combat discrimination based on sex, racial or ethnic origin, religion or belief, disability, age or sexual orientation.'

4   The first paragraph of the new Art. K1 reads: 'Without prejudice to the powers of the European Community, the Union's objective shall be to provide citizens with a high level of safety within an area of freedom, security and justice by developing common action among the Member States in the fields of police and judicial cooperation in criminal matters *and by preventing and combating racism and xenophobia*' (emphasis added).

5   The actual text of Art. 40(2) reads as follows: 'When ... disputes are not ... settled within six months, the Member States who are parties to the dispute shall decide, by agreement among themselves, the modalities to which they shall be settled'.

6   The following Declaration pertaining to Art. 40(2) appears at the end of the Europol Convention: 'The following Member States agree that in such cases they will systematically submit the dispute

to the Court of Justice of the European Communities'. The Declaration is followed by the names of all member states except the United Kingdom. See the Europol website, *www.europol.eu.int*.

7   Paragraph 5 of the new Art. K7 of the TEU reads: 'The Court of Justice shall have *no* jurisdiction to review the validity or proportionality of operations carried out by the police or other law enforcement agencies of a Member State or the exercise of the responsibilities incumbent upon Member States *with regard to the maintenance of law and order and the safeguarding of internal security*' (emphasis added).

8   The areas include visa policy, the terms for issuing residence permits to immigrants, asylum procedures, and rules governing judicial cooperation in civil matters (European Union, 1997).

9   Paragraph 2 of Art. F reads: 'The Union shall respect fundamental rights, as guaranteed by the European Convention for the Protection of Human Rights and Fundamental Freedoms signed in Rome on 4 November 1950 and as they result from the constitutional traditions common to the Member States, as general principles of Community law.'

10   'Protection of Fundamental Rights Within the Union: Current Situation and Outlook', web document, dated 22 March 2000, at *www.europa.eu.int/scadplus/leg/en/lvb/l33021/htm*. For a more skeptical view, see *The Economist*, 'The EU and Human Rights. Necessary?', 5–11 February 2000, p. 26. Thanks to Peter Chalk for this last reference.

11   The *Statewatch* report is about a book entitled *Haal De Was Maar Binnen* (Bring the Washing In), by Belgian journalist, Chris De Stoop. While a full reference is not given, De Stoop works for *Knack Magazine* and the *Statewatch* report is an excerpt from *Knack Magazine*, 17–23 January 1996.

References

Amnesty International. 1994a. *Switzerland – Allegations of Ill-Treatment in Police Custody*. London: Amnesty International, International Secretariat. AI Index: EUR 43/02/94.

Amnesty International. 1994b. *France – Shootings, Killings and Alleged Ill-Treatment by Law Enforcement Officers*. London: Amnesty International, International Secretariat. AI Index: EUR 21/02/94.

Amnesty International. 1994c. *Austria – The Alleged Ill-Treatment of*

Foreigners: A Summary of Concerns. London: Amnesty International, International Secretariat. AI Index: EUR 13/02/94.

Amnesty International. 1994d. *United Kingdom – Cruel, Inhuman or Degrading Treatment During Forcible Deportation*. London: Amnesty International, International Secretariat. AI Index: EUR 45/05/94.

Amnesty International. 1995a. *Federal Republic of Germany – Failed by the System: Police Ill-Treatment of Foreigners*. London: Amnesty International, International Secretariat. AI Index: EUR 23/06/95.

Amnesty International. 1995b. *Italy – Alleged Torture and Ill-Treatment by Law Enforcement and Prison Officers*. London: Amnesty International, International Secretariat. AI Index: EUR 30/01/95.

Brodeur, Jean-Paul. 1983. 'High Policing and Low Policing: Remarks about the Policing of Political Activities'. *Social Problems* 30: 507–20.

Chalk, Peter. 1994. 'EU Counter-Terrorism, the Maastricht Third Pillar and Liberal Democratic Acceptability'. *Terrorism and Political Violence* 6: 103–45.

Clutterbuck, Richard. 1994. *Terrorism in an Unstable World*. London: Routledge.

Cohen, Stanley and Daphan Golan. 1991. *The Interrogation of Palestinians During the Intifada: Ill-treatment, 'Moderate Physical Pressure' or Torture?* Jerusalem: B'TSELEM, The Israeli Information Center for Human Rights in the Occupied Territories.

Crelinsten, Ronald D. 1980. 'Prepared statement for International Scientific Conference on Terrorism, Berlin, November 1978'. *Terrorism* 3: 203–14.

Crelinsten, Ronald D. 1989. 'Terrorism, Counter-Terrorism and Democracy: The Assessment of National Security Threats'. *Terrorism and Political Violence* 1: 242–69.

Crelinsten, Ronald D. 1994. 'The Impact of Television on Terrorism and Crisis Situations: Implications for Public Policy'. *Journal of Contingencies and Crisis Management* 2: 61–72.

Crelinsten, Ronald D. 1995. 'In Their Own Words: The World of the Torturer'. In *The Politics of Pain: Torturers and Their Masters*, edited by Ronald D. Crelinsten and Alex P. Schmid. Boulder: Westview Press.

Crelinsten, Ronald D. 1997. 'Television and Terrorism: Implications for Crisis Management and Policy-Making'. *Terrorism and Political Violence* 9: 8–32.

Crelinsten, Ronald D. and Alex P. Schmid. 1993. 'Western Responses to Terrorism: A Twenty-Five Year Balance Sheet'. In *Western Responses to Terrorism*, edited by Alex P. Schmid and Ronald D. Crelinsten. London: Frank Cass.

European Union. 1997. *Amsterdam: A New Treaty for Europe: A Citizen's Guide*. Luxembourg: Office of the Official Publications of the European Communities.

Franks, C.E.S. 1989. 'Accountability of the Canadian Security Intelligence Service'. In *National Security: Surveillance and Accountability in a Democratic Society*, edited by P. Hanks and J.D. McCamus. Cowansville: Les Editions Yvons Blais.

Gould, Stephen Jay. 1981. *The Mismeasure of Man*. New York: W.W. Norton.

Kelman, Herbert C. 1995. 'The Social Context of Torture: Policy Process and Authority Structure'. In *The Politics of Pain: Torturers and Their Masters*, edited by Ronald D. Crelinsten and Alex P. Schmid. Boulder: Westview Press.

Kelman, Herbert C. and V. Lee Hamilton. 1989. *Crimes of Obedience: Toward A Social Psychology of Authority and Responsibility*. New Haven: Yale University Press.

Lacaze, Jeannou. 1994. *Report of the Committee on Foreign Affairs and Security on terrorism and its effects on security in Europe*. Strasbourg: European Parliament Session Documents, 2 February, A3-0058/94.

Lustgarten, Laurence and Ian Leigh. 1994. *In From the Cold: National Security and Parliamentary Democracy*. Oxford: Clarendon Press.

Rimington, Stella. 1995. 'National Security and International Understanding'. Speech to the English-speaking Union, on 4 October 1995.

Robles Piquer, Carlos. 1993. *Report of the Committee on Civil Liberties and Internal Affairs on cooperation in the field of justice and internal affairs under the Treaty on European Union (Title VI and other provisions)*. Strasbourg: European Parliament Session Documents, 1 July, A3-0215/93.

Rogers, Rita R. 1990. 'Intergenerational Transmission of Historical Enmity'. In *The Psychodynamics of International Relations: Concepts and Theories*, edited by Vamik T. Volkan, Demetrios A. Julius and Joseph V. Montville. Lexington, Mass: Lexington Books.

Salisch, Heinke. 1994. 'Opinion of the Committee on Civil Liberties and Internal Affairs for the Committee on Foreign Affairs and Security'. In *Report of the Committee on Foreign Affairs and Security on terrorism and its effects on security in Europe*, reported by Jeannou Lacaze. Strasbourg: European Parliament Session Documents, 2 February, A3-0058/94, pp. 14–17.

Statewatch. 1994. 'MI5 Director's speech: Extracts from Stella Rimington's lecture on "Intelligence, Security and the Law". The James Smart Lecture', 3 November. Vol. 4, no. 6 (November–December).

Statewatch. 1995a. 'Policing immigration: Britain and Europe'. Vol. 5, no. 2 (March–April).

Statewatch. 1995b. 'EU: Justice & Home Affairs Council'. Vol. 5, no. 3 (May–June).

Statewatch. 1996a. Vol. 6, no. 1 (January–February).

Statewatch. 1996b. Vol. 6, no. 2 (March–April).

Van Boven, Theo. 1993. 'The European Context for Intercultural Education'. Paper presented at the conference, 'Social Diversity and Discrimination in the Common Curriculum', 27–30 January, Bergen, The Netherlands.

Wilkinson, Paul. 1987. 'Pathways Out of Terrorism for Liberal Democracies'. In *Contemporary Research on Terrorism*, edited by P. Wilkinson and A.M. Stewart. Aberdeen: University of Aberdeen Press.

Woolacott, Martin. 1996. 'The Long Army [sic] of the Law'. *The Globe and Mail* (Toronto), 27 January, p. D4; reprinted from *The Guardian* (date unknown).

The Authors

Ronald D. Crelinsten is Professor of Criminology at the University of Ottawa, Canada. He is currently Visiting Professor in Political Science and International Relations at the Middle East Technical University in Ankara, Turkey.

Iffet Özkut teaches and conducts research in linguistics, cross-cultural communication, teacher training and media studies.

Index